# KEY CONCEPTS IN LANGUAGE AND LINGUISTICS

'This is brilliant book. It combines the readability of Pinker with the breadth and erudition of Crystal, and deserves a place of honour as a summary of the best of twentieth-century linguistics – liberal, scholarly, forward-looking, undogmatic, sensible, practical and above all wide ranging. Every linguist will be pleased with most of it . . . and every student will cling to it and love it.'

Richard Hudson, *University College London*

*Key Concepts in Language and Linguistics* is an A–Z guide to the main terms and concepts used in the study of language and linguistics. The book includes definitions of:

- terms used in grammatical analysis from phoneme to componential analysis;
- branches of linguistics from semantics to neurolinguistics;
- approaches used in studying language from critical discourse analysis to Systemic Linguistics;
- linguistic phenomena from code-switching to conversational implicature;
- language varieties from pidgin to standard language.

Each entry begins with a brief definition of the term followed by a more detailed description. Entries trace the origin of the concept, mention the key associated individuals, provide a guide to further reading and are extensively cross-referenced.

**R.L. Trask** is Professor of Linguistics at the University of Sussex. His numerous publications include *The History of Basque* (1996), *Language: The Basics* (1995), *A Dictionary of Phonetics and Phonology* (1995) and *A Dictionary of Grammatical Terms* (1993).

# KEY CONCEPTS SERIES

# KEY CONCEPTS IN LANGUAGE AND LINGUISTICS

R.L. Trask

London and New York

Chia-yiz R

2003 1 A
Penn. Philadelphia.
PA.

First published 1999
by Routledge
11 New Fetter Lane, London EC4P 4EE

Simultaneously published in the USA and Canada
by Routledge
29 West 35th Street, New York, NY 10001

Typeset in Bembo by The Florence Group,
Stoodleigh, Devon

Printed and bound in Great Britain by Clays Ltd., St. Ives PLC

*British Library Cataloguing in Publication Data*
A catalogue record for this book is available from the British
Library

*Library of Congress Cataloguing in Publication Data*
Trask, R. L. (Robert Lawrence) 1944–
    Key concepts in language and linguistics / R.L. Trask.
        p. cm.  (Key concepts)
    Includes bibliographical references and index.
    ISBN 0–415–15741–2 (HB). – ISBN 0–415–15742–0 (PB).
    1. Linguistics – Dictionaries.  I. Title.  II. Series.
P29.T687 1998
410′.3–dc21                                           98–24025
                                                          CIP

ISBN 0–415–15742–0 (Pbk)
ISBN 0–415–15741–2 (Hbk)

# CONTENTS

# PREFACE

The book in your hand is neither a dictionary nor an encyclopedia, but something in between. As its title suggests, it provides
fairly detailed coverage of nearly 300 key concepts in the study
of language. The named concepts selected for inclusion are all
among the most important in the field, and among those which
every beginning student is likely to encounter.

The concepts are taken from every area of language study,
from traditional grammar to contemporary grammatical theory,
from child language to language and brain, from lexicography
to the linguistic study of literary texts, from men's and women's
speech to language and power. Each entry provides a brief
definition of the term entered and then goes on to explain
the concept in some detail – often with numerous examples –
and it also introduces and explains related terms, which are
given in bold italics. Wherever possible, the historical origins of
the concept are described, including the time of introduction and the names of individuals who have made the concept
prominent. When a concept is controversial, the entry says so.
Cross-references to other concepts with their own entries are
frequent, and are always given in boldface. In most cases, the
entry concludes with cross-references to other entries which are
related, and with a list of suggested further reading, usually
arranged from briefest and most elementary to most advanced
and comprehensive. A complete bibliography of the suggested
reading is provided after the main part of the book. Where little

or no further reading is suggested, this usually means that the concept, though fundamental, is often maddeningly difficult to look up in textbooks, and here I have been at pains to provide the kind of explanation not readily available elsewhere.

At the front of the book you will find an alphabetical list of all the concepts with their own entries. At the end, you will find a detailed index; this includes not only the terms entered as headwords but also all other terms introduced within entries. So, if you don't find the term you're looking for in the main list, be sure to check the index, which includes hundreds of additional terms. The index also includes references to individuals named in the entries.

I hope that this book will prove to be of great utility to students undertaking the study of almost any aspect of language for the first time, either at undergraduate level or at postgraduate level.

## Acknowledgements

I am indebted to Kieron Corless for inviting me to write this book, and to Nicola Woods, Lyn Pemberton and Richard Coates for various types of advice and assistance in the writing of it.

*R.L. Trask*
*Brighton, UK*
*October 1997*

# KEY CONCEPTS

## A

accent
adjective
adverb
affix
agreement
airstream mechanism
alternation
ambiguity
analogy
anaphor
animal communication
anthropological linguistics
aphasia
apparent time
applied linguistics
arbitrariness
argument
artificial language
aspect
autonomy of language
auxiliary

# B

basic word order
behaviourism
bilingualism
bioprogram hypothesis
Black English

# C

caregiver speech
case
clause
code-switching
cognitive linguistics
cognitive science
coherence
cohesion
colloquial speech
communicative competence
comparative reconstruction
competence
complement
componential analysis
computational linguistics
conjunction
connotation
consonant
constituent structure
control
conversational implicature
conversation analysis
cooperative principle
coordinate structure
copula
corpus
creole
critical discourse analysis
critical period hypothesis

# D

dead language
deep structure
deficit hypothesis
deictic category
denotation
dependency
derivation
descriptivism
design features
determiner
diachrony
dialect
diglossia
discourse
discourse analysis
displacement
distinctive feature
distribution
duality of patterning
dyslexia

# E

ellipsis
entailment
ethnography of speaking
etymology
experimental approach

# F

finite
focus
folk linguistics
functionalism
functions of language

# G

gap
gender
generative grammar
genetic hypothesis of language
genetic relationship
genre
given/new
government
Government-and-Binding Theory
grammar
grammatical category
grammatical relation
grapheme

# H

head
historical linguistics

# I

iconicity
idiom
immigrant language
Indo-European
inflection
innateness hypothesis
internal reconstruction
international language
International Phonetic Alphabet
intertextuality
intonation
intuition

# K

kinship terms
knowledge about language

# L

language
language acquisition
language acquisition device
language and ethnicity
language and identity
language and ideology
language and power
language areas
language change
language contact
language death
language disability
language faculty
language family
language instinct
language in use
language myths
language planning
language processing
*langue*
lateralization
Lexical-Functional Grammar
lexicography
lexicon
*lingua franca*
linguistic area
linguistic relativity hypothesis
linguistics
linguistic sign
literacy
loan word

localization
logonomic rules

## M

manner of articulation
markedness
meaning
medium
mentalism
metalanguage
metaphor
minimal pair
minority language
modality
modifier
modularity
mood
morpheme
morphology
movement

## N

name
narrative
national language
natural class
natural language
natural-language processing
neurolinguistics
neutralization
nominalization
non-verbal communication
notational convention
noun
noun phrase
number
number of languages

# O

official language
onomastics
open-endedness
oracy
origin and evolution of language
orthography

# P

paradigm
paradigmatic relation
paralanguage
*parole*
part of speech
perceptual strategy
performance
performative
person
philology
philosophy of language
phonation type
phoneme
phonetics
phonology
phonotactics
phrase
phrase-structure grammar
pidgin
place of articulation
politeness
pragmatics
predicate
preposition
prescriptivism
presupposition
productivity

pronoun
prosody
proto-language
protolanguage hypothesis
psycholinguistics
punctuation
purism

## Q

qualitative approach
quantitative approach

## R

raising
reconstruction
recursion
reference
root
rule

## S

sandhi
Saussurean paradox
segment
selection restriction
semantic role
semantics
semiotics
sense
sense relation
sentence
sex differences in language
sexist language
sign language
slang

tone language
topic
traditional grammar
transcription
transformational grammar
transitivity
tree
turn-taking
typology

## U

universal
universal grammar
usage
utterance

## V

variation
verb
verb phrase
vernacular
vocal tract
voice
voicing
vowel

## W

well-formedness
word
word-formation
writing system

**accent**  A particular way of pronouncing a language. For any language with more than a handful of speakers, there are prominent regional, social and individual differences in the way the language is pronounced by different people; sometimes these differences are dramatic. Each distinguishable type of pronunciation is called an *accent*. Depending on where we come from and what experience we have, we will be able to identify accents different from our own with more or less precision: in the case of English this may be an American accent, a Deep South accent, a Scottish accent, a working-class London accent, a French accent (from a non-native speaker) and so on. Speakers of all languages can do the same.

It is important to realize that *everybody* has an accent: it is not possible to speak a language without using some accent or other. Of course, every one of us regards some accents as more familiar than others, or as more prestigious than others, but that is a different matter: we are merely more sensitive to accents which differ strongly from our own. A friend of mine with an impeccable middle-class south-of-England accent which attracts no attention in London once visited Yorkshire, where a wide-eyed little girl, after listening to him for a few minutes, finally confided to him, in a broad Yorkshire accent, 'Ee – tha talks *funny*.'

In Britain, the single most prestigious accent is **Received Pronunciation**, or RP, an accent which seems to have arisen

1

in the prestigious 'public schools' (private schools) in the nineteenth century. This accent is not associated with any particular region, though it is structurally most similar to certain accents of the southeast of England. No more than three per cent of Britons speak with an RP accent, though many more have a **near-RP** accent which differs only in a few particulars. RP is the accent usually taught to foreign learners of English in Britain. Nevertheless, regional and social variation in accents in Britain is very great, greater than anywhere else in the English-speaking world, and the urban accents of Newcastle, Glasgow or Liverpool may be unintelligible to outsiders.

In the USA, distinctive and readily identifiable regional accents of English are confined to New England, the east coast and the south, the areas which have been settled longest. West of the Appalachians, the differences level out into the great continuum of **General American** accents, with minimal local variation apart from a few large cities.

Regional accents of English are prominent in Ireland, less so in the Caribbean, still less so in Canada, and least prominent of all in the southern Hemisphere countries, the most recent to be settled.

A conspicuous difference among accents of English is that between **rhotic** and **non-rhotic accents**. In a rhotic accent, the historical /r/ is retained in all positions, so that *farther* does not sound like *father* and *tar* does not rhyme with *Shah*. In a non-rhotic accent, the historical /r/ has been lost everywhere except before a vowel, and so *farther* sounds just like *father* and *tar* does rhyme with *Shah*.

A striking way of testing accents is to check whether certain pairs of words are pronounced identically or differently. Here are some useful pairs; in each case, the words are pronounced identically by some speakers but differently by others: *horse/hoarse, threw/through, dew/do, nose/knows, pull/pool, poor/pour, whine/wine, winter/winner, court/caught, caught/cot, farther/father, god/guard, hair/air, three/free, stir/stare, buck/book, higher/hire, marry/merry/Mary*.

Observe that, in the USA, an **accent** is usually considered to be just one aspect of a **dialect**; in Britain, the two are regarded as largely independent, at least in principle.

(Note that the word *accent* is also used, very informally, to mean *diacritic*: one of the little marks placed on a letter to indicate something about its pronunciation, as in *café*, *learnèd*, *bête noire* and *Zoë*.)

*See:* **dialect**; **phonology**
*Further reading:* P. Hawkins (1984: ch. 8), Hughes and Trudgill (1996), Trudgill and Hannah (1994), Wells (1982)

**adjective** The **part of speech** which includes words like *big* and *beautiful*. English and many other languages have a large and growing class of adjectives, though in still other languages the class of adjectives is tiny and closed or absent altogether. (In these languages, the meanings expressed by adjectives in English are expressed by other parts of speech.)

In English, adjectives may be identified by a number of criteria. Not every adjective exhibits every single one of the typical adjectival properties, but a word that exhibits most of them must still be classed as an adjective. Here are some tests for adjectives.

Distribution: An adjective can typically appear in each of the following slots to produce a good sentence: *This is a(n) ___ book*; *This book is ___* ; *___ though this book is, it's not what we want.* (Try this with *new, interesting, expensive, beautiful*.)

Comparison: An adjective can be compared in one of the following two ways: *big/bigger/biggest*; *beautiful/more beautiful/ most beautiful*. It can also appear in the *as . . . as* construction: *as pretty as Lisa*.

Degree: An adjective can be modified by a *degree modifier* like *very, fairly, too, so* or *rather*: *very big, fairly nice, so good, rather interesting*.

Affixation: An adjective may take the prefix *un-* or *in-* to form another adjective, the suffix *-ly* to form an **adverb**, or the suffix *-ness* or *-ity* to form a **noun**, among other possibilities: *happy/unhappy/happily/happiness*; *possible/impossible/ possibly/possibility*.

3

Negative properties: An adjective cannot be marked for **number** (singular versus plural) or for **tense** (past versus nonpast), nor can it take the suffix *-ing* which goes onto **verb**s.

The meaning of an adjective is most typically a temporary or permanent state or condition: *big, human, young, red, happy, drunk, shiny, intelligent, asleep*. Many adjectives express subjective perceptions, rather than objective facts: *interesting, beautiful, disgusting*. A few adjectives express very unusual types of meaning: *mere, utter*, the *heavy* of *She's a heavy smoker*.

*See:* **adverb**; **part of speech**

*Further reading:* Collins Cobuild, 1990: ch. 2; Crystal, 1996: units 48–51; Greenbaum and Quirk, 1990: ch. 7; Hurford, 1994: 8–10.

**adverb** The **part of speech** which includes words like *soon* and *slowly*. English has a fairly large class of adverbs, as do many other languages (though not all). Most commonly, an adverb describes the circumstances of an action: where it is done (*here, elsewhere, overhead*), when it is done (*tomorrow, often, rarely, never*) or how it is done (*fast, well, carefully, dramatically, resentfully*). But some adverbs have less usual kinds of meaning, and, as always, we can only identify adverbs with confidence by their grammatical properties.

A typical property of adverbs is their position in the sentence. Consider the sentence *She poured the wine*. A typical adverb like *carefully* can be inserted into any one of three positions: *Carefully she poured the wine; She carefully poured the wine; She poured the wine carefully*. The same is true of many other adverbs, like *often, angrily* and *skilfully*. But not all adverbs are so flexible: *yesterday* and *downstairs* can only fit into the first and third of these positions, while *fast* can only fit into the last. (Naturally, some adverbs, such as *uphill*, have meanings which do not allow them to fit sensibly into this example, but consider another example like *She threw the ball*.) Adverbs with negative or interrogative meanings do something odd when they come first: we can't say *\*Seldom she poured the wine* or *\*Why she poured the wine?* but must say instead *Seldom* *did she pour the wine* and *Why did she pour the wine?* (the asterisk marks ungrammaticality).

Two other typical properties of adverbs are their ability to be compared with *more* or *most* and their ability to be modified by words expressing degree, such as *very, rather, too* and *so*: *more carefully, most often, very skilfully, rather casually, too fast, so well*. This is usually only possible with adverbs describing how something is done, though there are a few exceptions, like *often*. These adverbs can also appear in the *as . . . as* construction, as in *Susie drives as well as Esther*.

Adverbs have few other grammatical properties. They never change their form for any reason at all: for example, they cannot be marked for **tense**, and they have no separate plural form.

English has a subclass of adverbs, called *sentence adverbs*, which are rather different from ordinary adverbs. While ordinary adverbs describe some aspect of the action, the sentence adverbs express the speaker's view of the whole rest of the sentence. For example, in *She probably poured the wine*, the sentence adverb *probably* says nothing about her pouring of the wine, but rather expresses the speaker's view of the likely truth of the statement *She poured the wine*. Other sentence adverbs are *maybe, certainly, frankly, mercifully, honestly, hopefully* and *fortunately*. Some of these can also be used as ordinary adverbs: compare *Frankly, she must tell us about it* (sentence adverb expressing the speaker's view) with *She must tell us about it frankly* (ordinary adverb describing her telling). There is almost never any ambiguity.

Observe that many adverbs describing how something is done (the *adverbs of manner*) are derived from **adjectives** by means of the suffix *-ly*: *eager/eagerly, furious/furiously*. But other adverbs, including *adverbs of time* and *adverbs of place*, are usually simple words, not derived from anything.

Earlier grammarians often had the bad habit of assigning the label 'adverb' to almost any troublesome word they didn't know what to do with, such as *not, almost* and *very*. Some dictionaries and other books still continue this unfortunate practice today, but in fact these words do not behave like

5

adverbs and are not adverbs: some of them (like *very*) belong to other parts of speech entirely, while others (like *not*) exhibit unique behaviour and cannot be sensibly assigned to any part of speech at all.

*See:* **adjective**; **part of speech**

*Further reading:* Collins Cobuild, 1990: ch. 6; Crystal, 1996: units 52–58; Greenbaum and Quirk, 1990: ch. 7; Hurford, 1994: 10–13.

**affix**    A grammatical element which cannot form a word by itself. Most (but not all) of the world's languages contain grammatical *affixes* used for various purposes. English has fewer affixes than some other languages, but it still has some. For example, nouns exhibit the plural affix *-s*, as in singular *dog* but plural *dogs*, while adjectives exhibit the comparative afffix *-er* and the superlative affix *-est*, as in *wide, wider, widest*.

Verbs in English exhibit a somewhat larger number of affixes, as shown by *paint*, which has grammatical forms like *paints* (*She paints pictures*), *painted* (*She painted a picture*) and the quite different (*She has painted a picture*) and *painting* (*She is painting a picture*). Other affixes can be added to the verb *paint* to obtain the verb *repaint* and the nouns *painter* and *painting* (as in *This is a nice painting*).

An affix that goes on the end, like *-s* and *-ing*, is a *suffix*, while one that goes on the beginning, like *re-*, is a *prefix*. Other types of affix exist, such as *infixes*: observe that the Tagalog verb *sulat* 'write' has inflected forms *sumulat* 'wrote' and *sinulat* 'was written', with infixes *-um-* and *-in-* inserted into the middle of the verbal **root**. There are also *superfixes*, which are placed 'on top of' a word: note the English nouns '*record* and '*contest*, distinguished from the related verbs *re'cord* and *con'test* only by a change in the placement of the stress.

*See:* **derivation**; **inflection**; **morpheme**

*Further reading:* Bauer, 1988: ch. 3; Katamba, 1994: ch. 4.

**agreement**  The grammatical phenomenon in which the *form* of one word in a sentence is determined by the *form* of another word which is grammatically linked to it. Agreement, which is also called **concord**, is an exceedingly common phenomenon in languages generally, but it is not present equally in all of them. Swahili, Russian, Latin and German have a great deal of agreement; French and Spanish have somewhat less; English has very little; Chinese has none at all.

Certain types of agreement are especially frequent. A finite verb may agree in **person** and **number** with its subject. This happens in Basque; here are the present-tense forms of *joan* 'go' (the pronouns are in brackets since they are optional):

| | | |
|---|---|---|
| (*ni*) *noa* | 'I go' | |
| (*hi*) *hoa* | 'you go' | (singular intimate) |
| *Ana doa* | 'Ann goes' | |
| (*gu*) *goaz* | 'we go' | |
| (*zu*) *zoaz* | 'you go' | (singular polite) |
| (*zuek*) *zoazte* | 'you go' | (plural) |
| *Neskak doaz* | 'The girls go' | |

In each case the form of the verb marks the subject as first, second or third person and as singular or plural, and we say that the verb-form *agrees* with the subject in person and number. As you can see from the English glosses, English has only a tiny amount of agreement of this kind: only the third-singular *goes* is explicitly distinguished, all other persons and numbers taking an invariable *go*.

Much less frequently, a verb may agree in person and number with its object. This also happens in Basque. The form (*zuk*) (*ni*) *ikusi nauzu* 'you saw me' carries agreement both for the subject 'you' (*-zu*) and for the object 'me' (*n-*); compare (*zuk*) (*gu*) *ikusi gaituzu* 'you saw us' and *neskek* (*ni*) *ikusi naute* 'the girls saw me'.

Adjectives and determiners may agree in number with their head noun. Basque does not have this, but Spanish does: compare *la casa vieja* 'the old house' with *las casas viejas* 'the

7

old houses', in which both the determiner *la(s)* 'the' and the adjective *vieja(s)* 'old' show agreement with singular *casa* 'house' and plural *casas* 'houses'. As the English glosses suggest, this kind of agreement is generally absent from English, but we do have a trace of it in cases like *this old house* versus *these old houses*, in which the determiner agrees (but not the adjective).

A determiner or an adjective may also agree in **case** with its head noun. This occurs in German: in *mit diesem Mann(e)* 'with this man' (the *e* is optional and is therefore in brackets), the noun *Mann(e)* stands in the dative case, and the determiner *diesem* 'this' agrees with it in case, while in *für diesen Mann*, *Mann* stands in the accusative case, and the determiner now agrees with that.

The Spanish and German examples also illustrate what might be called agreement in **gender**. For example, the Spanish noun *casa* 'house' is feminine in gender; if we use instead a masculine noun, such as *libro* 'book', we get *el libro viejo* 'the old book' and *los libros viejos* 'the old books', showing that the determiner and the adjective are 'agreeing' in gender as well as in number. Such gender matching is traditionally regarded as another variety of agreement; strictly speaking, however, this is not agreement but **government**, since a single noun like *casa* or *libro* has only one possible gender, and hence in these cases it is not the *form* of the noun which determines the forms of the other words, but its very *presence* – the defining criterion for government. Some linguists apply to such cases the label *governmental concord*.

*See:* **government**
*Further reading:* Hurford, 1994: 13–14.

**airstream mechanism** Any way of producing a stream of air for use in speech. We produce speech by using our vocal organs to modify a stream of air flowing through some part of the vocal tract, and all speech sounds require this airstream for their production. There are several very different ways of producing an airstream, only some of which are used in languages, and only one of which is used in all languages.

To begin with, an airstream may be either *egressive* (flowing out of the mouth) or *ingressive* (flowing into the mouth). Further, the air which is moving may be lung air (this is the *pulmonic* mechanism), pharynx air (the *glottalic* mechanism) or mouth air (the *velaric* mechanism). This gives six possible combinations, only four of which are used in speech.

In the *pulmonic egressive* airstream mechanism, air is squeezed out of the lungs by the diaphragm and the rib muscles and passes out through the mouth (and possibly the nose). This is the principal mechanism in all languages and the only one used in most languages (including English). In the *pulmonic ingressive* mechanism, air is drawn in from the outside through the mouth into the lungs; no language uses this, but you may hear it intermittently from a child sobbing and talking at the same time.

In the *glottalic egressive* mechanism, the glottis is closed and the larynx is driven up in the throat like a piston, pushing the air of the pharynx out through the mouth. The sounds produced are *ejectives*, which occur in only a few languages. If the larynx is driven downward instead, outside air is pulled into the mouth and pharynx, and we have the *glottalic ingressive* mechanism. The sounds produced are *injectives* (or *voiceless implosives*); these are very rare in their pure form, but, if the glottis is left open slightly, so that air can leak out from the lungs, we get a complex ingressive-egressive mechanism, producing *voiced implosives*, which are much commoner.

In the *velaric egressive* mechanism, the back of the tongue is pressed against the velum and another closure is made in front of this; the tongue body is pushed up, so that, when the front closure is released, mouth air is driven outward. The resulting sounds are *reverse clicks*, which do not occur in any language. If, instead, the tongue body is pulled downward, when the front closure is released, air is pulled into the mouth; this is the *velaric ingressive* mechanism, and the resulting sounds are *clicks*. Clicks occur as speech sounds in some languages of southern Africa; elsewhere, these sounds occur only paralinguistically, as in the English *tsk tsk* noise and as in the sound of a kiss made with the lips tightly pursed.

There is one other airstream mechanism, which is very unusual. Persons who have had their larynxes removed surgically can learn to produce an airstream by swallowing air and then forcing it up through the oesophagus; this **oesophagic egressive** airstream is effectively a controlled belch.

*See:* **phonation type**
*Further reading:* Crystal, 1997a: ch. 22; Ladefoged and Maddieson, 1996: section 3.2; Laver, 1994: ch. 6.

**alternation** A variation in the form of a linguistic element depending on where it occurs. Certain English nouns ending in the consonant /f/ form their plurals with /v/ instead: *leaf* but *leaves*, *knife* but *knives*. We say that such items exhibit an /f/–/v/ alternation. For most (not all) speakers a similar alternation occurs in singular *house* (with /s/) but plural *houses* (with /z/), though here our spelling system does not represent the alternation explicitly.

A somewhat different sort of alternation is found in related words like *electric* (which ends in /k/) and *electricity* (which has /s/ instead of /k/ in the same position).

More subtle is the three-way alternation occurring in the English plural marker. The noun *cat* has plural *cats*, pronounced with /s/, but *dog* has plural *dogs*, pronounced with /z/ (though again the spelling fails to show this), and *fox* has plural *foxes*, with /z/ preceded by an extra vowel. This alternation is regular and predictable; the choice among the three **alternants** (as they are called) is determined by the nature of the preceding sound.

Alternations are exceedingly common in the world's languages, and they are often of great interest to linguists trying to produce elegant descriptions of languages.

*See:* **sandhi**
*Further reading:* Bloomfield, 1933: ch. 13; Hockett, 1958: ch. 33; Sommerstein, 1977: 41–45.

**ambiguity**   Two or more sharply distinct meanings for a single string of words. The simplest type of ambiguity is a *lexical ambiguity*, which results merely from the existence of two different meanings for a single word. Example: *The sailors enjoyed the port*. Here *port* can mean either 'fortified wine' or 'city by the sea', and the entire string of words accordingly has two different interpretations, but the structure of the sentence is exactly the same in both cases.

More interesting are *structural ambiguities*, in which the words have the same meanings, but quite different structures can be assigned to the entire string of words, producing different meanings. Examples: *Small boys and girls are easily frightened*; *Exploding mines can be dangerous*; *The shooting of the hunters was appalling*; *Anne likes horses more than Mark*. In the first two of these, the different structures can be easily represented by **tree** diagrams, and such cases are called *surface-structure ambiguities*. In the last two, the tree structures appear to be identical in both readings (interpretations), and we need to appeal to more abstract levels of representation to identify the differences in structure; these are *deep-structure ambiguities*.

Complex cases are possible, involving both lexical and structural ambiguities, as in the classic *Janet made the robot fast*, which has an astonishing number of quite different readings.

The concept of ambiguity can be extended to cases which are only ambiguous when spoken, and not when written. Simple cases of this are *an ice-box* versus *a nice box* and, for some speakers only, *a slide-rule* versus *a sly drool*. French provides a classic example:

> *Gal, amant de la Reine, alla (tour magnanime!)*
> *Galamment de l'arène à la Tour Magne, à Nîmes.*

> Gal, lover of the Queen, went (magnanimous journey!)
> Gallantly from the arena to the Great Tower, in Nîmes.

*See:* **meaning**; **structure**
*Further reading:* Cruse, 1986: ch. 3; Kempson, 1977: ch. 8.

**analogy** A type of **language change** in which some forms are changed merely to make them look more like other forms. The ordinary processes of language change, including perfectly regular changes in pronunciation, can have the effect of introducing irregularities. Speakers sometimes react to the presence of irregularities in their language by eliminating them and making the irregular forms regular; this is one kind of *analogy*.

For example, when Latin was changing into French, the pronunciation of stressed /a/ and that of unstressed /a/ developed differently, in a perfectly regular manner: stressed /a/ became the diphthong /ai/, while unstressed /a/ remained /a/. This led to apparently irregular variations in the stems of certain verbs, as with the verb meaning 'love'; compare the first two columns in the following table (here an acute accent marks the position of the Latin stress):

|      | *Latin* | *Old French* | *Mod. French* |
|------|---------|--------------|----------------|
| 1Sg  | ámo     | aim          | aime           |
| 2Sg  | ámas    | aimes        | aimes          |
| 3Sg  | ámat    | aimet        | aime           |
| 1Pl  | amámus  | amons        | aimons         |
| 2Pl  | amátis  | amez         | aimez          |
| 3Pl  | ámant   | aiment       | aiment         |

As you can see, the stem of the verb fluctuated between *aim-* and *am-* in Old French in a seemingly unpredictable way (the Latin stress was also lost in Old French). As a result, speakers subjected the forms in *am-* to analogy, producing the modern French forms shown in the third column (there have been further changes in pronunciation, of course, but these are not relevant here).

Analogy can be far less systematic than this, and it can even turn regular forms into irregular ones. Many formerly irregular English verbs have been turned into regular verbs by the analogy of cases like *love/loved*; an example is *work/wrought*, which has been analogized to *work/worked*. On the other hand, in Early Modern English, the past tense of *catch* was the regular *catched*, but this has been replaced by *caught*, apparently by analogy with *taught*, and many Americans have replaced *dive/dived* with *dive/dove*, by analogy with verbs like *drive/drove*.

*Further reading:* Trask, 1996: 105–115.

**anaphor**  A linguistic item which takes its interpretation from something else in the same sentence or discourse. In the sentence *Susie wants to get a job in Paris, but she needs to improve her French first*, the item *she*, in the most obvious interpretation, means *Susie*. We say that *she* is an **anaphor**, and that *Susie* is the **antecedent** of *she*; the relationship between these two items is one of **anaphora**, or **binding**, and *she* is **bound** by *Susie*.

Further examples of anaphors include *herself* in *Susie injured herself* (antecedent *Susie*) and *each other* in *Susie and Mike are seeing a lot of each other* (antecedent *Susie and Mike*).

The antecedent of an anaphor need not be in the same sentence. Consider this: *Susie is looking run-down. I think she needs a holiday.* Here the antecedent *Susie* is in a different sentence from the anaphor *she* which points to it.

It is possible for a **zero-element** (a null element) to be an anaphor: instead of saying *Susie needs a new car but she doesn't have the money*, we can say *Susie needs a new car but doesn't have the money*. In the second version, instead of the overt anaphor *she*, we have only a piece of silence, but the interpretation is the same. For linguistic purposes, we often write the second version with the symbol Ø (meaning 'zero') or *e* (for 'empty') in the appropriate place: *Susie needs a new car but e doesn't have the money.* The zero anaphor represented as *e* is often called an **empty category**.

In linguistic descriptions, it is common practice to use **referential indices**, usually subscript letters, to indicate explicitly which anaphors have which antecedents; items which are **coindexed** (have the same subscripts) are **coreferential** (refer to the same thing), while those which have different subscripts refer to different things. So, for example, *Mike$_i$ has found his$_i$ dog* means 'Mike has found his own dog', while *Mike$_i$ has found his$_j$ dog* means 'Mike has found somebody else's dog' (here the preceding context – i.e. what has been said or written before – must make it clear who owns the dog).

Anaphora in general, and empty categories in particular, pose many intricate problems of linguistic analysis, and in recent years they have been the object of intensive investigations. Theoretical linguists are fascinated by the seemingly complex nature of the rules governing the use of anaphors, and grammatical theorists have often seen the elucidation of these rules as a matter of fundamental importance, especially since the American linguist Noam Chomsky began drawing attention to them in the 1960s. At the same time, functional linguists are deeply interested in the way in which anaphors are used to structure discourses, and linguists with typological or anthropological interests have devoted considerable attention to the various ways in which anaphors are employed in different languages.

*See:* **gap**; **pronoun**
*Further reading:* Huddleston, 1984: ch. 7.


**animal communication** The signalling systems used by non-human creatures. Most of the other creatures on the planet can communicate with other members of their species in one way or another, and often by specialized vocal noises termed *calls*. But the signalling systems of these creatures are vastly different from human language. First, they lack **duality of patterning**: they are based on the principle of "one sound, one meaning", and neither sounds nor meanings can be modified or combined. Consequently, they lack **open-endedness**: only a tiny number of different meanings can be expressed. They lack **displacement**: "utterances" are confined to the here and now. They lack **stimulus-freedom**: a call is produced always and only when the appropriate stimulus is present, and there is no choice.

Hence non-human creatures live in a communicative world which is alien to us: it is bounded by the horizon, lacking a past or a future, consisting only of the endless repetition of a few familiar messages about what's going on at the moment. Moreover, unlike human languages, with their ceaseless and rapid changes, the signals used by other species never change by any process faster than evolutionary change.

There are marginal exceptions: honeybee dances contain a limited amount of displacement; bird songs possibly contain an element of duality; whale songs change from year to year; a fox may occasionally give a danger call in the absence of any danger merely to distract her cubs from a meal she is trying to eat. But these exceptions are inconsequential: animal signals do not remotely approximate to human language, and they cannot be regarded as simpler versions of it.

Since all these statements are true of our closest living relatives, the apes, it follows that our non-human ancestors of a few million years ago also had such a limited system. Attempts at teaching scaled-down versions of human language to apes and other creatures have often been vitiated by poor procedure, but there is now a small amount of evidence suggesting that these creatures, when intensively trained under laboratory conditions, can learn at least the rudiments of a human language, though no more.

*See:* **design features**; **origin and evolution of language**; **protolanguage hypothesis**
*Further reading:* Crystal, 1997a: ch. 64; Malmkjær, 1991: 10–16; Steinberg, 1993: ch. 2; Trask, 1995: ch. 1; Wallman, 1992.

**anthropological linguistics** The study of the relation between language and culture. Anthropologists generally find it necessary to learn the languages of the people they are studying, and they realized early that the languages themselves might provide valuable clues about the cultures under investigation. In the late nineteenth century, the anthropologist Franz Boas in the USA laid particular stress upon the importance of native American languages in the study of native American cultures and, thanks to his influence and that of his student Edward Sapir, American linguistics was largely born out of anthropology. As a result, American linguistics long retained an anthropological orientation, and indeed most linguists worked in anthropology departments until the middle of the twentieth century.

In Britain, the anthropologist Bronislaw Malinowski drew comparable attention to the study of languages in the early twentieth century, and his ideas greatly influenced J.R. Firth, widely regarded as the founder of linguistics in Britain.

The explosive growth of areas like sociolinguistics, psycho-linguistcs and linguistic theory during the last few decades has not obliterated interest in anthropological linguistics, which is now recognized as a distinctive discipline in its own right; it is sometimes also called *linguistic anthropology*. Anthropological linguists have been greatly interested in such topics as **kinship systems**, colour terms, **metaphors**, systems for conferring **names** upon people and places, connections between languages and myths, *folk taxonomies* (systems for classifying animals and plants), the treatment of space and time in languages, the expression of sex differences and social differences in speech, and the structure of **narratives**; more than most linguists, they have been intrigued by the **linguistic relativity hypothesis**.

*See:* **cognitive linguistics**; **ethnography of speaking**; **linguistic relativity hypothesis**

*Further reading:* Bonvillain, 1993; Crystal, 1997a: chs. 2–5; Duranti, 1997; W.A. Foley, 1997; G. Palmer, 1996.

**aphasia**  Disordered language resulting from brain damage. Strictly speaking, we should say *dysphasia* (which means 'disordered speech') for damage to the language faculties and reserve *aphasia* (which means 'absence of speech') for cases in which the victim's language faculties are totally destroyed. However, in practice the two terms are used interchangeably, and the most profound and severe cases are distinguished as *global aphasia*.

That damage to the head can produce language disorders has been known since ancient times. But it was only in the mid-nineteenth century that scientists began to investigate the problem systematically, by studying the symptoms of brain-damaged patients and then, after the victims' deaths, by carrying out post-mortem examinations to see which areas of the brain had been damaged. The French surgeon Paul Broca found that damage to a particular area of the brain, with a high degree of consistency, produced an aphasia characterized by painful, halting speech and a near-total absence of grammar; today the area he identified is called **Broca's area**, and the associated aphasia is called **Broca's aphasia**. A few years later, the German neurologist Carl Wernicke identified a second area of the brain, damage to which consistently produces a different aphasia, characterized by fluent but senseless speech and grave difficulties in comprehension; we now speak of **Wernicke's area** and **Wernicke's aphasia**. Broca's area and Wernicke's area are now known to be two of the most important **language areas** in the brain, each with responsibilities for specific aspects of language.

In practice, no victim ever suffers damage exclusively to one neatly defined area of the brain, and consequently every sufferer exhibits a somewhat distinctive range of symptoms. The complexity of aphasia rather discouraged further research during much of the twentieth century. However, in the middle of that century the American neurologist Norman Geschwind revived interest in the subject, confirmed the existence of distinct language areas in the brain, and developed a classification of aphasias which is now more or less standard. For example, Broca's and Wernicke's areas are connected by a bundle of fibres called the **arcuate fasciculus**, and damage to this produces a third type of aphasia, **conduction aphasia**, with specific symptoms of its own.

More recently, it has been discovered that brain damage affects users of **sign language** in precisely the same way as it affects users of spoken language. This confirms that what injury to the brain damages is **language**, and not merely the ability to speak or to perceive speech. It is crucial to distinguish aphasia from *speech defects*, which result merely from damage to the nerves or muscles controlling the speech organs, and have no consequences for the language faculty itself.

*See:* **language areas**; **language disability**; **neurolinguistics**
*Further reading:* Crystal, 1997a: ch. 46; Malmkjær, 1991: 16–20; O'Grądy *et al.*, 1996: ch. 10 [ch. 11 in the American edition].

**apparent time**   A technique for studying **language change** in progress. One way of studying language change in a community is to examine the speech of that community at intervals over several generations. But such *real-time* studies are often not practical, for obvious reasons.

An alternative is the use of *apparent time*. In this approach, we begin by assuming that individuals normally acquire their speech habits early in life and thereafter rarely change them. If this is so, then a comparison of the speech of elderly, middle-aged and younger speakers in a community will reveal any linguistic changes which are in progress: the younger the speakers, the more conspicuously their speech will be affected by any changes in progress.

Pioneered by the American linguist William Labov in the 1960s, apparent-time studies have proved to be a powerful tool in examining language change, even though it has been found that, in certain circumstances, older speakers actually *do* change their speech later in life.

*See:* **language change**; **quantitative approach**; **sociolinguistics**
*Further reading:* Labov, 1994: ch. 3.

**applied linguistics**   The application of the concepts and methods of **linguistics** to any of various practical problems involving language. The term *applied linguistics* is most often encountered in connection with foreign-language teaching. Linguistic concepts find a number of uses here, for example in *contrastive linguistics* – the systematic comparison of the sounds, the words and the grammatical systems of the mother tongue and the language being learned – with the intention of bringing out the important differences which need to be mastered.

But linguistics has also proved useful in a variety of other practical domains, such as mother-tongue teaching, **lexico-graphy**, translation, the teaching of reading, and the diagnosis and treatment of **language disability**. Today all these are understood as forming part of applied linguistics.

*Further reading:* Corder, 1975; Crystal, 1997a: chs. 18, 44, 46, 57, 61, 62; O'Grady *et al.*, 1996: ch. 13; Richards *et al.*, 1992.

**arbitrariness** The absence of any necessary connection between the form of a word and its meaning. Every language typically has a distinct word to denote every object, activity and concept its speakers want to talk about. Each such word must be formed in a valid manner according to the **phonology** of the language. But, in most cases, there is absolutely no reason why a given meaning should be denoted by one sequence of sounds rather than another. In practice, the particular sequence of sounds selected in a given language is completely arbitrary: anything will do, so long as speakers agree about it.

Speakers of different languages, of course, make different choices. A certain large snouted animal is called a *pig* in English, a *Schwein* in German, a *cochon* in French, a *cerdo* in Spanish, a *mochyn* in Welsh, a *txerri* in Basque, a *numbran* in Yimas (a language of New Guinea), and so on across the world. None of these names is more suitable than any other: each works fine as long as speakers are in agreement.

Such agreement need not be for all time. The animal was formerly called a *swine* in English, but this word has dropped out of use as a name for the animal and been replaced by *pig*.

Arbitrariness can be demonstrated the other way round. Many languages allow a word to have the phonetic form [min], but there is no earthly way of predicting the meaning of this word if it should exist. In English, [min] (spelled *mean*) exists and has several unrelated meanings: 'tight-fisted', 'cruel', 'average', 'signify'. French *mine* means '(coal) mine'; Welsh *min* is 'edge'; Irish *min* is 'meal'; Basque *min* is 'pain'; Arabic *min* is 'from'. There is nothing about this sequence of sounds that makes one meaning more likely than another.

It is the presence of such massive arbitrariness which makes impossible the **universal translator** beloved of science-fiction films. Because of arbitrariness, even the most powerful computer program can have no way of guessing the meaning of a word it has not encountered before.

On a more realistic scale, even if you have learned a couple of thousand words of Basque, if someone says to you 'Watch out! You might run into a *lupu* out there', where *lupu* is a word you don't know, you have no way of guessing what it might mean. In fact, it means 'scorpion' – but, in a now extinct variety of Basque, recorded in the sixteenth century, an identical word *lupu* meant 'wolf'.

Arbitrariness is pervasive in human languages (and also in **animal communication**), but there does nonetheless exist a certain amount of **iconicity**, cases in which the relation between form and meaning is not totally arbitrary.

Linguists have long realized the importance of arbitrariness, but it was particularly stressed by the Swiss linguist Ferdinand de Saussure in the early twentieth century, with his concept of the **linguistic sign**.

*See:* **design features**; **iconicity**; **linguistic sign**; **sound symbolism**

**argument**   Any one of the **noun phrases** required by a particular **verb**. Each verb require some number of noun phrases to accompany it in a sentence, if the result is to be grammatical; these NPs are its **arguments**, and the number of NPs required by a verb is the **valency** of that verb. For example, the simple intransitive verbs *smile* and *arrive* are **monovalent**, requiring only one argument, the subject, as in *Susie smiled*. (Note that *★Susie smiled Natalie* is ungrammatical; the asterisk marks this.) In contrast, a simple transitive verb like *kiss* or *slap* is **divalent**, requiring a subject and one object, as in *Susie kissed Natalie*. (Note that *\*Susie kissed* is ungrammatical.) But a ditransitive verb like *give* or *show* is **trivalent**, requiring a subject and two objects, as in *Susie gave Mike a present*. A given English verb usually requires between one and three arguments, but note the unusual behaviour of the verb *rain*, which neither requires nor permits any arguments at all, except for the 'dummy' subject it, as in *It's raining*. This verb arguably has a valency of zero.

In addition to its arguments, a verb very often permits some further phrases which are optional. These optional phrases are **adjuncts**, and adjuncts in English are most often expressed as **prepositional phrases** or as **adverbial phrases**. For example, the minimal sentence *Susie kissed Natalie* can be expanded with some optional adjuncts to yield *Susie kissed Natalie on the neck in the kitchen this morning* (there are three adjuncts here).

*See:* **complement**; **grammatical relation**; **transitivity**

**artificial language**   A language deliberately invented by a particular person. Since the seventeenth century, hundreds of artificial languages have been invented; some of them were no more than sketches, while others were provided with extensive grammars and large vocabularies. Only a handful of these have ever gained any use.

Many of the earlier attempts were made by philosophers, and these were often *a priori* in nature, meaning that they paid no attention to existing languages but were put together according to whatever principles seemed good to the inventors. More than a few were intended to be 'universal' or 'logical' languages and were based on some grand scheme for classifying all human knowledge. All were deeply impractical. Among the more notable attempts were those of the Frenchman Descartes, the Scot Dalgarno and the Englishman Wilkins.

Since the nineteenth century, artificial languages have more usually been *a posteriori*, that is, derived in some way from existing languages, and they have been constructed by linguists, logicians, priests, politicians, oculists and businessmen. The German philosopher Leibniz had much earlier proposed a kind of regularized Latin with only a small number of endings, and the French politician Faiguet had likewise sketched out a kind of regularized French, in both cases to no effect. In 1880 the German priest Schleyer published Volapük, an enormously awkward and complex mixture of bits of several European languages with cumbersome grammatical endings of his own devising; the result resembled a kind of demented Swedish, but it attracted hundreds of thousands of followers for a few years. Then in 1887 the Polish oculist Zamenhof published Esperanto, a much simpler language also stitched together from bits and pieces of several European languages, and this has ever since been the world's single most widely learned and used artificial language.

Esperanto still has a number of cumbersome features, and simplified versions called Ido, Esperantido, Espido, Esperantuisho and Modern Esperanto have been constructed, with minimal success. The Danish linguist Jespersen constructed a greatly modified offshoot called Novial, which attracted little interest. The Italian logician Peano invented Latino Sine Flexione, a kind of simplified and regularized Latin, and the American writer Hogben followed with Interglossa, essentially a version of classical Greek with no word-endings at all. A kind of regularized common Romance called Interlingua was constructed by a group of people and has found some limited use, especially for scientific purposes. A modified and expanded version of Interglossa now called Glosa has recently been published. And dozens of other twentieth-century projects have been put forward only to sink without trace.

Worthy of mention is Basic English, a stripped-down version of English employing only 850 words and published in 1930 by the British scholar C.K. Ogden; this was popular for a while, but it proved unworkable and has disappeared.

The fantasy writer J.R.R. Tolkien invented not one but several languages for his novel *The Lord of the Rings*, and he even provided some of them with histories, sound changes, family trees and writing systems. The linguist Marc Okrand was commissioned to invent a Klingon language for the *Star Trek* films, and there are now perhaps more Americans learning Klingon than learning most of the modern languages of Europe.

*See:* **language**; **natural language**
*Further reading:* Bodmer, 1944: ch. XI; Crystal, 1997a: ch. 58; Large, 1985; Malmkjær, 1991: 38–42.

**aspect** The **grammatical category** representing distinctions in the temporal structure of an event. Quite independently of its location in time, an event may be viewed as having any of a number of different temporal organizations: it may be seen as having internal structure or as consisting of an unanalysable whole; it may be seen as extending over a period of time or as occurring in a single moment; it may be seen as a single occurrence or as a series of repeated occurrences; it may be seen as beginning, continuing or ending. All these and others are types of *aspect*.

Compared to many other languages, English has a rather modest aspectual system, but aspect is still important in English. Here are some examples. The sentence *She smoked* illustrates *perfective* aspect (the event is viewed as an unanalysable whole); *She was smoking* shows *continuous* (or *progressive*) aspect (the event is viewed as extending over time); *She used to smoke* exhibits *habitual* aspect (the event is viewed as a customary or habitual one); *She kept smoking* illustrates *iterative* aspect (the action is viewed as a series of repeated events); *She started smoking* exhibits *inchoative* aspect (the event is viewed as just beginning); and *She quit smoking* exhibits *conclusive* aspect (the event is viewed as drawing to a close). The second, third and fourth of these all represent differing types of *imperfective* aspect (the action is viewed as having some kind of internal structure).

Some other languages display further aspectual forms, such as the **punctual** aspect (the event is viewed as occurring in a single moment); English has no special form for this, and we use our perfective form, as in *She sneezed*. But compare Basque, which distinguishes *Agertu zen* 'She appeared' (for a moment) from *Agertzen zen* 'She appeared' (over a period of time).

English has another distinctive form, the **perfect**, which has several functions but most typically expresses a state resulting from an earlier event. For example, the perfect form *She had finished the wine* most obviously means 'There was no wine then because she drank the last of it earlier.' The perfect is often classed as an aspect, although it is decidedly unusual among aspects. (Note that **perfective** and **perfect** have very different meanings; even some textbooks get these two confused.)

Aspect must be carefully distinguished from **tense**, even though the formal expression of the two categories is often deeply intertwined in languages. All of the English examples above are in the past tense, and all of them have corresponding non-past ('present') forms, except that the perfective *She smoked* and the habitual *She used to smoke* both have the same present-tense counterpart, *She smokes*, which most often has the habitual sense.

Certain types of aspect-like distinctions may be expressed by lexical means, rather than grammatically; an example is the contrast among English *nibble, eat, devour*. A distinction expressed in this way is often called an **Aktionsart** (plural **Aktionsarten**).

*See:* **grammatical category**; **tense**
*Further reading:* Comrie, 1976; Dahl, 1985.

**autonomy of language**    The view that the human **language faculty** is independent of general mental and cognitive abilities. A young child is obliged to spend years learning to make sense of the world it is born into, and at the same time it must learn its first language. For decades there has been a controversy, sometimes called the *nature–nurture debate* or the *content–process debate*, over whether children are born with a distinctive and largely independent faculty for learning language, or whether they simply acquire a language in the same way they acquire other kinds of understanding and skills, by using their general all-purpose cognitive abilities.

The first view – represented by such proposals as the **genetic hypothesis of language** and the **innateness hypothesis** – is probably supported by a majority of linguists; certainly by Noam Chomsky and his followers, but also by others who have limited sympathy for Chomsky's ideas. The second has been supported by a number of psychologists, notably by Jean Piaget and Jerome Bruner, and more recently by Elizabeth Bates and her colleagues.

The first view holds that children are born with specialized structures or areas in their brains which are dedicated to the learning and use of languages; Chomsky's version further holds that important information about the nature of human languages is already present at birth. The second view denies this, and sees language acquisition as not different in kind from, say, learning to judge size and distance; some versions go further and claim that learning a first language is not different from learning to ice skate or to drive a car.

This last, extreme, view can probably be disposed of: the abundant evidence for the **critical period hypothesis**, demonstrating that first-language acquisition is rapid in children but impossible in adults, surely demonstrates that learning a first language is very different from learning to ice skate. Otherwise, though, the debate is still very much alive.

Linguists like to support the first view by pointing to the evidence from **language disability**: some disabilities, such as the *Williams syndrome*, appear to leave the language faculties intact while severely damaging other mental faculties; others, such as *Specific Language Impairment*, chiefly affect only linguistic behaviour while leaving other mental faculties largely unscathed.

*See:* **critical period hypothesis**; **genetic hypothesis of language**; **innateness hypothesis**; **language disability**; **language faculty**; **modularity**

*Further reading:* Bates, 1976; Bates *et al.*, 1979; 1988; Jackendoff, 1993; Macwhinney and Bates, 1989; Pinker, 1994.

**auxiliary**   A specialized grammatical item, most often a **verb**, which serves to express any of several **grammatical categories**. The English auxiliaries are specialized verbs; they chiefly serve to express **aspect**, **voice** and **modality**, and they commonly also carry markers of **tense** and **agreement**.

The English auxiliary verbs possess several properties (the NICE properties) not shared by ordinary verbs.

- Negation: *She is coming; She isn't coming/She is not coming.* Compare *She smokes;* \**She smokesn't;* \**She smokes not* (the asterisk marks ungrammaticality).
- Inversion: *She is coming; Is she coming?* Compare *She smokes;* \**Smokes she?*
- Code: *Susie is coming, but Janet isn't.*
- Emphasis: *She is coming.*

The English auxiliaries are of two types. The ***primary*** (or ***non-modal***) ***auxiliaries*** are *be* and *have*. These resemble ordinary verbs (***main verbs***) in having a full set of inflected forms (*have, has, had, having*), and a primary auxiliary can be the only verb in a sentence: *She is British; She has brown eyes.* The ***modal auxiliaries*** have only one or two forms each; most of them come in pairs, which can to some extent be regarded as differing in tense: *can/could, will/would; shall/should; may/ might; must.* These lack the *-s* ending of the third-singular present: \**She cans speak French.*

The verbs *need, dare* and *ought* sometimes exhibit some (but not all) of the properties of modal auxiliaries; these are called the ***semi-modals***. Examples: *Need she come? She dare not do it, but she ought to.*

The verb *do* serves as a 'dummy' auxiliary, inserted to carry the auxiliary properties when no other auxiliary is present.

Examples: *She doesn't smoke*; *Does she smoke?*; *Janet doesn't smoke, but Susie does*; *She* does *smoke*.

In some other languages, such as Australian languages, the auxiliaries are not verbs at all, but an entirely distinct part of speech. Some linguists prefer to take the same view of the English auxiliaries.

*See:* **subcategorization**; **verb**
*Further reading:* Hurford, 1994: 20–23.

# B

**basic word order** The most typical order of elements in the sentences of a language. Almost every language shows a strong preference to put the words of a sentence into a particular order; this preferred order may be virtually rigid – with almost no departures allowed – or it may be little more than a statistical preference. This preference is the *basic word order* of the language.

A convenient and widely used way of characterizing basic word order is in terms of just three major elements: Subject, Object and Verb, or S, O and V. The basic word order of English, in these terms, is SVO: we normally say *The Turks love backgammon*, while *Backgammon the Turks love* is unusual, and other orders, such as *★Love the Turks backgammon* or *★Backgammon love the Turks* are impossible. SVO order is also typical of French, Swahili and Chinese, among others.

Other languages have different basic word orders. VSO is found in Irish and Welsh, SOV in Japanese, Turkish, Basque and Quechua, and VOS in Malagasy (in Madagascar). The Amazonian language Hixkaryana is OVS, and there are reports that another Amazonian language, Apurinã, may be OSV (this is not confirmed).

It appears that SOV order is the most frequent on the planet, followed closely by SVO and more distantly by VSO. VOS is decidedly uncommon, and OVS and OSV are, at best, very rare. No one knows if these observations represent important human preferences in grammatical structure or if they are merely historical accidents resulting from the survival and spread of some languages at the expense of others.

Basic word order is the basis of the single most famous **typology** of modern times.

*See:* **typology**
*Further reading:* Comrie, 1989: ch. 4; Whaley, 1997: chs. 5–6.


**behaviourism**   The view that psychology should invoke only observable and measurable phenomena. Early in the twentieth century, psychology had become somewhat obscurantist and even metaphysical. Behaviourism originated as a healthy reaction to this state of affairs: the early behaviourists wanted to sweep away what they saw as empty speculation and the endless postulation of undetectable concepts. They therefore resolved to deal with nothing except what could be directly observed and preferably measured. Along with their rejection of the excess baggage of earlier approaches, they often went so far as to reject such intangible concepts as 'emotions', 'intentions', 'purposes' and even 'minds'.

Behaviourism exercised great influence over the linguist Leonard Bloomfield and the *American structuralists* who followed him: they, too, preferred to concentrate on directly observable linguistic behaviour and to refrain from abstract theorizing.

In 1957 the American psychologist B.F. Skinner published *Verbal Behavior*, an attempt at interpreting **language acquisition** strictly in terms of behaviourism, and by far the most radical attempt ever at treating language in a behaviourist framework. Skinner's book was savagely (some would say unfairly) reviewed by the young Noam Chomsky, who argued vigorously that Skinner's approach not only explained nothing but could not possibly explain anything of interest.

Fair or not, Chomsky's review persuaded a whole generation of linguists that the essentially atheoretical behaviourist approach had nothing to offer linguistics. As a result, the linguists influenced by Chomsky abandoned behaviourism and embraced **mentalism** instead, and linguistics was eventually integrated into the emerging discipline of **cognitive science**.

More recent work on acquisition has reinforced Chomsky's arguments by demonstrating that first-language acquisition is clearly not, as Skinner had maintained, an essentially passive affair, but that young children actively construct their language as they go.

*See:* **language acquisition**; **language instinct**; **mentalism**
*Further reading:* Malmkjær, 1991: 53–57; Pinker, 1994: ch. 13; Trask, 1995: ch. 7.

**bilingualism**  The ability to speak two languages. In modern western society, the ability to speak two languages is often seen as something of a remarkable achievement, particularly in the English-speaking countries. However, over 70% of the earth's population are thought to be bilingual or *multilingual* (able to speak three or more languages), and there is good reason to believe that bilingualism or multilingualism has been the norm for most human beings at least for the last few millennia. There is evidence that children raised bilingually tend to be more expressive, more original and better communicators than children raised with only one language.

In New Guinea, in southeast Asia, in India, in the Caucasus, in the Amazon rain forest, people routinely learn two or three neighbouring languages as well as their own, and the same was true of Australia before the European settlement. Even today, many millions of Europeans are at least bilingual, speaking both their own mother tongue and the national language of the country they live in, and many of them can additionally speak a *global language* or *world language* like English or French.

Bilingualism can be the property of an individual, but equally it can be the property of an entire speech community in which two or more languages are routinely used. The existence of bilingual and multilingual societies raises a number of important social, political and educational issues.

In what languages should education be delivered, and at what levels? What languages should be accepted for publication and broadcasting? In what languages should laws be written, and what languages should be accepted in court proceedings? Differences of opinion may lead to *language conflict*, as speakers jostle for the right to use their own mother tongues in the widest possible domain, possibly to the exclusion of other languages.

It is also possible for an individual to speak two different **dialects** of a single language – for example, her own regional dialect and the **standard language**. In this case, we speak of *bidialectalism*.

*See:* **code-switching**; **diglossia**; **immigrant language**; **minority language**

*Further reading:* Bonvillain, 1993: chs. 11, 12; Crystal, 1997a: ch. 60; Edwards, 1994; Malmkjær, 1991: 57–65; Romaine, 1995; Steinberg, 1993: ch. 12.


**bioprogram hypothesis**    The hypothesis that human beings are born with a 'default' structure for language built into their brains. Human languages differ rather substantially in their grammatical structures (for example, in their **basic word order**). However, **creoles** all over the world appear to be strikingly similar in their grammar: all creoles look pretty much alike, regardless of where they came into existence or of which languages provided most of the input into them.

The British-born American linguist Derek Bickerton has proposed an explanation for this observation. Since creoles are newly created languages, built out of the grammarless **pidgins** which preceded them, and since the children who create a creole are obliged to build its grammar for themselves, Bickerton argues that there must be some kind of innate machinery which determines the nature of that grammar. He calls this machinery the *bioprogram*, and he sees the bioprogram as an innate default structure for language which is always implemented by children unless they find themselves learning an adult language with a different structure, in which case they learn that instead.

The bioprogram hypothesis therefore represents a rather specific and distinctive version of the **innateness hypothesis**. It has attracted a great deal of attention, but it remains deeply controversial.

*See:* **genetic hypothesis of language**; **innateness hypothesis**
*Further reading:* Bickerton, 1981; 1984.


**Black English**   The distinctive varieties of English used by many native speakers of African or Caribbean origin. Several important English-speaking countries have sizeable populations of black people whose ancestry lies largely in Africa or the Caribbean; most prominent here are Britain and the USA. For various historical reasons, the majority of British and American blacks speak varieties of English which are quite distinctive, differing from other varieties in vocabulary, pronunciation, grammar and modes of discourse.

These varieties, which we may generically label *Black English*, have sometimes been given more particular names, such as *Black English Vernacular* (BEV) in the USA and *Black British English* (BBE) in Britain. Like any varieties of any language, these black varieties of English exhibit characteristics which are often of considerable linguistic interest: for example, many black varieties have highly distinctive verbal systems which make distinctions unknown in other types of English. It is possible that some of these features may continue characteristics of the **creoles** once used by the ancestors of the present-day speakers, and a few may even continue features present in the mother tongues of Africans sold into slavery long ago.

But the primary reasons for the recent interest in black varieties are not linguistic, but rather social, political and educational. Like speakers of other distinctive varieties, speakers of Black English often regard their mother tongue as a badge of identity and a matter of pride: abandoning it may be seen as an act of betrayal. At the same time, just as with other groups, failure to acquire a command of standard English is a serious obstacle to making a career in all but a few professions, and Black English itself may be strongly stigmatized among white speakers.

Consequently, politicians, academics, teachers and school administrators, both black and white, are faced with some difficult questions of how to regard Black English. Some people advocate the extreme position of recognizing and teaching only standard English and of attempting to stamp out Black English. Most linguists, and some others, would see this stance as unworkable and destructive, and would advocate the encouragement of *bidialectalism*: competence in both Black English and standard English.

Recently, however, a number of influential commentators, particularly in the USA, have been vigorously advocating another extreme position: Black English, now renamed *Ebonics*, should be recognized not only as the equal of standard English but even as a totally separate language, and it should be the language of instruction in schools and even a school subject itself, a policy already adopted (though perhaps only briefly) by at least one American school board.

Naturally, such proposals have generated a furious controversy, one which is still raging today, and no resolution is in sight.

*Further reading:* Holmes, 1992: 193–199.

**caregiver speech**   The distinctive style of speech used in addressing young children. Adults looking after very young children, and above all mothers doing this, typically talk to those children using a highly distinctive type of language. They use special words like *choo-choo*, including many diminutives like *horsie* and *doggie*; they confine themselves to the simplest grammatical forms and constructions; they use exaggerated intonation patterns; they frequently repeat themselves; and they often expand the child's utterances into longer adult utterances by responding, for example, to the child's 'Daddy sock' with 'Yes, Daddy is putting his socks on'.

This special type of speech is popularly known as 'baby-talk', but this term is never used in linguistics; instead, it is variously known as *caregiver speech*, *caretaker speech* or *motherese*. Linguists are still debating the importance of caregiver speech in allowing acquisition to occur.

*Further reading:* Aitchison, 1989: 148–152.

**case**   The **grammatical category** by which the form of a **noun phrase** varies for grammatical or semantic reasons. Not all languages have case, but quite a few do. Consider Basque. The Basque noun phrase *etxea* 'the house' has a number of different case-forms; here are a some of them:

| Name | Form | Function |
|------|------|----------|
| Absolutive | *etxea* | intransitive subject; direct object |
| Ergative | *etxeak* | transitive subject |
| Dative | *etxeari* | 'to the house' (abstract relation) |
| Genitive | *etxearen* | 'of the house' (possessor) |
| Instrumental | *etxeaz* | 'by means of the house' |
| Comitative | *etxearekin* | 'with the house' |
| Locative | *etxean* | 'in the house' (location) |
| Ablative | *etxetik* | 'from/out of the house' |
| Allative | *etxera* | 'to the house' (motion) |

A case-language must have at least two case-forms; most have three to six distinct cases, and some, like Basque and Finnish, have a dozen or more.

English has case only marginally, in that a few **pronouns** make case distinctions for grammatical purposes, such as *I/me* and *she/her*. *I saw her*, but *She saw me*.

In the **Government-and-Binding Theory**, the idea of case has been generalized and made abstract, and an (abstract) *Case* (with a capital letter) is assumed to belong to every noun phrase in every grammatical sentence.

*Further reading:* B. Blake, 1994; Hurford, 1994: 25–28.

**clause**  The largest grammatical unit smaller than a **sentence**. The *clause* is a traditional and fundamental unit of sentence structure, though the term is not used by all grammarians in exactly the same way.

Traditionally, a clause is a grammatical unit consisting of a subject and a predicate, and every sentence must consist of one or more clauses. In the following examples, each clause is marked off by brackets. A *simple sentence* consists only of a single clause: [*Susie has bought a skirt*]. A **compound sentence** consists of two or more clauses of equal rank, usually joined by a connecting word like *and*, *or* or *but*: [*Susie wants children*], but [*her career won't allow them*]. A **complex sentence** consists of two or more clauses of which one outranks the others, which are subordinated to it: [*After she got her promotion*], [*Susie bought a new house*].

A clause which is the highest-ranking, or only, clause in its sentence is a *main clause*; a clause which is subordinated to another is a *subordinate clause*. Traditional grammarians usually regarded a subordinate clause as entirely separate from the higher-ranking clause it is attached to, but today linguists normally regard a subordinate clause as forming a part of its higher clause, and the examples below show this.

There are several types of subordinate clause. An *adverbial clause* is related to its higher clause like an **adverb**: [*Susie develops a rash* [*whenever she eats strawberries*]]. A *complement clause* is attached to a preceding word (usually a verb or a noun) and 'completes' the sense of that word: [*Susie has decided* [*that she will look for a new job*]]; [*The rumour* [*that Susie is quitting*] *is not true*]. An *embedded question* is a question buried in a larger sentence: [*Susie has not decided* [*what she is going to do*]]. A *relative clause* modifies a noun: [*The skirt* [*that Susie bought*] *is too short*].

Recently some grammarians have been extending the term *clause* to every unit containing a **verb**, including many units traditionally regarded only as **phrases**. Examples: [*Susie's heavy smoking*] *is affecting her health*; *Susie wants* [*to buy a new car*]; [*Having finished her dinner*], *Susie reached for her cigarettes*. This extended usage is not standard, but it is now very widespread, and you may find that your syntax teacher prefers it.

*See:* **phrase**; **sentence**; **subordination**
*Further reading:* Collins Cobuild, 1990: ch. 8; Crystal, 1996: units 8–14; Hurford, 1994: 28–30.

**code-switching** Changing back and forth between two language varieties, especially in a single conversation. Sociolinguists use the term *code* to denote any identifiable speech variety, including both a particular language and a particular variety of a language. Many speakers have control over at least two varieties of their language (for example, a German-speaker may speak both his local variety of German and standard German), and many more have control over two languages (for example, Welsh/English bilinguals in Wales). Such speakers will shift back and forth between these varieties, depending on such factors as who they are talking to, where they are, and what they are talking about. This is *code-switching*.

Very often, code-switching occurs within a single conversation. Spanish-speakers in the USA and Gujarati-speakers in Britain may switch back and forth repeatedly during a single conversation, sometimes even changing languages in the middle of a sentence. Sociolinguists are interested in trying to identify the factors that determine the choice of language variety at a given point during an exchange.

*See:* **bilingualism**
*Further reading:* Crystal, 1997a: ch. 60; Holmes, 1992: 41–53; Romaine, 1994: 55–64.


**cognitive linguistics**   An approach to the study of language which is based upon human perception and conceptualization of the world. During the twentieth century the most influential approach to the study of language has been **structuralism**: linguists have largely devoted themselves to the purely structural aspects of language systems themselves, such as sound systems and grammatical systems. A key feature of structuralism is that it concentrates on the internal structure of a language, and not on the way in which the language relates to the non-linguistic world.

Naturally, links between languages and the world have not been neglected, and **anthropological linguistics** in particular has been devoted to studying links between language and culture. Since about 1980, however, a growing number of linguists have been devoting serious attention to a more ambitious project: the elucidation of the ways in which linguistic objects and structures reflect the manner in which human beings perceive, categorize and conceptualize the world. To this new enterprise we give the name *cognitive linguistics*.

Among the early contributors to the cognitive approach was the American theoretical linguist George Lakoff, who has written extensively on the importance of **metaphor** in shaping languages. More recently, a number of people with diverse backgrounds have been attempting to analyse linguistic structures in terms of conceptual and perceptual categories like *figure and ground*, *landmark and trajector* (something which moves), location in space, events and states, *frames and scripts* (mental models of real-world objects and events), and categories and hierarchies. The American linguist Ronald Langacker has even gone so far as to try to construct a theory of grammar, called *cognitive grammar*, on the basis of such notions.

Cognitive linguistics is still in its infancy, but it looks set to become an increasingly important part of the discipline.

*See:* **metaphor**
*Further reading:* Lakoff, 1987; Lakoff and Johnson, 1980; Langacker, 1987/91; 1990; G. Palmer, 1996; Ungerer and Schmid, 1996.

**cognitive science** The science of the mind. Until recently, few scientists believed we could seriously undertake a study of the human mind, and the topic was largely the preserve of philosophers. In the last few years, however, various strands of investigation have come together from linguistics, psychology, philosophy, computer science and artificial intelligence, and the result has been the emergence of the new interdisciplinary field of *cognitive science*. The goal of cognitive science is to understand the structure and functioning of the human mind, and to this end it uses a variety of approaches, from philosophical debate through the study of **language acquisition** to computer modelling of vision. A recurring theme in the field is the **modularity** of mind, the idea that the mind is not a seamless whole but rather a collection of more or less specialized components with strong interconnections among them.

Cognitive science is largely a creation of the second half of the twentieth century, but its origins cannot be pinned down with any precision. Today, though, it is a recognized discipline, and both university courses and textbooks exist in some numbers.

*See:* **mentalism**; **modularity**
*Further reading:* Hofstadter, 1979; Johnson–Laird, 1983; 1993; Stillings *et al.*, 1987.

**coherence** The degree to which a piece of **discourse** 'makes sense'. When you attempt to understand a connected piece of speech or writing, your degree of success will depend upon several factors. Some of these, such as your general knowledge of the subject matter, are obvious and of no linguistic interest. But a factor of considerable interest and importance is the *coherence* of the discourse, its underlying structure, organization and connectedness. A *coherent* discourse has a high degree of such connectedness; an *incoherent* discourse does not, and is accordingly hard to follow.

The notion of coherence is important within the various approaches to language called **functionalism**, and particularly within **Systemic Linguistics**. Some types of connectedness are provided very explicitly by overt linguistic devices like **anaphors**; these are singled out for special attention as **cohesion**. But there are also more general devices for providing structure which are not explicitly grammatical in nature, and these other devices are examined under the rubric of *coherence*.

Here is a simple example, taken from a newspaper article: *After ten years of standardization, there should be a healthy UK market for used models. Curiously, there seems to be only one big second-hand PC dealer in London.* The point of interest here is the word *curiously*, whose function is to relate the following sentence to the preceding one in a manner that is immediately obvious to the reader: given the content of the first sentence, the assertion made by the second one should seem surprising.

The skilful use of such connections has, of course, been recognized for a long time as an essential part of good speaking and writing. But now linguists are increasingly turning their

39

attention to the explicit analysis of these connective devices. The term itself was introduced by the British linguist Michael Halliday, who has been particularly prominent in investigating coherence within Halliday's **Systemic Linguistics**.

*See:* **cohesion; Systemic Linguistics; text**
*Further reading:* Thompson, 1996: ch. 7.

**cohesion**   The presence in a **discourse** of explicit linguistic links which provide structure. Quite apart from the more general kinds of devices for providing structure to a discourse or **text**, which belong to the domain of **coherence**, there are some very explicit linguistic devices, often of a grammatical nature, which serve to provide connectedness and structure. Among these devices are **anaphors** like *she, they, this* and *one another*, temporal connectives like *after* and *while*, and logical connectives like *but* and *therefore*. Every one of these items serves to provide some kind of specific link between two other smaller or larger pieces of discourse.

Consider a pair of examples. In the first, the cohesion has gone wrong: *The Egyptians and the Assyrians were carrying standards some 5,000 years ago. They were poles topped with metal figures of animals or gods.* Here the reader naturally takes *they* as referring to *the Egyptians and the Assyrians*, and is flummoxed by the continuation. The second version is different: *Some 5,000 years ago, the Egyptians and the Assyrians were carrying standards. These were poles topped with metal figures of animals or gods.* This time the item *these* immediately makes it clear that it is the standards which are being referred to, and the continuation is smooth and effortless.

Naturally, the proper use of cohesive devices has long been recognized as a fundamental aspect of good writing, but in recent years linguists have been turning their attention to the analysis of these devices. The term *cohesion* was coined by the British linguist Michael Halliday, and the study of cohesion is especially prominent within Halliday's **Systemic Linguistics**, but it is also now a familiar part of most linguistic analyses of texts and discourses.

*See:* **coherence**; **Systemic Linguistics**; **text**
*Further reading:* Halliday, 1994: ch. 9; Halliday and Hasan, 1976; Thompson, 1996: ch. 7.


**colloquial speech**   Ordinary, relaxed, informal speech. Most of us have some control over the kind of language appropriate in formal circumstances: writing essays, giving lectures, being interviewed for a job, and so on. But all of us fall back on a more informal variety of our language when we are completely relaxed and unselfconscious. In English, we make liberal use of contractions like *I've* and *she'd've*; we use connecting words and phrases like *yeah* and *y'know*; we use abbreviated utterances like *Sounds good*; we use many words and expressions we would avoid in formal contexts, such as *Beats me* instead of *I don't know* and *Gotta pee* instead of *Would you excuse me for a minute?*; we may use swear words with some freedom; and so on. This is *colloquial speech*, and it is important to realize that *every* normal speaker uses it when it is appropriate. Using nothing but formal speech in all circumstances would be highly abnormal, virtually pathological.

The linguists of the past often concentrated their attention upon the more formal varieties of language, but today's linguists are more likely to consider colloquial speech to be the primary object of study, or at least as no less important than formal speech or writing.

Colloquial speech is not the same thing as **slang**: many people, when speaking colloquially, make liberal use of slang, while others use little or no slang: in colloquial speech, slang is admissible but not obligatory.

*See:* **slang**; **vernacular**


**communicative competence**   The ability to use language appropriately in social situations. In order to speak a language successfully, you need to have purely *linguistic competence* in that language: mastery of pronunciation, of grammar and of vocabulary. But you need more than that: you also need *sociolinguistic competence*, knowledge of such things as how to begin and end conversations, how and when to be polite, and how to address people. In addition, you further need *strategic competence*, knowledge of how to organize a piece of speech in an effective manner and how to spot and compensate for any misunderstandings or other difficulties.

Depending on who is using it, the term *communicative competence* refers (more usually) to the last two of these or (less usually) to all three together. The concept and the term were introduced, in the narrower sense, by the American linguist Dell Hymes in the 1970s. Hymes was dismayed by what he saw as the excessively narrow concern of many linguists with nothing but internal linguistic structure, at the expense of communication, and he wished to draw attention to the importance of *appropriateness* of language use.

Today linguists of a theoretical orientation still prefer to focus on the purely structural aspects of language, but those with an interest in **anthropological linguistics**, in **functionalism**, in **language in use**, in language teaching, or in communication generally typically attach great importance to the examination and elucidation of communicative competence.

*See:* **ethnography of speaking**
*Further reading:* Bonvillain, 1993: ch. 10; W.A. Foley, 1997: part V.


**comparative reconstruction** The principal method used to find information about an unattested language which is the ancestor of several known languages. Every living language changes over time, but it does not change everywhere in the same way. A language spoken over a sizeable area may therefore break up, first into regional **dialects**, and eventually into several quite diverse daughter languages. When we find several languages, either spoken today or abundantly recorded in written texts, which clearly share a common ancestor, we have ways of working backwards to figure out what that unrecorded ancestor was like. Chief among these is *comparative reconstruction*, or the *comparative method*.

The comparative method deals with the phonological forms of words, and its successful use in a given case depends upon the correctness of three assumptions. First, we assume that a significant proportion of the words of the ancestral language still survive in the recorded daughter languages. Second, we assume that those surviving words in most cases have not changed their meanings too dramatically. Third, we assume that phonological change (change in the pronunciations of those words) is generally *regular* – that is, that a given sound in a given environment has consistently changed in exactly the same way in a single daughter language. Only when these three assumptions are substantially correct can we apply the comparative method.

Below is a modest example, showing the words for certain meanings in four European languages for which we have excellent reasons for believing that they share a common ancestor.

| English | Latin | Greek | Irish |
|---------|-------|-------|-------|
| fish | piscis | ikhthys | iasg |
| father | pater | pater | athair |
| foot | ped– | pod– | troigh |
| for | pro | para | do |
| six | sex | hexa | se |
| seven | septem | hepta | seacht |
| sweet | suavis | hedys | milis |
| salt | sal | hal | salann |
| new | novus | neos | nua |
| night | noct– | nykt– | (in)nocht 'tonight' |
| nine | novem | (en)nea | naoi |

The key point here is the **systematic correspondences** which we can see in many cases. For the first set, we observe that a native English word beginning with /f-/ is matched by a Latin word beginning with /p-/ and a Greek word beginning with /p-/. The Irish case is a little more difficult, but examination of further data reveals that the usual Irish correspondence here is zero: no initial consonant at all, as in the words for 'fish' and 'father'. The reason that the Irish words for 'foot' and 'for', and also the Greek word for 'fish', do not match is that the ancestral words for these senses have been replaced in these cases by different words. (Remember our first assumption: not too many ancestral words have been lost and replaced.)

Likewise, in the second set, we find initial /s-/ consistently in all the languages except Greek, where instead we find initial /h-/ with equal consistency. Again, the word for 'sweet' has been lost and replaced in Irish.

The third set exhibits initial /n-/ in all four languages, though the Greek word for 'nine' has acquired a prefix absent elsewhere. The Irish word for 'night' does not fit, but the Irish word for 'tonight' does fit, and we may reasonably assume that the word for 'tonight' contains an earlier word for 'night', now itself lost and replaced. (Recall our second assumption: we can tolerate a certain amount of change in meaning, but not too much.)

Now the explanation for these correspondences resides crucially in our third assumption: change in pronunciation has mostly been *regular* in all four languages. So, we conclude, the words in the first group all began with the same sound in the ancestral language, and that sound has developed regularly into /f-/ in English, into /p-/ in Latin and Greek, and into zero in Irish. Similarly, all the words in the second group began with a *different* same initial sound in the ancestral language, one which has regularly developed into /h-/ in Greek but into /s-/ in all the others. And all the words in the third group began with yet another same sound in the ancestral language, one which has developed into /n-/ in all four languages.

It remains only to decide what the ancestral sounds were in each case, and this is the central step in comparative reconstruction. By examining all the available evidence, and by knowing what kinds of phonological changes are frequent and natural in languages, specialists have determined that, in the ancestral language, all the words in the first group originally began with */p-/, those in the second with */s-/, and those in the third with */n-/. (The asterisk denotes a reconstructed sound.) The original */p-/ has changed to /f-/ in English and been lost in Irish, and the original */s-/ has changed to /h-/ in Greek, all of these being changes which are frequent in languages and easy to understand. Apart from these cases, the three ancestral sounds, in initial position, have remained unchanged in all four languages.

Of course, we do not apply the comparative method only to word-initial sounds: we must figure out, as far as possible, what the entire words looked like in the ancestral language, but here we lack the space to consider this. However, specialists have managed to determine that the forms of these words in the ancestral language were approximately as follows (endings omitted): *pisk-, *pəter, *ped-, *per, *sweks, *septm, *swad-, *sal-, *newo-, *nekwt- and *newn. The change in pronunciation in each of the four daughter languages has been largely regular, though naturally with a few complications here and there. And the unrecorded ancestral language in this case, of course, is **Proto-Indo-European**, the ancestor of the **Indo-European** family, to which all four languages belong.

The comparative method consists of the entire business of deciding that certain languages probably share a common ancestor, identifying systematic correspondences, and working backwards to identify the forms of the words in the ancestral language, and this method is the cornerstone of work in **historical linguistics**. If we can't find systematic correspondences, then we can't do comparative reconstruction, and any miscellaneous resemblances that we come across are very likely only the result of chance, or perhaps even of ancient **language contact**.

*See:* **internal reconstruction; reconstruction; systematic correspondence**

*Further reading:* Trask, 1996: ch. 8.

45

**competence**  Our ability to use language, viewed in the abstract. When we use our language, we commit all sorts of errors. We make slips of the tongue, we sometimes can't think of a word or name we know perfectly well, we interrupt ourselves, we mishear or misunderstand what others are saying, we may even lose the thread of what we ourselves are saying, there are limits upon our memories, and so on.

In the early 1960s, the American linguist Noam Chomsky began arguing that such errors should be dismissed from consideration in examining our ability to use language. Chomsky argued that every one of us possesses an abstract linguistic *competence* which is independent of the errors we sometimes make, and he argued further that the elucidation of this competence was, or should be, the principal business of linguistic theory. The errors he relegated to the quite different domain of **performance**, which he considered to be the proper subject-matter of a quite different discipline, having more to do with the study of the behaviour of nerves and muscles than with the study of language *per se*.

Chomsky's position here has been enormously influential in linguistics, and it has formed the basis of his research programme, dedicated to the identification of the highly abstract principles which he sees as making up our competence. Interestingly, Chomsky's distinction is strikingly reminiscent of the distinction between *langue* and *parole* introduced generations earlier by the Swiss linguist Ferdinand de Saussure, though not quite identical to it. Nevertheless, there are critics who see Chomsky's conception of competence as far too abstract, and who are inclined to doubt whether such a sharp line should or can be drawn between our ability to use language and our actual behaviour.

*See:* **langue**; **language faculty**; **performance**; **universal grammar**

*Further reading:* Harris, 1993: 96–100; Newmeyer, 1983: 35–38; Matthews, 1979: 31–40.

**complement** A grammatical unit which contains a **verb** and which forms part of a larger unit. The term *complement* has in fact been used by linguists in a variety of senses, but it is most commonly applied to a grammatical unit which contains a verb and which, in some sense, *completes* a larger grammatical unit which begins with some other words (this 'completing' is the reason it is called a *complement*).

Consider the sentence *The rumour that John is a Chinese spy amuses me*. Here everything before *amuses* is a single **noun phrase**, the subject of the sentence, and it contains a *noun-complement clause*, which is *that John is a Chinese spy*; this is attached to the noun *rumour*, and it completes the subject noun phrase.

Slightly different are *Susie told me that she would come* and *I don't know whether she's coming*, in which *that she would come* and *whether she's coming* are **verb-complement clauses** attached to the verbs *told* and *know*, respectively.

The items *that* and *whether*, which introduce complement clauses, are assigned to a **part of speech** called *complementizers*. (Traditional grammarians called them **conjunctions**, but we no longer do so.)

The complements illustrated above are all **finite**. But we also have non-finite complements: the sentence *Susie wants to buy a car* contains the **non-finite** complement *to buy a car*, which is attached to the verb *wants*. Note, however, the big difference between *Susie wants to earn some extra money*, in which *to earn some extra money* is a **direct complement** attached to *wants*, and *Susie moonlights to earn some extra money*, in which *to earn some extra money* is a **purpose complement**; the second, but not the first, is equivalent to *in order to earn some extra money*.

The term *complement* is also applied to a variety of other things which appear to 'complete' a sentence in some sense. For example, in *Susie is considered clever*, the item *clever* is sometimes called a **subject-complement** (it applies to *Susie*, the subject of the sentence), and, in *Susie finds Mike tiresome*, the item *tiresome* is sometimes called an **object-complement** (it applies to *Mike*, the object of the verb).

See: **argument**
*Further reading:* Greenbaum and Quirk, 1990: ch. 16; Hurford, 1994: 33–41.

**componential analysis** A certain technique for analysing the meanings of words.⋆ The central idea of *componential analysis* (CA) is that the meaning of a word can be usefully broken up into a small number of **semantic components** (or **semantic features**), each with a **value** (plus for present, minus for absent, sometimes also zero for irrelevant). The technique is most useful for highlighting the similarities and differences in meaning between a number of words of related meaning.

For example, we might analyse *stallion* as [+ horse, − female, + adult], *mare* as [+ horse, + female, + adult], *colt* as [+ horse, − female, − adult], *filly* as [+ horse, + female, − adult]. The residue represented by [+ horse] does not lend itself to CA, and hence words for non-horses cannot readily be brought into the same description, except to show parallelism, as with *bull, cow, heifer, bullock.*

CA may be useful in identifying the existence of **lexical gaps**. The feature complex [+ horse, − adult] is possibly represented by *foal*, but English has no everyday word for [+ horse, + adult] or [+ horse, − female].

See: **meaning**; **semantics**; **sense relation**
*Further reading:* Leech, 1974: ch. 6; Malmkjær, 1991: 395–398; Nida, 1975.

**computational linguistics** The use of computers to perform various tasks involving language. The introduction of digital computers has made possible a number of approaches to descriptive and practical problems of language which could not previously be addressed adequately or at all.

One obvious use of computers is to store a **corpus** of spoken or written texts. Such a machine-readable corpus can be rapidly searched and interrogated in order to obtain such information as the frequency of occurrence of certain words, forms or constructions. In this way we can obtain hard data about real language use which would not otherwise be accessible, and we can further make comparisons between, say, spoken and written English, or between American and British English.

Another use of computers is the preparation of *concordances*. A concordance is an orderly list of every occurrence of every individual word found in some body of writing (say, the works of Shakespeare), and it allows scholars a quick way of locating all the passages pertaining to the topics they are interested in.

A combination of these two approaches is sometimes valuable in identifying the author of a disputed text: individual writers have a tendency to use certain words and forms more frequently than others, and a statistical examination of a disputed text may reveal clearly that it matches the known style of one author but not of another.

Yet another application lies in *machine translation* – the development of computer programs which can take a text written in one language and convert it into a different language. At present, all such programs require that their output should be edited by a human being, but they can still save a great deal of time and drudgery.

Computers can also perform *speech synthesis*: converting written input into an intelligible imitation of human speech. This technique has several applications, for example in providing a 'voice' to a disabled person who cannot speak.

One more increasingly important application is *computer-assisted language learning* (CALL), in which a student learns a foreign language largely by interacting with a computer program which sets tasks, assigns scores, and adjusts its behaviour according to the level of successs being achieved by the student.

These days, however, by far the largest amount of work in computational linguistics is devoted to **natural-language processing**, the construction of programs which can accept typed input (and sometimes also speech), interpret it, and respond appropriately. This area provides the principal contribution of linguistics to the creation of *artificial intelligence*.

*See:* **corpus**; **natural-language processing**
*Further reading:* Crystal, 1997a: 416–418; Malmkjær, 1991: 28–38; O'Grady *et al.*, 1996: ch. 17.

**conjunction**   The **part of speech** which includes words like *and* and *or*. Today the label *conjunction* is normally only applied to a very small group of words, chiefly *and* and *or*, which were traditionally called the *coordinating conjunctions*. Most usually, a conjunction *conjoins* (joins) two or more instances of the same category. Examples: *Would you like a doughnut or a piece of pie?* (conjoined noun phrases); *Susie sipped her drink, lit a cigarette and opened her book* (conjoined verb phrases).

Traditional grammarians also included among the conjunctions another group of words, the *subordinating conjunctions* or *subordinators*. These are the words like *if*, *whenever*, *although* and *after*, which introduce adverbial clauses. Examples: *After she finished her essay, she headed for a shower; If she arrives in time, she can come with us.* But these words behave very differently from the true conjunctions, and today they are normally placed in a class by themselves.

Traditional grammarians also counted as conjunctions the *complementizers* like *that* and *whether*, as in *She said that she would come* and *I don't know whether she's coming.* But these words behave diffeently again, and today they are placed by themselves in yet a third class.

*See:* **coordinate structure**
*Further reading:* Collins Cobuild, 1990: 373–383; Crystal, 1996: units 64, 66; Hurford, 1994: 46–50.

**connotation** A non-central word meaning acquired through frequent associations. The word *rugby* has as its central sense a particular type of football game, but, depending on your experience of rugby, it may also conjure up in your mind such associations as 'large men', 'manliness', 'boorish and bawdy behaviour', or 'public schools' (that is, expensive and prestigious private schools); it may remind you of your pride in your local or national team, or it may remind you of a present or former boyfriend. All these associations are part of the *connotation* of the word.

Apart from purely grammatical words like *of* and strictly technical terms like *thermoluminescence*, almost all words carry connotations for us, and, as you can see, these connotations may vary substantially from person to person. Particularly emotive words like *foxhunting, lesbian, multinational* and even *vegetarian* may produce connotations for different people which are almost wildly different. For some words, such as *pornography*, the connotations may be so overwhelming that an agreed central sense of the term may be almost impossible to identify.

Most words, though, are less dramatic in their behaviour. Probably all of us agree at least roughly about the connotations of *bunny* as opposed to those of *rabbit*. Nevertheless, even a simple word like *cat* can have very different connotations for old Mrs Simpson, who has a house full of cats, and for Trevor, who can't stand the creatures and is moreover allergic to them.

*See:* **denotation**; **meaning**

**consonant** A **speech sound** produced by significantly obstructing the flow of air through the **vocal tract**. All speech sounds are produced by manipulating the vocal tract while air is flowing through it. If this manipulation does not produce any significant obstruction of the airstream, the result is a **vowel**; if it does produce obstruction, the result is a *consonant*.

Consonants are classified into several types, differing in the kind of obstruction involved. If the vocal tract is blocked completely, and then the closure is released suddenly, the result is a *plosive*, like [p] or [d]. If the vocal tract is blocked completely and the closure is released slowly, producing friction noise, the result is an *affricate*, like [ts] or [ʧ]. If the vocal tract is not completely blocked, but is reduced instead at some point to a tiny opening through which the air is forced, producing friction noise, the result is a *fricative*, like [f] or [z]. These three types together are *obstruents*; all other consonants are *resonants*.

If a complete closure is made in the mouth, but the velum is lowered so that air can flow out freely through the nose, the result is a *nasal*, like [m] or [n]. If a complete closure is made along the centre-line of the vocal tract, but space is left for the air to flow out along one or both sides, the result is a *lateral*, like [l]. If a speech organ is 'flicked' rapidly against another one, touching it briefly and then returning immediately to its starting point, the result is a *tap*, like the sound [ɾ] in Spanish *pero* 'but'. If a similar flicking movement is made, but the moving organ ends up in a different place from where it started, the result is a *flap*, as in the unusual kind of /r/-sound found in some languages of India. (Many books, especially in the USA, do not distinguish between taps and flaps, but it seems helpful to do so.) If a small opening is made in such a way that air forced through the opening causes some organ to vibrate vigorously, the result is a *trill*, as in the [r]-sound of Spanish *perro* 'dog'.

There is one more class of consonants, but these do not really fit our definition. The [j]-sound at the beginning of English *yes*, the [w]-sound in *wet*, and most of the several different sounds used by English-speakers to pronounce the /r/ of *red* are all strictly vowels by the definition, since they involve no significant obstruction. But the point is that these sounds *behave* like consonants in English and other languages, in spite of their vowel-like nature, and hence they are commonly regarded as a distinct group of consonants, the *approximants*. See the remarks under **vowel** for an explanation.

*See:* **speech sound**; **vowel**
*Further reading:* Ashby, 1995: ch. 7; Ladefoged, 1993: ch. 3.


**constituent structure** A type of hierarchical grammatical structure in a sentence. Consider the sentence *The little girl washed her doll.* In the view of most linguists, this consists of two pieces, or grammatical units: *the little girl* and *washed her doll.* The first of these in turn consists of *the* plus *little girl*, and this last consists of *little* plus *girl.* The second likewise consists of *washed* plus *her doll*; of these, the first consists of *wash* plus *-ed* and the second of *her* plus *doll.*

This is the sort of grammatical (syntactic) structure exhibited by all sentences in English and in most other languages, and we call it *constituent structure*. Constituent structure is hierarchical: a sentence consists of a couple of large pieces, each of which consists of some smaller pieces, each of which in turn consists of some still smaller pieces, and so on, until we reach the smallest pieces of all, the **words** or **morphemes**. And every one of these pieces is a *constituent* of the sentence. Moreover, every constituent must belong to some particular **syntactic category**: that is, the grammar of English (or of any language) allows only constituents belonging to certain categories to be combined into certain larger categories. An attempt at using a constituent of the wrong category produces an ungrammatical result, as in *★The under the bed washed her doll* (the asterisk marks ungrammaticality).

Sentence structure, or **syntax**, is thus a very orderly affair: every grammatical sentence is built up from smaller constituents combined into larger constituents, according to certain rigid **rules**, the rules of grammar for that particular language. The resulting structure of a sentence can be revealingly exhibited by a **tree**.

Oddly, some languages, including many Australian languages, seem not to have this sort of sentence structure; instead, they exhibit a much looser type of structure in which smaller units do not have to be combined into larger ones in such an orderly way. These are called *non-configurational languages*, or **W-star languages**. Languages like English, in contrast, are **configurational languages**.

*See:* **phrase**; **phrase-structure grammar**; **syntax**; **syntactic category**; **tree**
*Further reading:* Brown and Miller, 1991: part one; Burton-Roberts, 1986.

**control**   The phenomenon in which a **verb phrase** (VP) with no subject is interpreted as having some subject. In sentences like *John wants to go home* and *John promised Mary to go home* (the second is not grammatical for all speakers), we understand that it is John who is going home. That is, *John* is the 'understood' subject of the subjectless verb phrase *go home*, and so we say that *John*, the subject of *wants* and of *persuaded*, **controls** the VP *go home*. This is an example of **subject-control**. However, in the sentence *John persuaded Mary to go home*, it is Mary who is going home; this time *Mary*, the object of *persuaded*, controls the VP *go home*, and we have an instance of **object-control**.

There is one more possibility, illustrated by the sentence *Going home sounds like a good idea*. This time there is no **noun phrase** available at all to be interpreted as the subject of the VP *going home*, and we call one an instance of *arbitrary control*.

Control phenomena can be rather intricate, and many current theories of grammar devote a good deal of machinery to their treatment. Note that some writers refer to control as **sharing**.

Note that the term **control** has a second sense. In a number of languages, intransitive sentences are divided into two different grammatical types, distinguished by the degree of control exercised over the action by the subject. In such languages, sentences like *He went home* and *He stood up*, in which the subject has a high degree of control, are expressed with one construction, while others, like *He died* and *He sneezed*, in which the subject has a low degree of control, are expressed with a different construction.

*See:* **anaphor**; **raising**
*Further reading:* Borsley, 1991: ch. 11; F. Palmer, 1994: 70–73.


**conversational implicature** A certain type of inference.
Suppose Alice asks Bill 'Is Susie coming to Mike's party on
Saturday?', and Bill replies 'Dave wants to go to a concert.'
On the face of it, this is an idiotic response to a simple question: Bill has declined to mention Susie at all, and has instead
brought up Dave and a concert, neither of which was being
asked about. And yet this is a perfectly normal and satisfactory answer to the question: *providing* that Alice knows that
Dave is Susie's boyfriend, she can reason as follows: 'Bill
doesn't *know* whether Susie is coming to the party, or he
would simply have told me, but Dave is Susie's boyfriend,
and Bill tells me he wants to go to a concert; doubtless he
will want Susie to come with him, and the concert must be
on Saturday, or Bill wouldn't have mentioned it, and therefore I can conclude that Susie will probably be going to the
concert with Dave, and hence that she won't be coming to
the party.'

Alice's conclusion that Susie probably won't be coming to
the party is an example of a *conversational implicature*, or CI.
This conclusion has not been asserted by Bill, and it does not
logically follow from what Bill has said, and yet it is reasonable, and Alice will surely draw it. How can this be so?

The first key point here is the *context* of Bill's utterance.
Alice knows that Dave and Susie are a couple, and she knows
that people like their partners to accompany them to social
events, or at least that Dave does, and this contextual knowledge is crucial: without it, Alice would have little chance of
making sense of Bill's response. This is typically the case with
a CI: it can only be drawn by a hearer who has an adequate
knowledge of the context.

A second key point is that Alice assumes that Bill is being
*cooperative*. If Bill had known for certain that Susie was or
was not coming to the party, Alice would have expected him
to say so, and failure to do this would be uncooperative.

Moreover, Alice has every right to assume that the concert in question must be on the Saturday; had it been on the Friday, Bill's behaviour would have been very uncooperative indeed, not merely irrelevant but positively misleading. Alice therefore assumes that Bill is cooperating, and draws her conclusion accordingly.

A notable property of CIs is that they are *defeasible* – they can be explicitly denied without producing anomaly. Suppose Bill's reply had been 'Well, Dave wants to go to a concert, but Susie has decided to come to Mike's party anyway.' Here Bill is expressly denying the CI 'Susie probably won't be coming to the party', but the result is still fine. This demonstrates that CIs are not logically valid. Nevertheless, CIs are powerful inferences, and a CI which is not denied will be assumed by the hearer to be true.

Now it is certainly not possible to assert that Bill's response actually *means* 'Susie is probably not coming to the party.' Suppose Alice asks Bill a quite different question: 'I'd like to go to one of the outdoor concerts in the park next week. Is anybody else interested?' Bill replies 'Dave wants to go to a concert.' This time Alice is hardly likely to conclude that Susie is probably not coming to Mike's party, since such an inference would make no sense in this very different context.

CIs are therefore very different in nature from the two other major kinds of inference, **entailment** and **presupposition**; among other things, neither of these two can be denied without producing anomaly.

CIs therefore belong squarely to the domain of **pragmatics**, the study of how meanings are extracted from context. The existence of CIs was uncovered by the British philosopher Paul Grice in the 1960s, and Grice's **cooperative principle** represents the major attempt at explaining how speakers are successful in communicating such meanings.

*See:* **cooperative principle**; **entailment**; **pragmatics**; **presupposition**

*Further reading:* Hurford and Heasley, 1983: unit 26; Levinson, 1983: ch. 3; Thomas, 1995: ch. 3; Yule, 1996: ch. 5.

**conversation analysis** A particular and highly empirical approach to examining the structure of **discourse**. The term *conversation analysis*, which came into prominence in the 1970s, sounds straightforward enough, but it is used in two rather different ways. Some people use it in a very broad sense, to include all possible approaches to the study of conversational structure. Much more commonly, however, the term is used more narrowly to denote a very particular approach to the subject matter: specifically, one which rejects the use of traditional and widely used grammatical concepts and terms, and attempts instead to work out from observation what speakers are doing and how they are doing it, with any required concepts and terms being derived purely from observation. The leading figure in the development of this approach was the American sociologist Harvey Sacks.

The approach is particularly associated with a general approach to social sciences called *ethnomethodology*, whose proponents argue that the proper object of sociological study is the set of techniques that the members of a society use to interpret their world and to act within it. In practice, this means a minimum of theorizing and a strong emphasis upon raw data and on the patterns that emerge from the data. Consequently, *conversation analysis*, in this narrow sense, contrasts most obviously with **discourse analysis**, which operates from the beginning with the familiar concepts and terms of general linguistics and attempts to examine the role of these concepts in discourses, including conversations.

*See:* **discourse analysis**
*Further reading:* Duranti, 1997: ch. 8; Levinson, 1983: ch. 6; Mey, 1993: chs. 10–12; Schiffrin, 1994: ch. 7; Yule, 1996: ch. 8.

**cooperative principle** A fundamental principle governing conversational exchanges. In the 1960s, the British philosopher Paul Grice undertook an examination of the way people behave in conversation. His fundamental conclusion was that conversational exchanges were governed by an overarching principle, which he named the ***cooperative principle***. Essentially, this principle holds that people in a conversation normally cooperate with one another, and, crucially, that they *assume* that the others are cooperating. That is, when you say something, and another person makes a response, you assume that the response is intended as a maximally cooperative one, and you interpret it accordingly.

It is this principle which is responsible for the existence of **conversational implicatures**, powerful inferences which are not logically valid but which are derived from the assumption that the other person is cooperating to a maximum extent.

Grice further decomposed his principle into a number of more specific components, the ***maxims of conversation***, such as 'Make your contribution as informative as is required' and 'Do not say that for which you lack adequate evidence'.

One of these maxims runs 'Make your contribution relevant'. In the 1980s, the British linguist Deirdre Wilson and the French philosopher Dan Sperber proposed that this maxim alone could be invoked to account for almost everything of interest: their ***Relevance Theory*** holds that utterances are interpreted in such a way that they combine with the context to produce the maximum amount of new information with the minimum amount of processing effort. Relevance Theory has been influential but is controversial.

*See:* **conversational implicature**

*Further reading:* Blakemore, 1992; Hurford and Heasley, 1983: unit 26; Sperber and Wilson, 1995; Thomas, 1995: ch. 3; Yule, 1996: ch. 5.

**coordinate structure**   A grammatical structure consisting of two or more units of equal rank joined by a connecting word. In English, a coordinate structure most usually consists of some grammatical units connected by a **conjunction** like *and* or *or*. As a rule, the two units, or ***conjuncts***, which are combined, or ***conjoined***, must belong to the same **syntactic category**. Here are some examples, in which the coordinate structures are bracketed and so are the conjuncts they consist of: [[*Susie*] *and* [*her parents*]] *are coming* (conjoined noun phrases); *Susie* [[*undressed*] *and* [*took a shower*]] (conjoined verb phrases); *Hungarian is spoken* [[*in Hungary*], [*in much of Romania*] *and* [*in part of Serbia*]] (conjoined prepositional phrases); *Does she drive* [[*well*] *or* [*badly*]]*?* (conjoined adverbs).

In certain circumstances, we can conjoin two units of different categories: *She polished the table* [[*lovingly*] *and* [*with great care*]] (adverb conjoined with prepositional phrase). But in most cases this is not possible: *★She smokes* [[*Marlboros*] *and* [*too much*]] (noun phrase wrongly conjoined with adverb phrase) (the asterisk marks ungrammaticality).

A few coordinate structures exhibit more complex patterns, as in *Susie is* [*neither* [*Irish*] *nor* [*Welsh*]]. And a few constructions that look broadly like coordinations have decidedly unusual structures, such as [*Janet prepared*] *and* [*Zelda served*] [*the sandwiches*] (this is called **right-node raising**), and [*Esther ordered chicken Kashmir*] *and* [*Larry, lamb rogon josh*] (this is called **gapping**); such constructions present formidable difficulties of analysis.

*See:* **conjunction**

*Further reading:* Collins Cobuild, 1990: 373–383; Crystal, 1996: units 63–64; Hurford, 1994: 46–50.

**copula**  A specialized grammatical item, often a **verb**, which serves only to express identity or class membership. The English copula is *be*, and this verb has two main functions. First, as the verb in an **equational sentence**, it expresses identity and functions rather like an equal sign in mathematics: *The largest planet in our solar system is Jupiter.* Such a sentence can be readily reversed: *Jupiter is the largest planet in our solar system.* Second, as the verb in an **ascriptive sentence**, it ascribes some property to its subject, or, in other words, it assigns its subject to membership in some class: *Susie is clever; Susie is sleepy; Susie is a linguist.* Here certain properties are being ascribed to Susie (cleverness, sleepiness, being a linguist), or, equivalently, Susie is being assigned to the class of clever people, to the class of sleepy people, or to the class of linguists. Such sentences become unnatural or worse when reversed: ??*Clever is Susie*; ??*A linguist is Susie.*

A sentence whose main verb is a copula is a *copular sentence*.

(Of course, English *be* can also function as an **auxiliary**, and in that case it is not serving as a copula.)

*Further reading:* Hurford, 1994: 51–53.


**corpus** A body of spoken or written texts in a language which is available for analysis. The study of *corpora* (this is the plural of *corpus*) presents many advantages. Instead of consulting our intuitions, or of extracting information painstakingly from speakers a bit at a time, we can examine a very large body of material which has been produced spontaneously by speakers or writers, and hence we can make accurate observations about the real linguistic behaviour of real people. Corpora can thus provide us with highly reliable information about the facts of a language, free of judgements and opinions.

Before the advent of powerful high-speed computers, the examination of corpora was laborious and time-consuming. Today, however, we can put a corpus onto a computer or a CD-ROM and treat it as a *database* which we can *interrogate*: that is, we can ask any question we are interested in, such as 'What are the relative frequencies of construction X and construction Y?', and get an accurate answer very quickly. Consequently, the study of corpora, now called *corpus linguistics*, has now become an important branch of the discipline. Both grammarians and lexicographers today routinely base their grammatical descriptions and their dictionaries on the data extracted from vast corpora.

Written texts are fairly easy to place into a computer memory, while spoken texts require more work: these must first be tape-recorded and then transcribed, usually by hand, into a more permanent form; consequently, most major corpora of English are still based on written texts. But, for many purposes, all corpora must be *tagged* before they can be used successfully; this means that a human investigator must label every word for its **part of speech** and usually also for other grammatical information.

A number of large corpora now exist, each stored on a computer somewhere in the world; many of these can be accessed via the Internet, but you normally need the permission of the owner before undertaking any work on a corpus.

*See:* **computational linguistics**; **natural-language processing**
*Further reading:* Crystal, 1997a: 414–415; Malmkjær, 1991: 73–80; Sinclair, 1991.


**creole** A language descended from a **pidgin**. A pidgin is not a natural language, but only a crude system of communication stitched together by people who have no language in common. If a pidgin establishes itself in a multilingual society, then there may well come a time when a generation of children is produced who have only the pidgin to use among themselves. In this case, the children will almost inevitably take the pidgin and turn it into a real language, complete with a large vocabulary and a rich grammatical system. This new natural language is a **creole**, and the children who create it are the first native speakers of the creole. The process of turning a pidgin into a creole is *creolization*.

Countless creoles have come into existence during the last few centuries, often because of the activities of European colonists. Speakers of English, French, Spanish, Portuguese and Dutch have established colonies in Africa, Asia and the Americas, in areas where the local languages were very different, and in many cases the Europeans imported African slaves speaking any of dozens of African languages.

The Caribbean has been a particularly fertile area for creoles, as Europeans and Africans (and to a lesser extent native Americans) were forced to construct innumerable local pidgins, very many of which went on to be converted to creoles.

At one time, there was a widespread belief that all creoles were descended from a single ancestral creole by massive vocabulary replacement (*relexification*), but this idea is no longer taken seriously.

When a creole remains in contact with the prestige language from which it was largely constructed, it may undergo significant *decreolization* – adjustment toward that prestige standard – and the result may be a *creole continuum*, a range of varieties from a highly conservative version of the creole (the *basilect*) through increasingly decreolized versions (the *mesolects*) to something more or less identical to the prestige standard (the *acrolect*).

The study of creoles was pioneered by the Trinidadian John Thomas, the American Addison Van Name and the German Hugo Schuchardt in the late nineteenth century, and the topic has never since been really neglected, but it has prospered particularly since the 1970s, and it is now regarded as a major area of investigation. Linguists studying contemporary **language change** have found creolization to be a rich source of information, particularly from the point of view of the construction of new grammatical systems. The remarkable similarities in grammar among creoles all over the world have led to the proposing of the **bioprogram hypothesis**.

*See:* **bioprogram hypothesis**; **pidgin**
*Further reading:* Crystal, 1997a: ch. 55; Holm, 1988–89; Malmkjær, 1991: 81–89; Romaine, 1988; Sebba, 1997.

**critical discourse analysis**   The analysis of **texts** within their social context. It is possible, of course, to examine a text from a purely structural point of view: the vocabulary and constructions it employs, the linguistic devices it uses to relate one part to another, and so on. But the approach called *critical discourse analysis* is rather different. In this approach, we are primarily interested in the social context in which a text is written.

Why was this text constructed at all? To whom is it addressed, and why? Does the writer or speaker have concealed purposes, and, if so, what are they? What hidden assumptions and biases underlie the text? These are the sorts of questions pursued in critical discourse analysis. The linguistic techniques involved in such analysis are often called *critical linguistics*, and the educational policy of teaching people to be alert to such matters is *critical language awareness*.

A simple example is provided by headlines and stories in different newspapers reporting the same story. One paper might print the headline *Striking workers protest Acme job losses*, while a second might print instead *Acme announces job losses; workers strike in protest*. These headlines suggest two very different views of what is going on: the first appears to lay the responsibility for the trouble on the workers, while the second assigns major responsibility to the company. Indeed, comparing the coverage of a single story in two or three newspapers of differing political stances can be an illuminating exercise.

Critical discourse analysis has been principally developed since the 1980s by the British sociolinguist Norman Fairclough. Critical linguistics has been more generally developed by a group of British linguists at the University of East Anglia and by Michael Halliday.

*See:* **discourse**; **text**
*Further reading:* Carter, 1997: 118–121; Fairclough, 1989; 1992; 1995; Malmkjær, 1991: 89–93.


**critical period hypothesis** The hypothesis that a first language can only be acquired during the first few years of life. Young children learn perfectly any language to which they are adequately exposed, and they do this without explicit teaching. Few adults can perform the same feat. In the 1960s the American neurologist Eric Lenneberg proposed an explanation: we are born with a singular ability to learn languages, but this ability is 'shut down', probably by some genetic programming, at around age thirteen, the *cutoff age* for first-language acquisition.

Strong support for Lenneberg's hypothesis comes from the observation of *feral children*: children who, for some reason, have been denied normal access to language in early life. In the eighteenth century, a young teen-aged French boy later named Victor was discovered living wild. He had no language and failed to learn much after being taken into care. More recently, a French girl known as Isabelle and an American girl known as Genie were prevented by psychopathic parents from hearing any language. After discovery and rescue, Isabelle, who was six, learned French rapidly, and quickly caught up with other children of her age, but Genie, nearly fourteen when discovered, never learned more than a minimal amount of English, in spite of intensive therapy. An American woman known as Chelsea was born nearly deaf, but was misdiagnosed as mentally retarded. Only at age thirty-one was she correctly diagnosed and given a hearing aid; she then began learning English but she too never made more than minimal progress.

*See:* **language acquisition**; **language instinct**
*Further reading:* Aitchison, 1989: ch. 4; Steinberg, 1993: ch. 3.

**dead language** A language which is no longer spoken. The term *dead language* is applied to two quite different cases, which you should be careful to distinguish.

In the first case, a dead language is a language which has disappeared as a mother tongue because its speakers abandoned it in favour of some other language (or, rarely, because its speakers were all killed). This has happened countless times. A number of languages of ancient Anatolia and the Middle East have disappeared in this way, including Hittite, Sumerian and Akkadian. An unknown number of European languages disappeared in favour of Latin during the Roman Empire, including Etruscan in Italy, Gaulish in Gaul and Iberian in Spain. In the British Isles, Cornish and Manx have vanished in modern times in favour of English. And hundreds of indigenous languages in Australia and the Americas have been abandoned in favour of English, Spanish and Portuguese.

A slight complication is that one or two of these truly dead languages, such as Cornish, have today a few speakers; these people speak the dead language as a second language, having learned it from books. Whether we continue to regard such a language as dead is a matter of taste, but most linguists would probably regard Cornish as dead, since it perhaps has no native speakers (though I am told that a few Cornish parents have taught their children Cornish as a first language). A few dead languages may continue to find some use as religious or literary languages, but again, in the absence of native speakers, they may be regarded as dead.

In the second case, the language in question never ceases to be spoken as a mother tongue, but over a period of time it changes so substantially that its later forms are so different from the earlier form (and often from one another) that it no longer makes sense to apply the same name. This has happened to Latin. Latin has never ceased to be spoken in Portugal, Spain, France and Italy, but the modern forms of Latin are so different from the language of the Romans, and from one another, that we no longer find it convenient to call them 'Latin'. Hence we speak of *French* rather than 'Paris Latin', *Catalan* rather than 'Barcelona Latin', and so on.

*See:* **language death**
*Further reading:* Holmes, 1992: 61–64; Romaine, 1994: 48–55.

**deep structure**  An abstract representation of the structure of a sentence posited by a linguist for analytical purposes. The concept of deep structure was a central part of the first versions of **transformational grammar**, introduced by Noam Chomsky in the 1950s. Chomsky's idea was that certain important generalizations about the structures of the sentences in a particular language were difficult to state in terms of the **surface structure** of sentences, but that these generalizations could be readily expressed in a theoretical framework in which sentences were assumed to have abstract underlying forms which were very different from their surface forms.

Chomsky defended his idea by appealing to examples like *John is eager to please* and *John is easy to please*. On the surface, these may appear to have identical structures, but, crucially, they receive very different interpretations. Using the symbol NP for a **noun phrase** which is in some sense 'missing' on the surface, we might therefore posit deep structures for these two sentences of approximately the following forms: *John is [eager to please NP]*, but *[NP to please John] is easy*. These representations now allow us to explain the meaning of each sentence, but they must be modified by the action of powerful rules called *transformations* in order to produce the correct surface forms in each case.

The conception of deep structure has changed substantially over the years, as Chomsky and his colleagues have continued to modify their ideas, and the several successive versions of transformational grammar (and its successor **Government-and-Binding Theory**) have involved very different views of deep structure, which has more recently been called *D-structure*. Consequently, different textbooks will present significantly different versions of it, and the more recent versions are often very abstract indeed. Most theories of grammar other than transformational grammar have declined to recognize a concept of deep structure, preferring instead to work solely with surface structures.

When deep structure was first introduced, there was some enthusiasm for seeing it as representing a mental reality, something actually present within speakers' brains. This idea has gradually been abandoned, and today only a minority of linguists would want to see D-structure as anything more than an analytical convenience.

*See:* **ambiguity**; **surface structure**; **transformational grammar**
*Further reading:* Lyons, 1991: ch. 7.


**deficit hypothesis**   The hypothesis that working-class children have an inadequate command of grammar and vocabulary to express complex ideas. In the 1960s, the British educational theorist Basil Bernstein proposed that a given language can be regarded as possessing two fundamentally different styles, or *codes*. A *restricted code*, in this view, has a limited vocabulary and a limited range of grammatical constructions; it is adequate for talking to people with very similar backgrounds about everyday experiences, but it is highly inexplicit and depends for success upon a large degree of shared experience. It is too inexplicit and too limited to express complex and unfamiliar ideas in a coherent manner. An *elaborated code*, in contrast, possesses a large vocabulary and a wide range of grammatical constructions, and it is entirely suitable for communicating complex ideas, in a fully explicit manner, to people who do not share the speaker's background.

Bernstein's *deficit hypothesis* holds that, while middle-class children have full control over both codes, working-class children have access only to the restricted code. Hence working-class children cannot communicate effectively in the manner expected in educational institutions, and so they cannot hope to succeed in school.

This hypothesis has generated a storm of discussion and debate. Linguists, led by William Labov, have mostly been critical and dismissive of it. They defend instead the *difference hypothesis* – by which working-class speech is merely different from middle-class speech, and not inferior to it in expressiveness – and, hence, that working-class children in school are penalized only for being different, and not for being incompetent.

*See:* **standard language**
*Further reading:* Holmes, 1992: 360–366.

**deictic category** Any **grammatical category** which expresses distinctions pertaining to the time and place of speaking or to the differing roles of participants. The word *deixis* means 'linguistic pointing', and we are engaging in the use of deixis whenever we use items like *there*, *this*, *you* or *then*. There are several types of deixis in languages, and we accordingly recognize several *deictic categories*. A deictic category is literally a 'pointing' category: it allows a speaker to 'point' at particular times, places and individuals. The reference points are always the identity of the speaker and the time and place of speaking. For example, the category called *deictic position* permits distinctions like those between *here* and *there*, *this* and *that*, which express differing distances from the speaker. The category of **person** allows distinctions among the speaker, the addressee, and everyone else. The category of **tense** allows the speaker to point in time: the past tense usually means 'before the moment of speaking', the future tense 'after the moment of speaking', and so on.

Languages may differ substantially in the distinctions expressed by their deictic categories: two, three or more deictic positions, two, three, four or more tenses (or none at all), and so on. English has just two deictic positions, three persons and two tenses. Other grammatical categories – such as **number**, **gender**, **aspect** and **mood** – are not deictic in nature.

*See:* **grammatical category**
*Further reading:* Lyons, 1968: 275–280.


**denotation**    The central meaning of a linguistic form, regarded as the set of things it could possibly refer to. The study of **meaning** is a complex affair, and several quite different kinds of meaning have to be carefully distinguished before we can hope to make much progress. For example, when you say *The cat is scratching the sofa*, you clearly have some particular, individual cat in mind, and the relation between *the cat* and that animal is one of **reference**. Now the word *cat* itself cannot normally refer to any particular entity in this way. However, one way of looking at the central meaning of *cat* is to see this as consisting of all the cats in the (real or conceptual) world – that is, as the totality of things to which the word *cat* might reasonably be applied. This interpretation is called the *denotation* of the word *cat*.

Denotation is a difficult concept to work with, since concepts like 'all the cats in the world' are almost impossible to pin down. Among 'all the cats in the world', should we include all those cats which have not yet been born, and all those which died millions of years ago? Nevertheless, denotation is often invoked in **semantics**, and formal versions of semantics often try to formalize denotation as what is called *extension*: the extension of *cat* is the *set* (in the formal mathematical sense) of all the entities in the universe of discourse (the totality of things we can talk about) to which *cat* can be applied.

Denotation is most frequently contrasted with **connotation**, but it has important similarities to **sense**, which is essentially a more directly linguistic way of interpreting the same kind of meaning. (And some writers have a habit of using *denotation* almost interchangeably with *reference*, but this is inappropriate.)

*See:* **connotation**; **reference**; **sense**

*Further reading:* Frawley, 1992: 274–291; Hofmann, 1993: ch. 10; Saeed, 1997: ch. 10.

**dependency** A grammatical link between two (or more) different points in a sentence. In a *dependency*, the presence, absence or form of an item at one point in a sentence is directly linked to the presence, absence or form of a second item at a different point in the same sentence. There are several types of dependency. When the presence of one item requires the presence or absence of another, we have **subcategorization** (for example, the verb *slap* requires an object noun phrase, while *smile* does not allow one). When the presence of one item requires a particular form on a second item, we have **government** (for example, the German preposition *mit* 'with' requires its object to take the dative case). When the form of one item requires a particular form on a second item, we have **agreement** (for example, a plural subject requires a plural verb-form).

All these are *local dependencies*, in which the two ends of the dependency are not allowed to be separated by more than a certain amount. In an *unbounded dependency* (or *extraction*), there is no limit on how far apart the two ends can be. The example *★Susie slapped* is ungrammatical (marked by the asterisk), since the verb lacks the object it requires. Likewise, *★Who did Susie slap Louise?* is ungrammatical, since *who* cannot be used unless there is a suitable **gap**, or 'hole', elsewhere in the sentence. But *Who did Susie slap e?* is fine, since *who* and the missing object (marked by the symbol *e*) permit each other to occur. And the question word and the gap can be arbitrarily far apart: *Who did Archie say that Bill thought that Claire believed that Donna suspected Susie slapped* e?

*See:* **agreement**; **government**; **subcategorization**
*Further reading:* Brown and Miller, 1991: ch. 17.

**derivation** (1) Constructing new words by adding **affixes** to existing words. In most languages, *derivation* is one of the principal ways of obtaining new words from existing words, and its study is one of the major branches of **morphology**.

The key point is to distinguish derivation from **inflection**. When we add certain affixes to *write*, producing forms like *writes*, *writing* and *written* (and also, in a more complex manner, *wrote*), we do not get any new words, but only grammatically distinct forms of the same word: this is *inflection*. You wouldn't expect to find different dictionary entries for all these forms: there would just be the one entry for all of them, under *write*. However, other affixes produce genuinely different words, such as *rewrite*, *underwrite* and *writer*, and these are examples of derivation. This time you *would* expect to find separate dictionary entries for these words, though a small dictionary might not bother with *rewrite*, since its meaning is so obvious.

Like many languages, English is rich in both derivational prefixes and derivational suffixes. Examples of the first are *re-*, *anti-*, *syn-*, *counter-*, *non-*, *un-*, *trans-*, *pre-* and *mis-*. Examples of the second are *-ness*, *-ity*, *-less*, *-wise*, *-ize*, *-dom*, *-ly* (two different ones), *-er* and *-(at)ion*. Multiple affixes are possible, though normally there are strict rules governing the order in which affixes may be added. Starting from *happy*, we can derive first *unhappy* and then *unhappiness*. Starting with *derive*, we can obtain first *derivation*, then *derivational*, and finally the very obscure technical term in linguistics *transderivational*. Starting with *exist*, we can successively derive *existent*, *existence*, *existential* and *existentialism*. In every case, at every stage, the result is a new word which deserves its own entry in the dictionary.

(2) In **transformational grammar**, the complete set of stages linking the **deep structure** of a sentence to its **surface structure**. Among the various theories of grammar, *transformational grammar* is distinguished by its claim that the syntactic structure of a sentence is not a single **tree**, but rather a series of trees. The most fundamental level of structure is the *deep structure* of the sentence, and the most superficial, the *surface structure*. These two levels of representation are typically linked by a whole series of trees, each one resulting from the application of a *transformation* to the preceding one. The ordered series of trees which results is the *derivation* of that particular sentence.

In this sense, the term *derivation* is also applied to the series of stages involved in process-based theories of phonology like *generative phonology* in converting an *underlying form* into a surface form.

*See:* (1) **affix**; **inflection**; **morphology**; (2) **phonology**; **transformational grammar**; **word-formation**

*Further reading:* Brown and Miller, 1991: ch. 15; Katamba, 1994: ch. 4.


**descriptivism**   The policy of describing languages as they are found to exist. A prominent feature of **traditional grammar** is the frequent presence of **prescriptivism**: identifying and recommending forms and usages favoured by the analyst and condemning others not favoured by the analyst. Excepting only in certain educational contexts, modern linguists utterly reject prescriptivism, and their investigations are based instead upon *descriptivism*. In a descriptivist approach, we try to describe the facts of linguistic behaviour exactly as we find them, and we refrain from making value judgements about the speech of native speakers. Of course, our descriptions sometimes include the observation that speakers themselves regard certain usages as good or bad, but that is a very different thing from expressing our own opinions.

Descriptivism is a central tenet of what we regard as a scientific approach to the study of language: the very first requirement in any scholarly investigation is to get the facts right. Prescriptivism, in great contrast, is not a scientific approach. The strong opinions of prescriptivists may be variously regarded as recommendations about good style, as an aspect of social mores, as a consequence of our educational system, or perhaps even as a matter of morality, but they are not statements about actual behaviour, and hence they are not scientific.

For a prescriptivist, the so-called *split infinitive* is a matter of what people *ought* to say; for a descriptivist, it is a matter of what people *do* say. Since the overwhelming majority of native English-speakers, educated or not, routinely say things like *Susie decided to never touch another cigarette*, in which the sequence *to never touch* is the so-called 'split infinitive', then this construction is by definition a normal and grammatical part of English, and that is the end of the matter: objecting to it is a little like objecting to the law of gravity, since denying the facts is a hopeless way of going about things.

*See:* **prescriptivism**
*Further reading:* Pinker, 1994: ch. 12; Trask, 1995: ch. 8.

**design features**  An informal list of the seemingly universal properties of human languages. The idea of design features was introduced by the American linguist Charles Hockett in 1960; both Hockett and others have occasionally proposed revisions to the original list, and several versions are in print. All contain the fundamental features of **arbitrariness**, **duality of patterning**, **displacement**, **open-endedness** and **stimulus-freedom**. Of these five, only the first is also normally found in **animal communication**.

**Sign languages** present a few complications. They clearly do not possess the secondary design feature of using the *vocal-auditory channel* as their primary medium, and it is debatable whether they possess duality of patterning.

*See:* **animal communication**; **arbitrariness**; **duality of patterning**; **displacement**; **open-endedness**; **stimulus-freedom**
*Further reading:* Crystal, 1997a: 400–401; Hockett, 1960; Trask, 1995: ch. 1.

**determiner** The **part of speech** which includes words like *the* and *my*. The English determiners are a smallish class of chiefly grammatical items which have only a single function: they typically occur as the first item in a **noun phrase**. Here is a simple test for determiners. Any single word which can fit into the blank in the following frame to produce a noun phrase is a determiner: ___ *new book*. Examples: *the, a, this, that, some, every, no, my, her, which*. There are some further determiners which can only fit into plural noun phrases, as in ___ *new books*. Examples: *these, most, both, all, few, several*. But be careful here: certain words which are not determiners will also fit into this second blank (*entirely, attractive, other*), but these items require entirely different syntactic structures to fit into this string of words.

The two most highly grammatical determiners, *the* and *a(n)*, are called *articles*. The ones like *my* and *her* are traditionally called ***possessive pronouns***, but grammatically they are determiners, not **pronouns**.

A noun phrase which is headed by a singular uncountable noun or by any plural noun need not have an overt determiner: *French wine, new books*. Some linguists prefer to say that such noun phrases contain a ***zero determiner***.

Normally a noun phrase contains only one determiner. But certain noun phrases appear to contain two: *all my children, both these books*. In such cases, the first item is often called a ***predeterminer***.

Some (not all) determiners have meanings involving quantity, such as *many, several* and *all*. These are called ***quantifiers***, and some linguists prefer to separate the quantifiers into a separate part of speech from determiners, but there is little or no grammatical justification for this.

*See:* **noun phrase**

*Further reading:* Collins Cobuild, 1990: 42–60; Greenbaum and Quirk, 1990: 72–92.


**diachrony** The time dimension in language. It was the Swiss linguist Ferdinand de Saussure, in the early twentieth century, who first emphasized the fundamental difference between **synchrony** and *diachrony* in the study of language. In a *diachronic* approach, we look at how a language has changed over some period of time. Most work in **historical linguistics** is diachronic in nature, but not all of it: a linguist might well be interested in constructing a purely synchronic description of, say, the Old English of King Alfred's day or the Latin of Caesar's day, without considering how the language had developed from an earlier form or what happened to it later.

*See:* **historical linguistics**; **language change**; **Saussurean paradox**; **synchrony**

**dialect**   A more or less identifiable regional or social variety of a language. Every language that is spoken over any significant area is spoken in somewhat different forms in different places; these are its *regional dialects*. Moreover, even in a single community, the language may be spoken differently by members of different social groups; these different forms are *social dialects* or *sociolects*.

For example, the English of London is noticeably different from the English of Birmingham, Liverpool, Glasgow, New York, New Orleans or Sydney, and even within London stockbrokers do not speak like motor mechanics.

It is important to realize that everybody speaks some dialect or other; it is not possible to speak a language without using some dialect. Informally, we often reserve the label *dialect* for a speech variety which is noticeably different from our own, or which is lacking in prestige, but this is not the way the term is used in linguistics.

In British usage, the term *dialect* includes only features of grammar and vocabulary, while features of pronunciation are treated under the quite different heading of **accent**. In American usage, an accent is usually considered to be just one part of a dialect.

The study of regional dialects, known as *dialect geography*, has been a major part of linguistics since the late nineteenth century; there have been many studies of regional variation, often resulting in the publication of *dialect atlases* containing a series of *dialect maps*, each showing the variation in respect of a single feature. In contrast, social dialects have only been seriously studied since the 1960s; the pioneering work here was done by the American linguist William Labov.

A **standard language** is a rather special dialect of some language, one which has been codified and elaborated for use in a wide variety of domains.

Linguistically unsophisticated people sometimes apply the term *dialect* to a regional language of low prestige, but the term is never so used in linguistics, in which a dialect is always a variety of a language which has other varieties.

*See:* **accent**; **standard language**
*Further reading:* Crystal, 1997a: ch. 8; Malmkjær, 1991: 93–98.


**diglossia** Marked specialization of function between two language varieties in a single speech community. It is by no means rare for two or more distinct languages or language varieties to be used side by side within a single community, with or without a high degree of **bilingualism**. For example, many citizens of Spain routinely switch between Basque, Catalan or Galician on the one hand and Castilian Spanish on the other, depending on the circumstances; German-speakers in Germany, Switzerland and Austria likewise switch between standard German and their own local varieties of German, which are often not comprehensible to other speakers; all of English, Malay, Cantonese Chinese and Tamil are widely spoken in Singapore, though very few people there can speak all four.

In most such cases, people naturally prefer to speak their own mother tongue whenever they can, and they switch to another language or variety only when they have to. In a few communities, however, something very different happens: the languages or language varieties come to be perceived as having different functions in the community as a whole, and hence each variety is used more or less exclusively for those functions in which it is deemed appropriate. Normally only two language varieties are involved in such a case, and the result is *diglossia*.

Diglossia was first identified as a distinctive phenomenon by the American linguist Charles Ferguson in the 1960s. Ferguson's initial characterization has since been modified very slightly, but the characteristics of a diglossic society are essentially the ones he identified.

There is a clear difference in prestige between the two language varieties: one, called High (or H), enjoys great prestige, while the other, called Low (or L), enjoys little or no prestige; in extreme cases, speakers may deny the very existence of L. In all cases, L is the mother tongue of all or most speakers, while H is learned only through formal education. Speakers of limited education may have a very inadequate command of H, and they may even have trouble understanding it.

The specialization of function is highly predictable from one diglossic society to another. The L variety is used for ordinary conversation and for the more popular types of entertainment (such as soap operas and commentary on sports events); it is rarely written, and may well lack a recognized written form. However, it may be used in comic strips, in captions to political cartoons, in scurrilous publications, and perhaps in personal letters. The H variety is used in newspapers and most other publications, for all serious literature, for university lectures, for news broadcasts and other formal types of radio and television broadcasts, and (usually) for religious purposes.

So well entrenched is this perceived specialization that using the 'wrong' variety for a particular purpose will be seen as comical or offensive: even speakers with a minimal command of H prefer to hear H when H is appropriate, since the use here of L, which they can understand perfectly well, is felt to be undignified or worse. In one famous incident, there were riots in the streets of Athens in 1901 upon the publication of a translation of the New Testament into the Low variety of Greek: thousands of Greeks were enraged by the use of L in such a solemn religious context, and they insisted upon an H version which many of them could not understand.

Among the diglossic societies identified several decades ago were

- Greece – H = Katharévusa, a kind of fake classical Greek, L = Dhimotikí, ordinary spoken Greek
- German Switzerland – H = standard German, L = Swiss German
- the Arab countries – H = the classical Arabic of the Koran, L = ordinary spoken Arabic
- Paraguay – H = Spanish, L = Guaraní, the mother tongue of most of the population and a native American language.

Changing political circumstances have brought diglossia to an end in Greece, and there are signs that the Arab countries may be going the same way (though diglossia is far from dead here); Switzerland and Paraguay continue much as before.

Other instances of diglossia have arisen in the past and have often proved highly stable. A good example is medieval Europe, in which Latin (H) was used for all serious purposes, while the innumerable local vernaculars (L) remained the everyday speech of the entire population, most of whom knew nothing of Latin. This state of affairs persisted for centuries before Latin finally gave way to the new national languages like French, Spanish, Italian and German, which had previously been regarded as unfit for serious purposes.

*See:* **bilingualism**
*Further reading:* Ferguson, 1959; Holmes, 1992: 32–40; Malmkjær, 1991: 99–100.


**discourse** Any connected piece of speech or writing. A discourse may be produced by a single speaker or writer, or by two or more people engaging in a conversation or (rarely) in a written exchange. The study of discourse has become prominent in recent years, and the approaches are many and varied. While usage varies, we most commonly apply the label **discourse analysis** to an approach which is based heavily upon traditional grammatical concepts, **conversation analysis** to an empirical approach which rejects traditional concepts and seeks to extract patterns from data, and **text linguistics** to the study of large units of language each of which has a definable communicative function.

Two fundamental terms in the study of discourse are **cohesion** and **coherence**. Cohesion is the presence of explicit linguistic links which provide recognizable structure, such as *she*, *this*, *after*, *therefore* and *but*. Coherence is the degree to which a discourse makes sense in terms of our knowledge of the world. For example, in response to the question *Who's going to drive to the Christmas party?*, the remark *Susie's on antibiotics* might seem irrelevant and uncooperative, but of course it makes perfect sense if we know about the real-world links between alcohol and Christmas parties, alcohol and driving, and alcohol and antibiotics.

*See:* **coherence**; **cohesion**; **critical discourse analysis**; **discourse analysis**

*Further reading:* Allen and Guy, 1974; Carter, 1997; Coulthard, 1985; Crystal, 1997a: 20; Nofsinger, 1991; Schiffrin, 1994; Sinclair and Coulthard, 1975.

**discourse analysis** An approach to the study of **discourse** which is based upon traditional grammatical concepts and terms. In principle, we might apply the label *discourse analysis*, or DA, to any kind of investigation of the structure of discourse, but in practice the label is most commonly reserved for an approach based upon familiar grammatical concepts. That is, a proponent of discourse analysis comes to the analytical task with a complete battery of grammatical concepts and terms of the sort familiar to any student of grammar, and attempts to see how these concepts are involved in structuring discourses. To put it another way, DA is an attempt to extend our highly successful analysis of sentence structure to units larger than the sentence.

Though there is considerable variation in practice, DA often begins by trying to identify minimal units of discourse and then by looking for rules governing how these minimal units can be strung together in sequence to produce well-formed discourses, much as smaller syntactic units are combined into sentences according to the rules of syntax. DA thus contrasts strongly with the alternative approach known as **conversation analysis**. Proponents of DA complain that conversation analysis is hugely inexplicit and *ad hoc*, and lacking in any identifiable underpinning, while the practitioners of the other approach in turn accuse DA of being excessively *a priori* and of paying too little attention to real texts, as opposed to deliberately constructed ones.

DA has been prominent since the 1970s; it is particularly important in Germany and the Netherlands, where it is often almost indistinguishable from **text linguistics**, but it has also been pursued with some vigour in the English-speaking countries.

*See:* **conversation analysis**; **text linguistics**
*Further reading:* Brown and Yule, 1983; Carter, 1997: 111–122; Levinson, 1983: 286–294; McCarthy, 1991; Malmkjær, 1991: 100–110.

**displacement**　The ability to speak about things other than the here and now. With just a single known exception (see below), every signal used by a non-human creature to communicate pertains wholly and directly to the immediate time and place of signalling. No non-human signal, with the marginal exception of scent markings left to define territory or to provide a trail, ever refers to the past or the future, to hypothetical or counterfactual states of affairs, or to anything not directly perceptible to the creature signalling. To put this more picturesquely, mice do not swap stories about their close encounters with cats, nor do bears soberly discuss the severity of the coming winter; rabbits do not engage in heated discussions about what might lie on the far side of the hill, nor do geese draw up plans for their next migration.

Human language is utterly different. We have not the slightest difficulty in talking about last night's football game, or our own childhood, or the behaviour of dinosaurs which lived over 100 million years ago; with equal ease, we can discuss political events in Peru or the atmosphere of the planet Neptune. And, of course, we can discuss what might have happened if the South had won the American Civil War, and we can produce fables and fantasies involving hobbits, dragons, talking animals and intergalactic wars. All this is displacement: the ability to talk about things other than what we can see, hear, feel and smell at the moment.

This displacement, which we take utterly for granted, is one of the most momentous differences between human languages and the signalling systems of all other species. They can't do it at all; we do it almost every time we open our mouths.

There is just one striking exception. A honeybee scout which has discovered a source of nectar returns to its hive and performs a dance, watched by the other bees. This *bee dance* tells the watching bees what direction the nectar lies in, how far away it is, and how much nectar there is. And this is displacement: the dancing bee is passing on information about a site which it visited some time ago and which it now cannot see, and the watching bees respond by flying off to locate the nectar.

Startling though it is, the bee dance is, so far at least, absolutely unique in the non-human world: no other creatures, not even apes, can communicate anything of the sort, and even the bee dance is severely limited in its expressive powers: it cannot cope with the slightest novelty.

The importance of displacement was first pointed out by the American linguist Charles Hockett in 1960.

*See:* **design features**; **open-endedness**; **stimulus-freedom**

**distinctive feature**　Any one of a number of minimal phonological elements of which **speech sounds** or **phonemes** are composed. For decades after the **phoneme** concept was introduced into linguistics, linguists tended to assume that each phoneme was an independent unit which could not be analysed into any smaller units. But this view, while profitable, ran into serious difficulties in some respects. Most obviously, it provided no basis for recognizing the **natural classes** of phonemes which often need to be singled out in describing languages.

Eventually, therefore, phonologists ceased to regard phonemes as indivisible, and to treat them instead as *bundles*, or *matrices*, of smaller components. These smaller components are *distinctive features*, or *features* for short. In most cases, the features invoked are *binary*, meaning that a feature can only be either present (marked by [+]) or absent (marked by [−]).

For example, all sounds which are produced with **voicing**, such as [a m z d], carry the *feature specification* [+ voice], while voiceless sounds, such as [p f h], are [− voice]. Similarly, sounds produced with the velum lowered, like [m n ã], are [+ nasal], while all others are [− nasal]. A suitable set of such features, typically around fifteen or so, is adequate both to distinguish every phoneme in a language from every other, and also to characterize the required natural classes: for example, the set /p t k/, which is a natural class in English, might be singled out as [− continuant, − friction, − voice], the class of voiceless frictionless stops.

The set of feature specifications identifying a particular segment or class was long regarded as a mere unordered collection of items with no internal structure, but, since the 1980s, there has been a marked tendency to assign to each set of features a kind of hierarchical structure, in which some features are treated as subordinate to other features; this approach is called *feature geometry*.

The idea of distinctive features was first developed by the European linguists of the Prague School in the 1930s, most prominently by the Russian Nikolai Trubetzkoy, but it was another member of the school, the Russian Roman Jakobson. Jakobson later emigrated to the USA, and there, in collaboration with the Swede Gunnar Fant and the American Morris

Halle, put together the first complete theory of distinctive features, in the 1950s. This first effort was formulated in terms of *acoustic features* reflecting things that could be seen in a sound spectrogram, but in the 1960s Halle and Noam Chomsky proposed a very different set of *articulatory features*, based chiefly on the activities of the speech organs. Features of this sort have predominated in phonology ever since, though phonologists continue to propose modifications to the system even today.

*See:* **natural class**; **phoneme**

*Further reading:* Clark and Yallop, 1995: ch. 9, appendix 2; Giegerich, 1992: chs. 4–5; P. Hawkins, 1984: ch. 3; Katamba, 1989: ch. 3; Malmkjær, 1991: 110–115.


**distribution**   The set of positions in which a given linguistic element or form can appear in a language. The notion of *distribution* is a central feature of the approach to language study called **structuralism**, and it was outstandingly important in the version called *American structuralism*.

Distribution is a simple notion. Any given linguistic element which is present in a language, whether a speech sound, a phoneme, a morpheme, a word, or whatever, can occur in certain positions but not in other positions. A statement of its possible positions is its distribution, and this distribution is usually an important fact about its place in the language.

For example, distribution is important in identifying **parts of speech**. In English, any word which can occur in the slot in *This ___ is nice* must be a **noun**, because English allows only nouns to occur in this position. And larger **syntactic categories** can be partly identified in the same way: anything that can occur in the slot in *___ is nice* must be a **noun phrase**.

But distribution is perhaps most prominent in **phonology**. Consider the English labiodental fricatives [f] and [v]. Simplifying slightly, in Old English, the sound [v] could only occur between vowels, while [f] could never appear between vowels. Hence Old English allowed words like [fiːf] 'five', [fæːt] 'fat', [livian] 'live' (verb), and [ovər] 'over', but no words like *[væːt] or *[ofər]. We say that, in Old English, [f] and [v] were in *complementary distribution*, meaning that there was no position in which both could occur. Since the two sounds are phonetically similar, we can therefore assign both to a single **phoneme**, usually represented as /f/. Indeed, the Old English spellings of the four words were *fif*, *fatt*, *lifian* and *ofer*, reflecting the fact that only one phoneme existed.

In modern English, however, the distribution of these two sounds is very different: they can both occur in the same positions to make different words. We thus have **minimal pairs** like *fat* and *vat*, *fine* and *vine*, *rifle* and *rival*, and *strife* and *strive*. We therefore say that [f] and [v] are in *contrastive distribution*, and they must now be assigned to separate phonemes, /f/ and /v/, just as the modern spelling suggests.

*See:* **phoneme**; **phonotactics**

**duality of patterning**  A type of structure in which a small number of meaningless units are combined to produce a large number of meaningful units. Non-human creatures have signalling systems based upon 'one sound, one meaning', and hence they can express only a tiny number of meanings. Since we can scarcely produce more than 100 distinguishable speech sounds, and if our languages worked in the same way, it would follow that we would not be able to produce more than 100 distinct units of meaning.

But human languages are organized differently. Each spoken language possesses a small number of basic speech sounds: its **phonemes**. The number varies from a minimum of ten to a maximum of around 100, with the average being around thirty. Crucially, these phonemes are themselves meaningless, but they can be combined into sequences which are meaningful.

English has around forty phonemes (the precise number depending on the **accent**). Among these are the 'p-sound'

/p/, the 't-sound' /t/, the 'k-sound' /k/, and the 'short a' /æ/ (as in *cat*). Even just these four phonemes can be combined variously to produce a large number of words with very different meanings: /æt/ *at*, /ækt/ *act*, /kæt/ *cat*, /pæt/ *pat*, /tæp/ *tap*, /kæp/ *cap*, /pæp/ *pap*, /pækt/ *pact* or *packed*, /tækt/ *tact* or *tacked*, /kæpt/ *capped*, /tæpt/ *tapped*, and so on. Adding one more phoneme, the 'long a' /eɪ/, we can now get /peɪ/ *pay*, /keɪ/ *Kay*, /teɪp/ *tape*, /keɪk/ *cake*, /teɪk/ *take*, /keɪp/ *cape*, /teɪpt/ *taped*, and so on. With forty-odd phonemes, English can produce a huge number of one-syllable words, but of course English also has words that are several syllables long.

Duality thus allows a language to form many tens of thousands of different words, all of which can be produced by a **vocal tract** which can produce no more than a few dozens of distinguishable speech sounds. Duality is therefore of crucial importance in facilitating the existence of spoken languages. Together with the grammatical property of **recursion**, duality allows human languages the ability to produce an infinite number of utterances, all with different meanings, and hence makes **open-endedness** possible.

**Sign languages** perhaps lack duality; this has been much debated. It is not in doubt that the signs of sign languages can be decomposed into smaller meaningless elements, but it is not clear at present that these smaller elements from a system analogous to a set of phonemes in a spoken language.

The importance of duality was first pointed out by the French linguist André Martinet in the 1950s (he called it *double articulation*) and by the American linguist Charles Hockett in 1960; it was Hockett who coined the term duality.

*See:* **animal communication**; **design features**; **phoneme**; **phonotactics**

**dyslexia** A certain disability affecting reading and writing. Strictly, *dyslexia* (often informally called *word blindness*) is a disability with reading, while the related disability with writing is *dysgraphia*, but the two very commonly occur together. (The terms *alexia* and *agraphia* are often preferred in North America.) A sufferer has difficulty in perceiving a printed page: the words on the page often appear distorted, as though viewed through a misshapen lens; both the order and the shapes of the letters may be perceived wrongly. Similar problems affect writing: letters may be put down in the wrong order or turned upside-down or backwards. Both in reading and in writing, mirror-image letters like *b*, *d*, *g* and *q* may be confused. In more severe cases, called *deep dyslexia*, words may be confused with totally unrelated words, even those of very different appearance, which are somehow similar in sound, meaning or grammatical class: for example, *saw* with *was*, *dinner* with *food*, *rib* with *ride*, *bun* with *cake*, *saucer* with *sausage*, *for* with *and*.

As is usual with disabilities, individual sufferers vary significantly in the particular symptoms they exhibit, but specialists have nonetheless identified certain recurring patterns of disability and given them names. Also, as with other disabilities, dyslexia and dysgraphia may be present from early childhood in children showing no sign of brain damage, or they may be acquired in adulthood as a result of brain damage; the two cases are called *developmental dyslexia* and *acquired dyslexia*, respectively. The former belief that dyslexia could be traced to a single uniform cause is now known to be false: dyslexia can in fact result from any of a number of different causes, and many specialists suspect that any given case of dyslexia probably results from the interaction of several distinct factors.

Dyslexia is very commonly accompanied by some detectable degree of other types of language disability. In addition, there is evidence that it tends to be accompanied by certain non-linguistic features, such as poor or mixed handedness, poor short-term memory, clumsiness, and a poor sense of direction, including left–right confusion, though no single sufferer ever exhibits all of these traits.

Individuals with the milder kinds of dyslexia, especially the developmental kind, can often overcome their handicap and make successful careers in business, politics, entertainment, academia, or any other kind of work.

*See:* **aphasia**; **language disability**
*Further reading:* British Dyslexia Association, 1996; Crystal, 1997a: 274–277; Malmkjær, 1991: 115–120.

# E

**ellipsis**   The omission from a sentence or an utterance of material which is logically necessary but which is recoverable from the context. Traditional grammarians have for centuries applied the term *ellipsis* to a wide range of phenomena in which some part of a sentence or an utterance appears to be 'missing' or 'understood'. Contemporary linguists, however, generally prefer to use the term more narrowly to denote only the omission of material which can be unambiguously recovered from the context.

So, for example, consider the following exchange. Mike: *Where's Susie?* Sarah: *In the library*. Here, Sarah's response is unambiguously interpretable in the context as meaning *Susie is in the library*, and hence we speak of the ellipsis of the material *Susie is*. But now consider another exchange. Mike: *Here's the book I promised you*. Sarah: *Thanks*. This time Sarah's response cannot be specifically identified as a reduced form of any particular longer utterance, and so we would probably not speak of ellipsis here.

Various particular types of ellipsis can occur within a single utterance, and these often have individual names. Example: *Susie wants me to come to Greece with her, but I can't*. Here the missing continuation is clearly *come to Greece with her*, and this construction is called **VP-deletion**. Another example: *Somebody wants me out, and I know who*. The missing material is *wants me out*, and this construction is **sluicing**.

Ellipsis must be carefully distinguished from *elision*, w
is the removal of *sounds*, as when we pronounce *fish and chips*
as *fish 'n' chips*, or when a British speaker pronounces *library*
as *libry*. Sounds are elided; words are ellipted.

**entailment**   A particular type of inference. If I say to you
*Booth assassinated Lincoln*, then, assuming my statement is true,
you may safely draw certain conclusions, including *Lincoln is
dead* and *Booth killed somebody*. These are among the several
*entailments* of my original sentence.

We say that *statement P entails statement Q* whenever the
following inference holds: if P is true, then Q must also be
true. Note that any entailment of P never contains more
information than P, and in fact it usually contains less.

Normally, if P entails Q, then Q does not entail P (check
this with the examples). But it is possible for P and Q to entail
each other, and in this case we are looking at *paraphrases*.
Examples: *Sally sold a car to Mike*; *Mike bought a car from Sally*.

An entailment differs in several respects from a **presupposition** or a **conversational implicature**. For one thing,
an entailment is destroyed by negation: the sentence *Booth did
not assassinate Lincoln* does not entail either *Lincoln is dead* or
*Booth killed somebody* (presuppositions are different here). For
another, an entailment is totally independent of any context
(conversational implicatures are different in this respect).

*See:* **conversational implicature**; **presupposition**
*Further reading:* Hurford and Heasley, 1983: 107–112.

**ethnography of speaking**   The study of the norms of
communication in a speech community, including verbal,
non-verbal and social factors. Every society has its own norms
for communicative behaviour. If I am sitting at the dinner
table and I want the salt, which is out of reach, I might say
'Would you mind very much passing me the salt?' or 'Could
you pass the salt, please?' or 'Gimme that salt'; I might even
say nothing, but just reach over the person next to me to

grab the salt. Some of these behaviours are more acceptable than others, depending on the circumstances, and some would perhaps never be acceptable at all.

The key point is that the norms are not everywhere the same; instead, they vary substantially from culture to culture. In a traditional Basque household, the master of the house may indicate that he wants his wine glass refilled simply by banging it, without saying a word; this would probably never be acceptable in an English-speaking society (nor is it normal among younger Basques).

Anthropological linguists have long stressed the importance of examining communicative behaviour in the context of a culture, though the term *ethnography of speaking* (or *ethnography of communication*) itself was not coined until the 1970s, by the American anthropological linguist Dell Hymes. Investigators have looked at a broad range of variables in a number of speech communities: loudness of voice, pitch of voice, distance between speakers, expressions and postures, eye contact, terms of address, rules for initiating conversations, and many others.

Mexicans in conversation prefer to stand much closer together than do Americans, which can lead to comical results when a Mexican is talking to an American. English-speakers who meet each other but have nothing in particular to say will begin talking about the weather, since silence is considered unacceptable; but Chinese-speakers in the same position may choose to remain silent without giving offence. In Japanese and in Javanese, even the simplest utterance may assume any of a number of very different forms, depending on the relative status of the speaker, the addressee and the person being talked about, and also on the circumstances in which the conversation takes place. Italians punctuate their speech with animated gesticulations; Swedes do not. In the British House of Commons, it is considered technically improper for one MP to address another directly, and hence all speeches and remarks are formally directed at the Speaker, and all other MPs are referred to in the third person, with frozen locutions like 'the Honourable Member for Tatton'.

The study of the ethnography of communication seems capable of producing almost limitless surprises, and there is now a rich literature on the subject. However, integration of the findings has so far proved difficult, and there are few text-books.

*See:* **non-verbal communication**; **paralanguage**
*Further reading:* Bonvillain, 1993: ch. 4; Duranti, 1997: ch. 4; W.A. Foley, 1997: part V; Schiffrin, 1994: ch. 5.

**etymology**   The origin and history of a particular word, or the branch of linguistics that studies this. Every language has a vocabulary containing many thousands of words, and every one of those words has its own particular origin and history, that is its own *etymology*. Specialists in etymology make it their business to uncover the origins of words, one by one. Doing this successfully requires a prodigious knowledge of the language containing the word being investigated and of any neighbouring or related languages from which the data may be relevant. It also requires the scrutiny of any number of old documents, sometimes very old documents, in order to extract every available scrap of information about the word.

Sometimes the word in question has been in the language as long as the language has existed; in this case, the word has simply been inherited from some ancestral language. For example, English *three* derives from Old English *threo*, which in turn derives from Proto-Germanic *★thrijiz*, which in turn derives from Proto-Indo-European *★treyes*, which in turn probably derives from the word for 'three' in the unknown ancestor of Proto-Indo-European (The asterisk denotes a reconstructed form). The same Germanic source yields Gothic *threis*, Danish and Swedish *tre*, Dutch *drie*, German *drei*, and so on. The same Indo-European source yields Latin *tres*, itself the ancestor of Spanish *tres*, Italian *tre*, French *trois*, Romanian *trei*, and so on. Also from the same Indo-European source come Sanskrit *trayas*, Russian *tri*, Polish *trzy*, Lithuanian *trys*, Albanian *tre*, Irish *trí*, Welsh *tri*, and, less obviously, Persian *se* and Armenian *erek*. The last two may look dubious, but generations of patient and careful etymological work have established the histories of all these words beyond dispute.

In other cases the word in question has not been inherited from an ancestral language, but has instead entered the language at some point in time; it may simply have been 'borrowed' (copied) from a neighbouring language, or it may have been coined by speakers using the resources of the language. In these cases etymologists will be deeply interested in finding out, as far as they can, just when the word was first used, where and by whom, and in what sense. Without such evidence, etymology can be little more than guesswork.

Many thousands of English words have been (directly or indirectly) borrowed from other languages in which they already existed: *angel* from ancient Greek, *lettuce* from Latin, *knife* from Old Norse, *face* from Norman French, *cigarette* from modern French, *skunk* from Massachusett, *shampoo* from Hindi, *brandy* from Dutch, *mosquito* from Spanish, *poodle* from German, *umbrella* from Italian, *alcohol* from Arabic, *ski* from Norwegian, *yogurt* from Turkish, *ukulele* from Hawaiian, *whisky* from Scots Gaelic, *banana* from an African language, *kayak* from an Eskimo language, *kangaroo* from the Guugu–Yimidhirr language of Australia, and so on, and so on. In such cases, etymologists may be interested in going further, and in tracing the history of the word within the foreign language from which it is borrowed.

Many other English words have been constructed by English–speakers in any of a large number of ways. Such words as *gingerbread, paperback, scarecrow, spaghetti western, striptease, baby-sit, laptop, word processor, underfunding, bewitch, megastar, non-magnetic, miniskirt, edit, deli, flu, smog, burger, love-in, laser, giggle, bang, scrooge, quixotic, gothic* and *malapropism* have all been coined in English by one means or another – some of them centuries ago, others very recently – and etymologists are interested in all of them.

*See:* **loan word**; **onomastics**
*Further reading:* Hock and Joseph, 1996: ch. 9; Trask, 1996: 345–356.

**experimental approach**  An approach to the study of speech in which the investigator deliberately manipulates the speakers under study. The simple recording and analysis of a **corpus** of spontaneous speech yields valuable information, but it may not turn up answers to the particular questions the investigators are interested in. One solution is to question speakers directly about their **intuitions**, but it has been established that speakers often provide inaccurate answers about their own usage.

In the *experimental approach*, therefore, the investigators deliberately manipulate speakers in a calculated way. The idea is to construct scenarios in which speakers are induced to provide or to interpret utterances of a sort which will supply the required information, but without ever becoming aware of what that information is. This usually involves constructing well-designed tasks for speakers to perform; while performing these tasks, speakers inadvertently reveal the information being sought.

Constructing such tasks is, naturally, not trivial, and the originator of this approach – the American sociolinguist William Labov – has devoted a great deal of attention to their design.

*See:* **intuition**
Further reading: Labov, 1975.

# F

**finite**  Marked for **tense**. In many (not all) languages, a single **verb** may exhibit a number of different forms serving different grammatical functions, and these forms are often divided into two types called *finite* and *non-finite*. English, with its small number of grammatical markings, is not the ideal language to illustrate the difference, since some of the non-finite forms look just like some of the finite forms. But let's try.

A finite form is always marked for *tense*, and it also carries **agreement**, insofar as English has any agreement. Consider the verb *smoke*. Now this *citation form* of the verb, the form we use to name it and to enter it in a dictionary, is a non-finite form, the so-called *infinitive*. But the form *smokes*, as in *Susie smokes*, is finite: that -*s* on the end tells us that this form is marked for present tense and that it agrees with a third-person singular subject. Moreover, it is the only verb-form in the sentence, and only a finite form can stand as the only verb in a sentence. By the same reasoning, the form *smoke* which occurs in *I smoke* and *they smoke* is also finite, even though it carries no overt marking at all.

Also finite is the *smoked* of *Susie smoked*, which bears the past-tense suffix -*ed* and is again the only verb in the sentence. But present-tense *smokes* and *smoke* and past-tense *smoked* are the only finite forms the verb *smoke* has.

A non-finite form is not marked for tense, it shows no agreement, and it cannot be the only verb in a sentence.

An example is the form *smoking*, which has several functions. In *Susie is smoking*, it combines with the **auxiliary** *is*, which itself is finite. In *I have often seen Susie smoking*, it functions as a kind of **complement** (the finite form here is *have*). In *Smoking a guilty cigarette, Susie pondered the ruins of her love life*, it introduces a kind of **modifier** (the finite form here is *pondered*). In *Smoking is bad for you*, it functions as a kind of **nominalization**, the kind called a *gerund* (the finite form is *is*).

Also non-finite is *smoked* when it functions as a *past participle*, as in *Susie has smoked since she was fifteen* (the finite forms are *has* and *was*), or as a *passive participle*, as in *Cigars are rarely smoked by women* (the finite form is *are*).

The infinitive *smoke*, also non-finite, occurs in constructions like *Susie can't smoke in her office* (the finite form is *can*) and *Susie wants to smoke* (the finite form is *wants*).

If, as is sometimes done, we choose to regard sequences like *is smoking* (as in *Susie is smoking*) and *has smoked* (as in *Susie has smoked since she was fifteen*) as single verb-forms, then these are finite, since the first element is finite. It is more usual, though, to analyse such sequences into their finite and non-finite components. But not all such sequences are finite: in *Wanting to smoke a quick cigarette, Susie made a rush for the balcony*, the sequence *wanting to smoke* contains no finite forms at all (the only finite form in the sentence is *made*).

A clause or a sentence containing a finite verb-form is itself finite. Thus, *Susie smokes* is a finite sentence, while both clauses are finite in *Susie always smokes a cigarette after she finishes dinner*. But, in *Having finished her dinner, Susie decided to smoke a cigarette*, only *Susie decided to smoke a cigarette* is finite, while *having finished her dinner* and *to smoke a cigarette* contain no finite forms and are non-finite.

*See:* **tense**
*Further reading:* Hurford, 1994: 74–76.


**focus** Singling out some particular element of a sentence or an utterance as representing the most important new information. Consider the utterance *Susie needs a holiday*. Here it is not obvious that attention is being drawn to any particular part of the utterance. But now add **stress**: *SUSIE needs a holiday*. Now the utterance clearly means 'The one who needs a holiday is Susie, and not somebody else', and we say that *Susie* is in *focus*. If we stress something else, then that element is placed in focus: *Susie needs a HOLIDAY* (it's not something else that Susie needs).

In spoken English, we can always put a particular element in focus by stressing it. But both spoken and written English have another device for placing an element in focus: the use of any of several types of *cleft*. So, we might say, or write, *It's Susie who needs a holiday* (placing *Susie* in focus), or *What Susie needs is a holiday* (placing *a holiday* in focus).

Other languages may have other devices. For example, in Basque any element can be focused simply by placing it directly before the verb.

Focus must be clearly distinguished from **topic**: even professional linguists have been known to confuse these terms.

*See:* **given/new**; **topic**
*Further reading:* Greenbaum and Quirk, 1990: ch. 18.

**folk linguistics** Speakers' beliefs about their language or about language generally. In any given speech community, speakers will usually exhibit many beliefs about language: that one language is older, more beautiful, more expressive or more logical than another – or at least more suitable for certain purposes – or that certain forms and usages are 'correct' while others are 'wrong', 'ungrammatical' or 'illiterate'. They may even believe that their own language was a gift from a god or a hero.

Such beliefs rarely bear any resemblance to objective reality, except insofar as those beliefs *create* that reality: if enough English-speakers believe that *ain't* is unacceptable, then *ain't* is unacceptable, and, if enough Irish-speakers decide that English is a better or more useful language than Irish, then they will speak English, and Irish will die.

It is because of facts like these that a few linguists are now arguing that folk-linguistic beliefs should be taken seriously in our investigations – in great contrast to the usual position among linguists, which is that folk beliefs are no more than quaint bits of ignorant nonsense.

*See:* **language myths**; **prescriptivism**
*Further reading:* Crystal, 1997a: chs. 1–3.


**functionalism**   Any approach to the description of language structure which attaches importance to the purposes to which language is put. Many approaches to linguistics focus entirely on the purely structural characteristics of languages, ignoring the possible functions of language, and this approach has been very rewarding. But a large number of linguists have preferred to combine the investigation of structure with the investigation of function; an approach which does this is a *functionalist* approach.

There are very many functionalist approaches which have been put forward, and they are often very different from one another. Two prominent ones are *Role-and-Reference Grammar* (RRG), developed by William Foley and Robert Van Valin, and **Systemic Linguistics** (SL), developed by Michael Halliday. RRG approaches linguistic description by asking what communicative purposes need to be served and what grammatical devices are available to serve them. SL is chiefly interested in examining the structure of a large linguistic unit – a **text** or a **discourse** – and it attempts to integrate a great deal of structural information with other information (social information, for example) in the hope of constructing a coherent account of what speakers are doing.

Functionalist approaches have proved fruitful, but they are usually hard to formalize, and they often work with 'patterns', 'preferences', 'tendencies' and 'choices', in place of the explicit **rules** preferred by non-functionalist linguists.

*See:* **structuralism**; **Systemic Linguistics**
*Further reading:* Givón, 1995; Halliday, 1994; Malmkjær, 1991: 141–146, 158–161; Siewierska, 1991; Thompson, 1996.

**functions of language** The various purposes to which language may be put. We often tend to assume that 'the function of language is communication', but things are more complicated than that. Language serves a number of diverse functions, only some of which can reasonably be regarded as communicative. Here are some of the functions of language which we can distinguish:

1 We pass on factual information to other people.
2 We try to persuade other people to do something.
3 We entertain ourselves or other people.
4 We express our membership in a particular group.
5 We express our individuality.
6 We express our moods and emotions.
7 We maintain good (or bad) relations with other people.
8 We construct mental representations of the world.

All of these functions are important, and it is difficult to argue that some of them are more important, or more primary, than others. For example, studies of conversations in pubs and bars have revealed that very little information is typically exchanged on these occasions, and that the social functions are much more prominent. Of course, a university lecture or a newspaper story will typically be very different.

This diversity of function has complicated the investigation of the **origin and evolution of language**. Many particular hypotheses about the origin of language have tended to assume that just one of these diverse functions was originally paramount, and that language came into being specifically to serve that one function. Such assumptions are questionable, and hence so are the hypotheses based upon them.

Proponents of **functionalism** are often interested in providing classifications of the functions of languages or texts; see under **Systemic Linguistics** for a well-known example.

*See:* **language in use**; **qualitative approach**; **Systemic Linguistics**

*Further reading:* Crystal, 1997a: ch. 4.

**gap**  The absence in a sentence of a linguistic element which is in some sense logically required. Though linguists had long been aware of the existence of **ellipsis**, in the 1960s the American linguist Noam Chomsky and his students began to pay particular attention to certain types of 'missing' elements in the syntactic structures of sentences. These missing elements were dubbed *gaps*. Here are a few examples of English sentences containing gaps; as is conventional, the position of each gap is marked with the symbol *e* (for 'empty'): *Susie wants* e *to buy a car* (*to buy* has no subject); *Susie is hard to please* e (*please* has no object); *Who were you talking to* e *?* (*to* has no object); *Susie bought a necklace and Zelda* e *a bracelet* (the second clause has no verb); *Rod gave the museum a T-shirt and Elton* e e *a pair of glasses* (the second clause lacks both a verb and the phrase *the museum*).

The behaviour of gaps has increasingly been seen as crucial in formulating adequate theories of grammar, and recent theories of grammar often provide specific machinery for treating them. Recently the name *empty category* has often been preferred to *gap*, at least for those cases in which the 'missing' element is a **noun phrase**.

*See:* **anaphor**

**gender**  The classification of **nouns** into two or more classes
with different grammatical properties. In many of the world's
languages, all the **nouns** are divided into two or more classes
which require different grammatical forms on the noun
and/or on certain other words grammatically linked with the
noun or nouns in particular sentences. German, for example,
has three gender classes, which require different forms for
associated **determiners** and **adjectives**. Thus, 'the table' is
*der Tisch*, 'the pen' is *die Feder*, and 'the book' is *das Buch*,
where *der*, *die*, and *das* are all different forms of 'the'; 'an old
table' is *ein alter Tisch*, 'an old pen' is *eine alte Feder*, and 'an
old book' is *ein altes Buch*.

A gender language must have at least two gender classes, but
it may have more – eight, ten, or possibly even more. In some
gender languages, we can often guess from the form of a noun
which gender it belongs to; in others, we can often guess
from its meaning which gender it belongs to; in very many
languages, however, we cannot guess, because gender assignment is arbitrary. In German, for example, a noun which
denotes a male or a female *usually* (not always) goes into the
*der* gender or the *die* gender, respectively, and nouns with certain endings usually go into a predictable gender. After that,
though, the gender of the remaining nouns is impossible to
guess. In Navaho, nouns denoting humans usually go into one
gender, nouns denoting round things into a second gender,
nouns denoting long stiff things into a third gender, and so on,
but not all nouns can have their gender guessed in this way.

It is important to realize that grammatical gender need have
nothing to do with sex. In German (and other European
languages), there is a noticeable (but imperfect) correlation
between sex and gender assignment; however, most nouns
denote things that have no sex, and yet they must still be
assigned to a gender. In many other gender languages, sex
plays no part at all in gender assignment.

English, it is worth pointing out, has no gender. We
have a few sex-marked pronouns like *he* and *she*, and a few
sex-marked nouns like *duke* and *duchess*, but we have no
grammatical gender.

Sociolinguists (and others) often use the term *gender* in a very different way, meaning roughly 'a person's biological sex, especially from the point of view of the associated social role'. This usage must be carefully distinguished from the strictly grammatical sense of the term. A young lady in Germany belongs to the female gender (in this second sense), but the noun *Fräulein* 'young lady' is grammatically neuter. Non-linguists sometimes go further and use *gender* to mean 'sex-marked social role, regardless of biology'; in this usage, a biological male who dresses and lives as a woman belongs to the female gender.

*See:* **grammatical category**

*Further reading:* Corbett, 1991; Hurford, 1994: 78–81; Trask, 1995: 40–44.

**generative grammar**   A grammar of a particular language which is capable of defining all and only the grammatical sentences of that language. The notion of generative grammar was introduced by the American linguist Noam Chomsky in the 1950s, and it has been deeply influential. Earlier approaches to grammatical description had focused on drawing generalizations about the observed sentences of a language. Chomsky proposed to go further: once our generalizations are accurate and complete, we can turn them into a set of **rules** which can then be used to build up complete grammatical sentences from scratch.

A generative grammar is mechanical and mindless; once constructed, it requires no further human intervention. The rules of the grammar, if properly constructed, automatically define the entire set of the grammatical sentences of the language, without producing any ungrammatical garbage. Since the number of possible sentences in any human language is infinite, and since we do not want to write an infinitely long set of rules, a successful generative grammar must have the property of **recursion**: a single rule must be allowed to apply over and over in the construction of a single sentence.

Chomsky himself defined several quite different types of

generative grammar, and many other types have more recently been defined by others. A key characteristic of any generative grammar is its *power*: the larger the number of different kinds of grammatical phenomena the grammar can handle successfully, the more powerful is the grammar. But – and this is a fundamental point – we do not want our grammars to have limitless power. Instead, we want our grammars to be just powerful enough to handle successfully the things that actually happen in languages, but not powerful enough to handle things that do not happen in languages.

Within certain limits, all the different kinds of generative grammar can be arranged in a hierarchy, from least powerful to most powerful; this arrangement is called the *Chomsky hierarchy*. The goal of Chomsky's research programme, then, is to identify that class of generative grammars which matches the observed properties of human languages most perfectly. If we can do that, then the class of generative grammars we have identified must provide the best possible model for the grammars of human languages.

Two of the most important classes of generative grammars so far investigated are (context-free) **phrase structure grammar** and **transformational grammar**. The second is far more powerful than the first – and arguably too powerful to serve as an adequate model for human languages – while the first is now known to be just slightly too weak.

(Special note: in recent years, Chomsky and his followers have been applying the term *generative grammar* very loosely to the framework called **Government-and-Binding Theory** (GB), but it should be borne in mind that GB is not strictly a generative grammar in the original sense of the term, since it lacks the degree of rigorous formal underpinning which is normally considered essential in a generative grammar.)

*See:* **phrase-structure grammar; transformational grammar**
*Further reading:* Bach, 1974: chs. 2–3; Lyons, 1991: chs. 5–7; Malmkjær, 1991: 162–165.

**genetic hypothesis of language** The hypothesis that the human language faculty is rooted in our genes. This hypothesis holds that our distinctive language faculty is a trait which we have evolved over time, just like our upright posture and our opposable thumb. According to this view, language just *grows* in children, much as their teeth grow, except that language learning requires exposure to speech; that is, the hypothesis sees our language faculty as a distinct and specific part of our genetic endowment. It is seemingly supported by the nature of certain genetically based disabilities, which disrupt language while affecting little else, or which leave language largely unaffected while disrupting most other cognitive abilities. It is perhaps further supported by the existence of the astonishing **language instinct** in children. While controversial, this hypothesis is now widely accepted by linguists. The **innateness hypothesis** is a more specific version of it.

Nevertheless, the genetic hypothesis has been vigorously criticized by the British linguist-turned-computer-scientist Geoffrey Sampson and by the American psychologist Elizabeth Bates and her colleagues.

*See:* **autonomy of language**; **innateness hypothesis**; **language instinct**

*Further reading:* Bates, 1976; Bates *et al.*, 1979; Bates *et al.*, 1988; Macwhinney and Bates, 1989; Pinker, 1994: ch. 10; Sampson, 1997.

**genetic relationship** The relationship between languages which share a common ancestor. Living languages are always changing, and, when a single language extends over a significant geographical area, different changes inevitably occur in different places. Over time, then, the original language breaks up, first into a continuum of regional **dialects**, then eventually into several quite distinct languages. The several languages which result are the *daughter languages* of their common ancestor, and these daughters are *genetically related*.

Over millennia, this splitting may be repeated again and again, and that single ancestral language may thus give rise to a sizeable **language family**. All the languages in the family are genetically related; those which share a more recent common ancestor are more closely related than those whose last common ancestor is more distant.

One of the principal goals of **historical linguistics** is the identification of genetic relationships. This is often easy when the languages in question are closely related – that is, when their last common ancestor was spoken not more than two or three millennia ago. More distant genetic links, resulting from more remote common ancestry, are more difficult to identify with certainty and require careful analytical proce-dures to avoid being misled by chance resemblances and ancient instances of **language contact**. Eventually, at some time-depth, genetic links become impossible to identify at all, because the ceaseless processes of linguistic change will obliterate all traces of a common origin, or at least render them unrecognizable amid the background noise.

It is possible that all languages are ultimately descended from a single common ancestor – the ancestral speech of the first humans – and hence that all are genetically related, but we will never know about it.

*See:* **historical linguistics**; **language family**; **proto-language**;
   **reconstruction**

*Further reading:* Lehmann, 1992: ch. 5; Trask, 1994: ch. 10; Trask, 1996: ch. 7.


**genre**   A historically stable variety of **text** with conspicuous distinguishing features. The concept of *genre* is shared by (at least) linguistics, anthropology and literary criticism. Its study is well established but contentious, and figures ranging from the Russian linguist Roman Jakobson to the Russian Marxist literary critic Mikhail Bakhtin have made important contributions.

The key fact about a given genre is that it has some readily identifiable distinguishing features that set it off markedly from other genres, and that those features remain stable over a substantial period of time. In most cases, a particular genre also occupies a well-defined place in the culture of the people who make use of the genre.

Among the genres familiar to most of us are lyric poetry, religious liturgy, legal documents, proverbs, fairy tales, scholarly monographs, and news stories. Other societies may present further types, such as the illness-curing chants of Mayan shamans, and the oral epic poems of Serbian or ancient Greek bards. Very often mastery of a particular genre is seen as a requirement for a certain profession; this is so for lawyers, bards, academics, shamans, scientists and physicians, among others.

It is characteristic of every genre that the outward form of expression is of vital significance, and at least as important as the content; in some cases the form may actually be more important than the content, as is true of many types of poetry, such as French villanelles and Japanese haiku. In many communities, song and verse genres are characterized by such features as the use of totally different words from the everyday ones and the requirement that no word may ever be repeated. But even a scientific paper is subject to rigid rules of form: the order of presentation must be background / procedure / results / interpretation / conclusions; the paper must be written in an impersonal third person; and all mistakes, accidents and dead ends that cropped up during the work must be silently omitted. A chemist who volunteered in a paper 'At this point I dropped the beaker on the floor and had to start over' would not get his or her paper published.

*See:* **text**
*Further reading:* Bhatia, 1993; W.A. Foley, 1997: ch. 18; Malmkjær, 1991: 176–181.

**given/new** A way of classifying the elements of a sentence according to their information content. Most utterances are not produced in isolation: instead, each is produced in some context involving what has been said previously and what is known to, or believed by, the speaker and the listener. As a result, it is often the case that some part of an utterance serves only to tie it to this context, while another part introduces some kind of new information. We therefore speak of the *given/new* distinction.

The *given* part of an utterance represents the part which is already familiar to the listener in one way or another, while the *new* part represents the main contribution of the utterance. Consider the following exchange. Mike: *I don't know the woman in the white dress.* Susie: *Oh, she's the new Professor of Psychology.* Here Susie's reply can be analysed into the given part *she* and the new part *is the new Professor of Psychology.*

The analysis of sentences and utterances in terms of their organization of information was pioneered by the linguists of the *Prague school* in the early twentieth century, especially by the Czech Vilém Mathesius, under the name *functional sentence perspective*. Instead of *given* and *new*, Mathesius used the terms *theme* and *rheme*, and these are still in use today, especially by the proponents of **Systemic Linguistics**, though the terms are used here in a slightly specialized way. Still other linguists prefer the terms *topic* and *comment* in the same senses.

*See:* **topic**

*Further reading:* Brown and Miller, 1991: ch. 20; Greenbaum and Quirk, 1990: ch. 18; Thompson, 1996: ch. 6.

**government** The grammatical phenomenon in which the *presence* of a particular word in a sentence requires a second word which is grammatically linked with it to appear in a particular *form*. Most English personal pronouns occur in two different **case** forms, the *nominative* and the *objective*. Examples: *I/me, she/her, they/them*. When a preposition takes one of these pronouns as its object, that pronoun must appear in its objective form: *with me*, not *⋆with I*; *for her*, not *⋆for she*. We say that the preposition *governs* the case of its object, or simply that the preposition governs its object. What this means is that it is the very presence of the preposition which requires the objective case. This is not **agreement**: it makes no sense to say that the pronoun is 'agreeing' with the form of the preposition, because an English preposition has only a single form.

Government can be more complex. In German, for example, there are several different cases, and some prepositions govern one case, others another. For example, *mit* 'with' governs the dative case, and so German requires *mit mir* 'with me', with the dative case-form *mir* of the pronoun *ich* 'I'. But the preposition *für* 'for' governs the accusative case, and so 'for me' is *für mich*, with accusative *mich*. Each preposition in German governs some particular case, and a learner simply has to learn which prepositions require which cases.

Verbs can also govern case-forms. In Basque, for example, a particular verb may govern objects in any of several cases. Most govern the absolutive case; for example, *ikusi* 'see' does so: *neska ikusi dut* 'I saw the girl' (*neska* 'the girl', absolutive). But some govern the dative, such as *lagundu* 'help': *neskari lagundu diot* 'I helped the girl' (*neskari*, dative). And a few govern the instrumental, such as *gogoratu* 'remember': *neskaz gogoratu naiz* 'I remembered the girl' (*neskaz*, instrumental). In English, all verbs govern objects in the objective case.

For the somewhat special case of gender government, see under **agreement**. In the **Government–and–Binding Theory**, the concept of government is generalized and extended in certain ways that are central to the machinery of that framework.

*See:* **agreement**; **dependency**; **subcategorization**
*Further reading:* Gleason, 1961: 159–164.

**Government–and–Binding Theory** A particular theory of grammar, the descendant of **transformational grammar**. During the 1960s and 1970s, Noam Chomsky's transformational grammar went through a number of substantial revisions. In 1980, Chomsky gave a series of lectures in Pisa outlining a dramatic revision of his ideas; these lectures were published in 1981 as a book, *Lectures on Government and Binding*. The new framework presented there became known as the **Government-and-Binding Theory** (GB) or as the **Principles-and-Parameters** approach.

GB represents a great departure from its transformational ancestors; while it still retains a single transformational rule, the framework is so different from what preceded it that the name 'transformational grammar' is not normally applied to it.

As the alternative name suggests, GB is based squarely upon two ideas. First, the grammars of all languages are embedded in a **universal grammar**, conceived as a set of universal *principles* applying equally to the grammar of every language. Second, within universal grammar, the grammars of particular languages may differ only in small and specified respects; these possible variations are conceived as *parameters*, and the idea is that the grammar of any single language will be characterized by the use of a particular *setting* for each one of these parameters. The number of available settings for each parameter is small, usually only two or three.

GB is a *modular* framework. Its machinery is divided up into about eight distinct **modules**, or **components**. Each of these modules is responsible for treating different aspects of sentence structure, and each is subject to its own particular principles and constraints. A sentence structure is well-formed only if it simultaneously meets the independent requirements of every one of the modules. Two of those modules – those treating **government** and **binding** (the possibility that two **noun phrases** in a sentence refer to the same entity) – give GB its name.

Just like transformational grammar, GB sees every sentence as having both an abstract underlying structure (the former **deep structure**, now remaned *D-structure*) and a superficial structure (the former **surface structure**, now renamed *S-structure*). There is also a third level of representation, called *logical form* (LF). Certain requirements apply to each one of these three levels, while further requirements apply to the way in which the three of them are related.

The motivation for all this, of course, is the hope of reducing the grammars of all languages to nothing more than minor variations upon a single theme, the unvarying principles of universal grammar. But the task is far from easy, and Chomsky, confronted by recalcitrant data, has been forced into the position of claiming that the grammar of every language consists of two quite different parts: a *core* – which alone is subject to the principles of universal grammar – and a *periphery* – consisting of miscellaneous language-specific statements not subject to universal principles. This ploy has been seen by critics as a potentially catastrophic retreat from the whole basis of the Chomskyan research programme.

GB was an abstract framework to begin with, but it has become steadily more abstract, as its proponents, confronted by troublesome data, have tended to posit ever greater layers of abstraction, in the hope of getting their universal principles to apply successfully at some level of representation. Critics have not been slow to see this retreat into abstraction as a retreat from the data altogether, that is as an attempt to shoehorn the data into *a priori* principles which themselves are sacrosanct. The more outspoken critics have declared the GB framework to be more a religious movement than an empirical science. Nevertheless, GB has for years been by far the most influential and widely-practised theory of grammar in existence.

Recently, however, Chomsky has, to general surprise, initiated the *Minimalist Programme*, in which almost all of the elaborate machinery of GB is rejected in favour of a very different approach. It is too early to tell whether GB, like its transformational predecessors, is about to be consigned by its own proponents to the dustbin of history; if this does happen, those critics will surely become even more outspoken in their dismissal of the whole Chomskyan enterprise.

*See:* **modularity**; **transformational grammar**
*Further reading:* Cook, 1996; Cowper, 1992; Culicover, 1997; Haegeman, 1994; Horrocks, 1987: ch. 2; Ouhalla, 1994; Sells, 1985: ch. 2.

**grammar**   The rules for constructing words and sentences in a particular language, or the branch of linguistics studying this. Every language has a *grammar*; indeed, every language has quite a lot of grammar. Spoken languages like Latin, English, Chinese and Navaho differ rather substantially in their grammar, but they all have lots of it. The same is true of **creoles** and of true **sign languages** like ASL and BSL; it is even true of **artificial languages** like Esperanto, which has vastly more grammar than is hinted at in its inventor's celebrated 'sixteen rules'. On the other hand, **pidgins** have no grammar to speak of and consist merely of words supplemented by contextual clues.

The linguistic study of grammar is conventionally divided into two parts: **morphology** – the study of word structure – and **syntax** – the study of sentence structure.

The tradition of studying grammar is venerable: the ancient Indians, the ancient Greeks and Romans, and the medieval Chinese, Arabs and Jews all did important grammatical work on their favourite languages, and the Port-Royal grammarians in seventeenth-century France were already contemplating grammar from a universalist point of view. But the rise of modern linguistics in the early twentieth century gave new impetus to the study of grammar; by the 1930s and 1940s the American Leonard Bloomfield and his successors were doing important work in morphology, and in the 1950s Noam Chomsky made the study of syntax one of the most prominent of all areas of linguistics, by introducing the new approach called **generative grammar** and by reviving the search for **universal grammar**.

Approaches to the study of grammar are many and various. Pre-twentieth-century approaches represent **traditional grammar**, while most twentieth-century approaches are varieties of **structuralism**. The more formal approaches developed since the 1950s are known as *theories of grammar*; among the more prominent ones are the several versions of **phrase-structure grammar**, **Lexical-Functional Grammar**, and **transformational grammar** with its descendant **Government-and-Binding Theory**. Among the approaches embedded within **functionalism**, the most prominent is **Systemic Linguistics**.

(A note on usage. The term *grammar* is also applied to a particular description of the grammatical facts of a language, or to a book containing this. Moreover, a few linguists like to use the word *grammar* more broadly, to include *all* the structural characteristics of languages, including their **phonology**, **semantics** and even **pragmatics**. But this is not usual.)

*See:* **generative grammar**; **morphology**; **syntax**; **universal grammar**

*Further reading:* Brown and Miller, 1991; Crystal, 1997a: ch. 16; Hurford, 1994: 87–92; Pinker, 1994: ch. 4.

**grammatical category** A linguistic category which has the effect of modifying the forms of some class of words in a language. The words of every language are divided up into several *word classes*, or **parts of speech**, such as **nouns**, **verbs** and **adjectives**. It often happens that the words in a given class exhibit two or more forms used in somewhat different grammatical circumstances. In each such case, this variation in form is required by the presence in the language of one or more *grammatical categories* applying to that class of words.

English **nouns** are affected by only one grammatical category, that of **number**: we have singular *dog* but plural *dogs*, and so on for most (but not all) of the nouns in the language. These forms are not interchangeable, and each must be used always and only in specified grammatical circumstances. And here is a key point: we must *always* use a noun in either its singular form or its plural form, even when the choice seems irrelevant; there is no possibility of avoiding the choice, and there is no third form which is not marked one way or the other. This is typically the case with grammatical categories.

English **pronouns** sometimes vary for **case**, as with *I/me*, *she/her* and *they/them*, and again only one of the two forms is generally possible in a given position. English nouns lack the category of case, but nouns in Latin, German, Russian and many other languages do vary in form for case.

English **adjectives** vary for the grammatical category of *degree*, as with *big/bigger/biggest*, and yet again only one of the three forms is possible in a given position.

English **verbs** exhibit the category of **tense**, as with *love/loved, work/worked, see/saw, take/took, sit/sat* and *drive/drove*. (Quite a few of these are irregular, but that does not matter: what matters is that the first form is required in certain circumstances but the second in others, and so we have *I see her* [now] but *I saw her* [in the past].) (English verbs have other forms, of course, but these other forms are either not marked for tense, or not just for tense; instead they are marked for other grammatical categories like **aspect** and **voice**.)

Some grammatical categories, like number and tense, are extremely widespread in the world's languages (though by no means universal), while others are unusual and confined to a few languages. For example, some North American languages have a grammatical category of *visibility*, by which nouns and pronouns must be explicitly marked to indicate whether or not the speaker can see the things they refer to at the moment of speaking. And many languages have the category of *evidentiality*, by which every statement must be overtly marked to show the source of the speaker's information: 'I saw it myself', 'Somebody told me', 'I have inferred this from evidence', and sometimes further distinctions.

*See:* **aspect**; **case**; **deictic category**; **gender**; **mood**; **number**; **tense**; **person**; **voice**

*Further reading:* Crystal, 1997a: 93; Gleason, 1961: ch. 14; Lyons, 1968: ch. 7; F. Palmer, 1971: 8297.

**grammatical relation**   Any one of the ways in which a **noun phrase** may be related to a **verb** in a particular sentence. Grammatical relations have been recognized as fundamental since ancient times. Though they were noticeably ignored during the early days of **generative grammar**, they have once again come to be viewed as an essential part of the grammatical structure of a sentence.

Grammatical relations, which are sometimes called *grammatical functions*, are also surprisingly difficult to define explicitly. The most familiar grammatical relation is that of *subject*. In English, the subject of the sentence usually comes first, or at least before the verb, and it is the only thing the verb ever agrees with (English doesn't have much **agreement**, of course). The subjects of the following sentences are bracketed: [*Susie*] *smokes*; *Carefully* [*she*] *poured the wine*; [*My girl-friend's parents*] *are visiting us*; [*Most of my students*] *drink*; [*That you are worried*] *is obvious*. The part of the sentence that follows the subject is the **predicate** (in one sense of that term).

A noun phrase that follows a verb is in most cases a *direct object*. Examples: *She likes* [*me*]; *Susie wants* [*a new car*]; *Susie has visited* [*most of the countries in Europe*]. But, if the verb is one of a small group including *be* and *become*, the following noun phrase is not a direct object but a *predicate nominal*. Examples: *Susie is* [*the cleverest person I know*]; *Susie became* [*an atheist*].

An *oblique object* is less directly connected to the verb. In English, an oblique object surfaces as the object of a **preposition**, though some other languages use case-endings for the same purpose. Examples: *I went to Spain with* [*Lisa*]; *The cat is under* [*the bed*].

Another traditional grammatical relation is the *indirect object*, but it is not clear whether or not indirect objects exist in English. Traditional grammarians would say that *Lisa* is an indirect object in both *Mike gave this book to Lisa* and *Mike gave Lisa this book*, and some linguists agree. However, in the first it is hard to see that *Lisa* is anything other than an ordinary oblique object. In the second, somewhat surprisingly, *Lisa* is arguably a direct object: note the corresponding passive *Lisa was given this book by Mike*.

*Further reading:* Brown and Miller, 1991: ch. 19; Hurford, 1994: 66–68, 103–105, 226–229.

**grapheme**    A single character in a recognized **writing system**. Every established writing system necessarily makes use of some set of written characters. Depending both upon the nature of the system used and on the facts of the language being written, this number may range from a mere handful up to many thousands.

At the simplest level of analysis, for example, the version of the roman alphabet used for writing English makes use of some eighty-odd graphemes: the 26 capital letters <A>, <B>, <C>, . . . , the 26 small letters <a>, <b>, <c>, . . . the ten digits <0>, <1>, <2>, . . . , an assortment of punctuation marks like <.>, <,>, <?> and <;>, and the blank space < >. (It is conventional to enclose a grapheme in angle brackets.)

A more sophisticated analysis of English writing might prefer to set up some additional graphemes, notably the *digraphs* used for writing single sounds, such as the <sh> of *ship*, the <ch> of *chip*, the <th> of both *thin* and *then*, the <ng> of *sing* and the <ea> and <ee> of *bread* and *reed*.

Some other languages using the roman alphabet have additional graphemes involving *diacritics*, such as <ç>, <ş>, <ñ>, <é>, <â> and <ø> (plus their capital versions); these are sometimes counted as distinct letters of the alphabet and sometimes not, but they are still distinct graphemes. A few languages even add further letters, like Icelandic <þ> and German <ß>. The Arabic alphabet has no capital letters, but most letters have two or three different graphic forms, depending on where they occur in a word, and each of these different forms is a grapheme.

The non-alphabetic Chinese writing system uses several thousand graphemes for everyday purposes and thousands more for specialist purposes, and the complex mixed system represented by the Egyptian hieroglyphs used a total of nearly 5,000 graphemes.

The standard ASCII set of characters found on most computer keyboards contains 95 graphemes, including such symbols as <$>, <*>, <+>, <&> and <@>, which are not usually counted as graphemes in the English writing system.

*See:* **orthography**; **writing system**
*Further reading:* Crystal, 1997a: ch. 33.

**head**   That element in a **phrase** which is chiefly responsible for the nature of that phrase. Every phrase in every language is built up from smaller units according to certain rather rigid rules. The several different types of phrase are distinguished from one another to some extent by differences in structure but mainly by the nature of the item (usually a word) around which it is constructed; that item is the *lexical head*, or simply the *head*, of the phrase, and it usually provides the name for the kind of phrase built up around it.

For example, the **noun phrase** *the little girl in the blue dress* is built up around the **noun** *girl* as its head; the whole phrase denotes some kind of girl. Likewise, the **verb phrase** *sang quietly to herself* is built up around the **verb** *sang* as its head; the whole phrase denotes some specific kind of singing. The adjective phrase *pretty as a picture* is headed by the adjective *pretty*; the adverb phrase *very slowly* is headed by the adverb *slowly*; and the prepositional phrase *under the bed* is headed by the preposition *under*.

The concept of heads is an ancient one, but it largely disappeared from linguistics during earlier part of the twentieth century. Since the 1970s, however, heads have once again come to be seen as grammatically central, and many contemporary theories of grammar assign them a very prominent place; one or two theories even take headedness to be the most important grammatical notion of all.

*See:* **modifier; phrase**
*Further reading:* Brown and Miller, 1991: ch. 17; Hurford, 1994: 92–94.

**historical linguistics**   The study of **language change** and of its consequences. Historical linguistics was the first branch of linguistics to be placed on a firm scholarly footing. It is traditional to date the founding of the discipline to 1786, when the British amateur linguist Sir William Jones famously pointed out the clear common ancestry of Greek, Latin and Sanskrit, and hence of the existence of the vast **Indo-European** family of languages, all of which descend from a single common ancestor. At about the same time, however, several Hungarian linguists were establishing that Hungarian must likewise share a common origin with Finnish and several other languages, in a different family now called *Uralic*.

Historical linguistics was vigorously developed throughout the nineteenth century, chiefly by linguists who were German or trained in Germany. Most of the attention was on *comparative linguistics*: the business of deciding which languages shared a common ancestry and hence which **language families** existed, of performing **reconstruction** to work out the properties of unrecorded ancestral languages (**proto-languages**), and of identifying the various changes which had led each ancestral language to break up into its several divergent daughters.

In the latter part of the nineteenth century, a number of younger linguists decided that they had enough evidence to declare that sound change was invariably regular – that is, that a given sound in a given context in a given language always changed in the same way, without exception. This *Neogrammarian hypothesis* became the orthodoxy in the field for the next hundred years, and it proved very fruitful.

In the twentieth century, and especially in recent years, there has been an explosion of interest in all aspects of language change. In particular, linguists have been searching eagerly for principles governing language change: what makes some changes more likely than others? It has proved possible to study changes which are in progress in contemporary languages, including English, and such studies have turned up a number of startling phenomena, many of which are clearly incompatible with the Neogrammarian hypothesis. A key point has been the discovery of the crucial link between **variation** and change. Historical linguistics has once again become one of the liveliest areas in all of linguistics.

*See:* **comparative reconstruction**; **internal reconstruction**; **language change**; **language family**; **Saussurean paradox**; **systematic correspondence**

*Further reading:* Hock and Joseph, 1996; McMahon, 1994; Malmkjær, 1991: 189–216; Trask, 1996.

**iconicity** A direct correlation between the form of a word and its meaning. The overwhelming norm in languages is **arbitrariness**, by which the form of a word bears no relation to its meaning. But there are certain exceptions, and these exceptions exhibit varying degrees of *iconicity*.

The most familiar type of iconicity is *onomatopoeia*. An onomatopoeic word is one which denotes a sound and which has a linguistic form specifically designed to mimic that sound with some degree of recognizability. English examples include *clink*, *meow*, *hiss*, *bang*, *boom*, *hum*, *quack* and *woof*. But even onomatopoeic words exhibit a good deal of arbitrariness: the sound of a gunshot is represented as *bang* in English, but as *pum* in Spanish, *peng* in German, and *dzast* in Basque.

Other types of iconicity exist. For example, the Basque word *tximeleta* (roughly, chee-may-LAY-tah) means 'butterfly', and the light, fluttery sound of the word seems to mimic the light, fluttery appearance of the insect.

*See:* **arbitrariness**; **sound symbolism**
*Further reading:* Anttila, 1988: 12–20.

**idiom** An expression whose meaning cannot be worked out from the meanings of its constituent words. Even if you know the meanings of all the words in the phrase *let the cat out of the bag*, you cannot guess the idiomatic meaning of the whole expression: this you must learn separately. (It means, of course, to reveal something publicly which is supposed to be a secret.) Such an expression is an *idiom*, and English, like other languages, has lots of idioms. Among these are *buy a pig in a poke* (commit oneself to an irrevocable course of action without knowing the relevant facts), *the tip of the iceberg* (the small visible part of a large problem), *kick the bucket* (die), *three sheets to the wind* (drunk) and *stick to one's guns* (refuse to change one's mind or give up).

The meanings of all such idioms are unpredictable and must be learned separately. Many such idioms are so familiar that native speakers hardly realize they are using an idiom at all. Exposure to a foreign language quickly reveals the true position: for example, the Basque idiom *Ez kendu babak altzotik* is literally 'Don't take the beans out of your lap', but no non-speaker of Basque is likely to guess the idiomatic meaning. (It means 'Don't get up on your high horse', 'Don't lecture me', and perhaps you can now see the motivation for the idiom.)

A linguistically fascinating fact about idioms is that some of them (though not all of them) can undergo the ordinary syntactic processes of the language. For example, *let the cat out of the bag* can appear in sentences like *The cat has been well and truly let out of the bag*, in which the idiom has been broken up and its parts scattered about the sentence, and yet the idiomatic sense is still present. Such findings pose interesting problems both of syntax and of psycholinguistics.

*Further reading:* Fernando, 1996; Huddleston, 1984: 42–44.

**immigrant language**  A language spoken in a country by a sizeable number of people who have only recently immigrated there. For centuries large numbers of people have been leaving their homelands and migrating to other countries in the hope of finding a better life. In some cases, the chief languages of the immigrants have already displaced the indigenous languages of the receiving countries as the national languages: Portuguese in Brazil, English in Australia, New

Zealand, the USA and much of Canada, Spanish in most of the rest of Latin America. These languages can no longer be regarded as immigrant languages.

But other cases are different. More recent immigrations have often brought large, even huge, numbers of people into nation-states with established national languages: speakers of Ukrainian in Canada; of Spanish, Vietnamese, Korean and a dozen other languages in the USA; of Gujarati, Panjabi and Bengali in Britain; of Arabic in France; of Turkish in Germany; and so on. The result in each case is the presence in the country of a large community of immigrants whose mother tongue is something quite different from that of the people who were already there. Each of these new languages is an *immigrant language* in the receiving country.

Often these immigrants are welcomed for the labour they bring, but their presence brings with it difficult problems of education, medical treatment and policing, among other things. The new arrivals typically know not one word of their new country's language, and they may or may not eventually acquire an adequate command of it. Their children, especially if born in the new country, are more likely to acquire the host country's language, but they do not inevitably do so. The linguistic and cultural differences may make integration into the new country very difficult, and some immigrant parents may not actually want their children to become integrated into the strange new society: instead, they may want them brought up according to the traditions, and in the language, of the old country. A further factor favouring isolation of the newcomers is possible resentment from the new country's established citizens: especially in time of economic recession, the immigrants may find themselves the victims of hostility, discrimination, persecution and violence.

In such circumstances, it is often exceedingly difficult to come up with a language policy which satisfies everyone, or even anyone. Children arriving in school cannot understand a word the teachers say. Attempts at providing them with special teaching may meet opposition from other citizens, who must foot the bill, and from immigrant parents, who want their children educated in the immigrant language. Attempts at providing mother-tongue education may be resisted again by those paying for them, by people who fear that the children may thus be perpetually condemned to second-class status, and by other immigrant parents who are eager to see their children educated in the host country's language – though not necessarily to be integrated into the host country's culture. All these competing pressures are visited upon the children, who may come to feel that they belong to no community at all. These children may reject the culture of their parents, which they see as alien and backward, leading to fierce family conflicts; at the same time, the children may be likewise rejected by the neighbours into whose culture they are trying to assimilate.

The linguistic consequences may be formidable. Consider the case of second-generation Arabic-speakers in southern France. On the one hand, their French-influenced Arabic may be very different from the Arabic of their parents, who may thus regard the young people's Arabic as defective and unacceptable. On the other, the youngsters, rejected by the surrounding French-speakers, often deliberately cultivate a style of French which is largely incomprehensible to outsiders, in a defiant attempt at giving themselves a sense of identity.

These linguistic consequences are of great interest to linguists, but they are nonetheless often a reflection of large-scale human misery.

*See:* **minority language**
*Further reading:* Crystal, 1997a: ch. 9; Pavlinić, 1994; Wardhaugh, 1987: ch. 10

**Indo-European**   A vast **language family**. People have long been aware that certain languages are strikingly similar to certain other languages. In the late eighteenth century a few linguists began to realize that certain ancient languages of Europe and Asia, notably Latin, Greek and Sanskrit (in India), were so remarkably similar in their grammars that they must share a common origin. This observation, famously made by

Sir William Jones in 1786, marks the official beginning of the recognition of the Indo-European (IE) family. It was quickly realized that Gothic (and the other Germanic languages), Old Persian (and the other Iranian languages) and the Celtic languages also shared the same common origin, as well as the Baltic and Slavic languages, and Albanian and Armenian. Over a century later, texts written in several long-extinct languages were unearthed in Anatolia and central Asia; when deciphered, these too proved to be written in ancient Indo-European languages: Hittite (and several other Anatolian languages) in the first case and the Tocharian languages in the second. A very few other ancient Indo-European languages have turned up in inscriptions but are so poorly documented we know little about them.

By applying **comparative reconstruction** (which was largely developed and refined by its application here), linguists were eventually successful in carrying out a substantial reconstruction of the single language which was the remote ancestor of all these languages. This ancestor is called *Proto-Indo-European*, or PIE. The speakers of PIE were illiterate and left no records, but we nevertheless know a great deal about the phonology, grammar and vocabulary of PIE. For example, we are confident that a PIE root of the approximate form *kwel-* 'revolve, turn' (the asterisk indicates a reconstructed form) is the source of Latin *collum* 'neck', Greek *polos* 'pole' – borrowed as English (*north*) *pole* – and Old Church Slavonic *kolo* 'wheel' (among others), and that a reduplicated form of this *kwekwlo-* is the source of Greek *kuklos* 'circle, wheel' – borrowed as English *cycle* – Sanskrit *cakra-* 'wheel' and English *wheel* (Old English *hweowol*).

We think PIE was probably spoken around 6,000 years ago, but the place is unknown. Most people favour the south Russian steppes, but others have argued for the Balkans, Anatolia, the Middle East, the Caucasus, central Asia and other locations. In any case, the IE languages eventually spread over a huge area of Asia and most of Europe, repeatedly breaking up into clusters of daughter languages as they did so. In the process, the IE languages obliterated an unknown number of earlier languages, including all the earlier languages of Europe except for Basque in the west and Finnish and its relatives in the north. Until the eve of modern times, the family extended from India to western Europe (hence its name), but the European expansion has introduced IE languages like English, Spanish, French, Portuguese and Russian into vast areas of the globe, displacing many more languages in the process. Today about half the world's people speak IE languages, even though the number of living IE languages is below 200.

*See:* **comparative reconstruction**; **language family**; **reconstruction**

*Further reading:* Baldi, 1983; Beekes, 1995; Crystal, 1997a: ch. 51; Lehmann, 1967, 1993; Lockwood, 1969, 1972; Mallory, 1989; Szemerényi, 1996; Trask, 1996.

**inflection**   Variation in the form of a single word for grammatical purposes. In many (not all) languages, a single word can assume any of several different forms, or even dozens of different forms, the choice depending on the grammatical context in which it is used. This is *inflection*. A word may be inflected by adding **affixes** or by various types of internal change.

English has very little inflection, but it does have some. A typical **noun** has only two grammatical forms: singular *dog* and plural *dogs*, singular *child* and plural *children*, singular *foot* and plural *feet*. A typical **verb** has slightly more forms than a noun; for example, *write* has *write*, *writes*, *wrote*, *written*, *writing*, while *love* has only *love*, *loves*, *loved*, *loving*, and *put* has just *put*, *puts*, *putting*. (The number is larger if we count syntactic forms like *has written* as inflections, which we sometimes do but usually don't.) A typical **adjective** has three inflected forms: positive *big*, comparative *bigger*, superlative *biggest*.

Inflection is not universal. Vietnamese, for example, has no inflection at all, and every word is completely invariable in form. On the other hand, some North American languages have astonishingly complex inflectional systems, in which a single verb may appear in hundreds of different forms.

The key point about inflection is that applying it never gives you a new word, but only a different form of the same word. But **derivation**, in contrast, does produce new words which have to be entered separately in a dictionary.

*See:* **derivation**; **grammatical category**; **morphology**
*Further reading:* Bauer, 1988: ch. 6; Brown and Miller, 1991: chs. 12–14.

**innateness hypothesis**   The hypothesis that children are born knowing what human languages are like. It is obvious that *particular* languages are not innate and must be learned. Any child, regardless of ethnic background, will learn perfectly whatever language it is exposed to, and an isolated child prevented from any exposure to language will learn no language at all.

Nevertheless, modern linguists are often impressed by the striking resemblances among languages all over the globe. In spite of the obvious and seemingly dramatic differences among them, linguists are increasingly persuading themselves that the observed degree of variation in language structures is much less than we might have guessed in advance, and hence that there are important universal properties shared by all languages.

In the 1960s, the American linguist Noam Chomsky put forward a bold hypothesis to explain this apparent universality: according to his *innateness hypothesis*, a number of important characteristics of language are built into our brains at birth, as part of our genetic endowment, and hence we are born already 'knowing' what a human language can be like. In this view, then, learning a particular language is merely a matter of learning the details which distinguish that language from other languages, while the universal properties of languages are already present and need not be learned.

The innateness hypothesis was controversial from the start, and a number of critics, among them philosophers and psychologists, took vigorous issue with Chomsky's position, arguing that there is no evidence for innate linguistic knowledge, and that the acquisition of a first language could be satisfactorily explained in terms of the all-purpose cognitive faculties which the child uses to acquire other types of knowledge about the world. This controversy reached a head in 1975, when Chomsky debated the issue with one of his most distinguished critics, the Swiss psychologist Jean Piaget.

Chomsky and his supporters have responded in several ways. First, they attempt to point to identifiable universal properties of language, what they call **universal grammar** (itself a deeply controversial notion); these properties they claim to be arbitrary, unexpected and in no way deducible from general cognitive principles. Second, they point out that children *never* make certain types of errors which we might have expected. For example, having learned *The dog is hungry*, they can produce *They dog looks hungry*, yet, having learned *Susie is sleeping*, they *never* produce *\*Susie looks sleeping*. Third, they invoke the *poverty of the stimulus*. By this term they mean that the data available to the child are quite inadequate to account for the knowledge which the child eventually acquires. For example, the usual rules of question-formation in English seem to predict that a statement like *The girls who were throwing snowballs have been punished* should have a corresponding question *\*What have the girls who were throwing been punished?* In fact, every English-speaker knows that this is impossible, and no child or adult ever tries to construct such questions. However, there seems to be no way that this constraint could possibly be inferred from what the child hears, and Chomsky therefore invokes a universal principle, supported by comparable data from other languages, which he takes as part of our innate linguistic endowment.

The debate continues, and no resolution is in sight.

*See:* **genetic hypothesis of language**; **universal grammar**
*Further reading:* Aitchison, 1989: chs. 3–6; Piattelli-Palmarini, 1979; Sampson, 1997; Steinberg, 1993: ch. 7.

**internal reconstruction** A method in **historical linguistics** which can be applied to a single language to recover information about its past. The name *internal reconstruction* is given to several related but different procedures. What most of them have in common is this: we observe that a certain pattern exists in the language of interest, but that certain forms are exceptions to the pattern; we hypothesize that the exceptional forms were once regular, and we identify the changes which made them irregular.

A particularly famous example of internal reconstruction involves *Proto-Indo-European* (PIE), the unrecorded ancestor of the **Indo-European** languages. The young Ferdinand de Saussure observed that, while the vast majority of PIE verbal roots could be reconstructed with the general form *CeC-*, where *C* represents any consonant, there were a number with other forms: *eC-*, *aC-*, *oC-*, *Ce:-*, *Ca:-* or *Co:-*, the last three always with long vowels represented by a colon. Saussure therefore hypothesized that these exceptional roots had once been perfectly regular roots of the form *CeC-*, but that certain ancestral consonants had been categorically lost from the language, that some of these vanished consonants had first altered the quality of a neighbouring vowel *e* to *a* or *o*, and that all of them had, upon disappearance, induced lengthening of a preceding vowel. This analysis makes all the exceptional roots the result of regular phonological change applying to what were originally perfectly normal roots. These hypothetical lost consonants have become known as *laryngeals*, and Saussure's *laryngeal hypothesis* was eventually confirmed by the discovery that one Indo-European language, Hittite, actually preserves some of these consonants.

*See:* **comparative reconstruction**
*Further reading:* Terry Crowley, 1992: ch. 6; Fox, 1995: ch. 7; Hock, 1986: ch. 17; Trask, 1996: ch. 9.

**international language** A language which is widely used, for a variety of purposes, by people in different countries, especially by people for whom it is not a mother tongue. As a consequence of various political and social circumstances, a single language may come to be used extensively by people in a number of countries, most of whom speak various other languages as their mother tongues. In medieval Europe, Latin was everywhere the language of scholarship, science, diplomacy, religion and (usually) the law, and people working in these areas could all write (and sometimes speak) Latin. In eighteenth- and nineteenth-century Europe, French was the international language of diplomacy, of fine arts and high culture, and of polite society generally; most educated people could and did speak French, even if their mother tongue was (say) Russian or German. Chinese and Arabic have likewise served at times as international languages, in east Asia and in the Muslim world, respectively.

Today, however, English is beyond dispute the premier international language throughout the world. English is everywhere the first language in such domains as business, science, technology, communications and popular culture. When a Swedish manufacturing company negotiates a business deal in Thailand, the negotiations are conducted in English. When a Brazilian geneticist publishes his latest research, he publishes in English. When an Egyptian pilot flies into Moscow, he speaks to the control tower in English. When the Secretary-General of the United Nations, the chairman of the International Olympic Committee or the commanding officer of NATO makes an important announcement, he makes it in English. Even pop groups from Norway, Russia, France and Japan often sing in English.

This pre-eminence of English is rather recent; it largely dates from 1945. Though the British Empire had earlier introduced English, as a first or a second language, into huge areas of the world, it was chiefly the rise of American political and economic power, and the accompanying spread of American culture (hamburgers, jeans, Hollywood films, TV shows, rock music) after the Second World War which made a command of English such an attractive and valuable asset in the succeeding decades.

Indeed, English has now become the first *global language* or *world language* the planet has ever seen. That is, English now enjoys some kind of special status in almost every country in the world: as the sole official language, as a co-official language, or as the designated principal foreign language. Polyglot countries like Nigeria, India and Singapore use English for most administrative and commercial purposes; countries like Spain, Germany, Greece, Algeria, Korea and Japan have abandoned French or Chinese as the preferred foreign language in favour of English; many large German business forms now require their senior managers to conduct all internal business in English; Dutch universities have come close to adopting English as the sole language of instruction for all subjects, and may yet do so. It has been estimated that nearly one quarter of the earth's population – approaching 1.5 billion people – are now competent in English, and the number is growing all the time. Nothing like this has ever happened before.

*See:* **language and power**

*Further reading:* Crystal, 1997a: ch. 59, 1997b; Wardhaugh, 1987: ch. 10.


**International Phonetic Alphabet**   An agreed set of symbols for representing speech sounds. The languages of the world employ a rather large number of distinguishable speech sounds, and, for serious work in phonetics and linguistics, it is essential to have an agreed set of symbols for representing these sounds as explicitly as possible. The twenty-six letters of the roman alphabet are not nearly enough for the task, and consequently various systems have been invented for the purpose, most of them based upon the roman alphabet supplemented by various additional symbols and/or diacritics ('accents'). By far the most widely used system is the *International Phonetic Alphabet*, or *IPA*. The IPA was invented in 1888 by the International Phonetic Association, the professional body of phoneticians; the Association has frequently revised and expanded its alphabet, the most recent revision having taken place in 1993.

The policy of the Association is to keep the use of diacritics to a minimum, and hence the IPA employs a very large number of specially designed characters, such as [ʃ] for the consonant in English *shy*, [ŋ] for the velar nasal in English *singing*, [ɬ] for the sound spelled <ll> in Welsh, as in *Llanelli*, and [ʎ] for the sound spelled <gl> in Italian, as in *figlio* 'son'. This makes the alphabet cumbersome to print, but nevertheless the IPA is the most widely used phonetic alphabet in the world; even many good dictionaries of English and of other languages now often use the IPA for representing pronunciations.

The ordinary roman letters often have obvious values, as with [k], [s], [m] and [i] (this last is the vowel of Italian *si* 'yes'), but a few of these have values which are unexpected for English-speakers: [j] for the initial consonant of English *yes*, [y] for the vowel of French *tu* 'you', [x] for the final consonant of German *Bach* and [r] for the trill of Spanish *perro* 'dog'.

Double characters are used for certain purposes: for example, [t͡ʃ] for the affricate occurring twice in English *church* and [g͡b] for the consonant in the language-name *Igbo* (roughly, a [g] and a [b] pronounced simultaneously). Diacritics are used for a wide variety of purposes: for example, [tʷ] is a labialized (lip-rounded) version of [t], [tⁿ] is a nasally released version of [t] (released through the nose, not through the mouth), [b̰] is a creaky-voiced version of [b], and [i̠] is a retracted version of [i] (a vowel resembling [i] but pronounced a little further back in the mouth). Length is marked by a special colon, so that [iː] represents a long version of [i]. There are also symbols for representing various types of tones, pitches, boundaries and pauses.

Though they are primarily designed for representing speech sounds (objective physical events), the IPA symbols are naturally also widely used for representing the **phonemes** of particular languages. For example, the initial consonant of English *think* is phonetically the dental fricative [θ] for most speakers, and so the phoneme realized in this way is commonly represented as /θ/. But note carefully that a conventional phoneme symbol consisting of an IPA symbol in phoneme slashes may not in fact be pronounced in the way the IPA symbol would suggest; for example, the phoneme at the beginning of English *red* is customarily represented as /r/, for orthographical convenience, but probably no native speaker of English ever pronounces this word with the trill [r]: it's just that the IPA symbols that represent precisely what English-speakers say are awkward to print, and moreover different speakers of English use different pronunciations of /r/, pronunciations which would be represented by different IPA symbols. An IPA symbol in square brackets is (or should be) intended to represent a real speech sound accurately; an IPA symbol in phoneme slashes is just a convenient way of representing some phoneme in some language, and may not be a faithful guide to phonetic reality.

In the USA, many people use a different phonetic alphabet, called *American transcription*. This uses many different symbols from the IPA. For example, American [š] = IPA [ʃ]; American [č] = IPA [ʧ]; American [ü] = IPA [y]; American [ř] = IPA [r]; and so on. The American system is designed to use diacritics in preference to special characters, and it is more convenient for people writing on a typewriter. With the increasing use of computers and word processors which can produce IPA characters, the American system is slowly giving way to the IPA. Meanwhile, though, many American textbooks and scholarly publications continue to use American transcription, and you will have to become familiar with both systems.

No other phonetic alphabet finds any significant general use today. Note, though, that specialists in particular languages often have their own local conventions which depart widely from the IPA. For example, specialists in Tibeto-Burman languages often use the symbol <x> to represent the vowel schwa (IPA [ə]), and specialists in Pacific languages often use <q> to represent glottal stop (IPA [ʔ]). Romanized transcriptions of languages not normally written in the roman alphabet may also exhibit unexpected usages: for example, in the familiar **Pinyin** system of romanizing Mandarin Chinese, the letters <x> and <q> are used for Mandarin phonemes whose phonetic realizations are nowhere near those of IPA [x] and [q]. These odd usages are chosen purely to make printing as easy as possible.

*See:* **consonant**; **phonetics**; **speech sound**; **vowel**
*Further reading:* Malmkjær, 1991: 219–224; Pullum and Ladusaw, 1996.

**intertextuality**   Connections between **texts**. The concept of *intertextuality* was introduced in the 1960s by the French critic Julia Kristeva. Most obviously, the term can be applied to the prominent allusions made in one literary work to another work: for example, Tom Stoppard's play *Rosenkrantz and Guildenstern Are Dead* to Shakespeare's *Hamlet*; James Joyce's *Ulysses* to Homer's *Odyssey* (and others); William Golding's *Lord of the Flies* to R.M. Ballantyne's *The Coral Island*; David Lodge's *Nice Work* to the whole genre of novels studied by the chief character; and T.S. Eliot's *The Waste Land* to a large collection of works.

But Kristeva's intention is of much broader applicability: she sees every text as constituting an *intertext* in a succession of texts already written or yet to be written. A version of this idea has recently begun to be incorporated into the linguistic analysis of texts. The general idea is that a text does not exist in isolation and cannot be fully appreciated in isolation; instead, a full understanding of its origins, purposes and form may depend in important ways on a knowledge of other texts. A sonnet may depend upon the reader's familiarity with the sonnet-writing tradition; a newspaper story may depend upon previous news stories; a political speech may invoke earlier speeches and political statements; even a recipe may depend upon the reader's acquaintance with other recipes.

Intertextuality is still a very new idea in linguistic analysis, and it is too early to say how prominent it may prove to be.

*See:* **text**
*Further reading:* Fabb, 1997: 227–233; Thibault, 1994.

**intonation**   Variation in the pitch of the voice during speech. In science-fiction films, robots are often made to speak in a dead-level pitch, with no rises and falls. The (intended) effect is one of inhuman speech, for no healthy human being ever speaks in such a way. Instead, the pitch of our voice rises and falls in structured ways during each utterance, and the resulting pattern is the *intonation* pattern of the utterance.

Every utterance in every language, without exception, is produced with some intonation pattern imposed on it. These patterns are largely peculiar to individual languages and accents, though certain universal tendencies can be observed. For example, it is very common in languages for yes–no questions to be uttered with a final rise in pitch (as in *Are you coming with us?*), while statements tend more often to be uttered with a final fall (as in *This is my wife*) – but Australians and Americans often utter statements with a final rise, a phenomenon which is highly conspicuous to other speakers of English, and which has been dubbed 'uptalk'.

The intonation of English has been seriously studied since the 1920s, at least. The British tradition has been to analyse intonation in terms of *contours*, or *tunes*, superimposed on sizeable chunks of an utterance; the American tradition, in contrast, prefers to decompose intonation patterns in terms of jumps between several discrete *levels*.

*See:* **prosody**; **suprasegmental**
*Further reading:* Cruttenden, 1986; Crystal, 1997a: ch. 29; Malmkjær, 1991: 230–236; Tench, 1996.

**intuition**   Your 'gut feeling' about the facts of your native language. We all have intuitions about our own language: about what is normal, acceptable, unusual, strange or impossible, or about what a given form means and when we might use it, if at all. The issue, and it is a central one, is how

133

(if indeed any at all) much trust we should place in speakers' intuitions in compiling our descriptions of language.

The American linguists of the first half of the twentieth century, with their adherence to empiricism, generally preferred to base their descriptions entirely on the observed spontaneous usage of native speakers. At times they found it necessary (as we still do today) to interrogate speakers directly to obtain elusive information: 'How would you say X?'; 'Is Y a possible form?'; 'What does Z mean?' But, on the whole, they regarded speakers' judgements as a less secure source of information than spontaneous usage.

In the 1950s, the American linguist Noam Chomsky and his followers put forward a dramatic new proposal: that important facts about a language could be obtained directly from speakers' intuitions. That is, they proposed that you could find out important things about your own language by merely asking yourself questions like 'Is construction X possible, and, if so, what does it mean?' Since almost all the early Chomskyans were speakers of English, this meant that their descriptions of English were very largely based upon their own considered opinions about their own usage. And this policy has proved to be deeply controversial.

For one thing, it didn't take long for sceptical linguists to demonstrate conclusively that native speakers' intuitions were sometimes hopelessly wrong. Again and again, the sceptics found that native speakers of English and of other languages, on being asked 'Is construction X possible for you?', would assert strongly that X was not possible, and would sometimes further insist that they couldn't even understand X – and then, a few minutes later, these same speakers would use X in their own spontaneous speech. A good example is the northeastern American locution 'They're a lousy team any more', which, on interrogation, is sometimes rejected as ungrammatical and incomprehensible by people who nevertheless use this form freely in their own speech. (The example means 'They used to be a good team, but now they're lousy.')

For another thing, the linguists who were working on English often had a theoretical stake in the outcome of questions, and time and again a linguist pondering the status of a doubtful example would consult his (or her) own intuitions and find that those intuitions gave him just the answer he needed to make his current analysis work. For example, one linguist, pondering the case of 'I saw us in the mirror', reached the conclusion that this was ungrammatical – which was exactly the result he needed to make his new theory work. Yet most speakers of English who are unacquainted with the theoretical issue and have no stake in it not only agree that this sentence is perfectly grammatical but use such sentences freely in their spontaneous speech.

Consequently, many linguists not of a Chomskyan persuasion today reject intuitions as a reliable source of information. Some, led by the American sociolinguist William Labov, have devoted considerable attention to the problem of obtaining reliable information about usage that require neither direct questions nor merely waiting for the required information to turn up by chance, and they have developed some skilful techniques for doing this.

*See:* **experimental approach**
*Further reading:* Labov, 1975; Sampson, 1975: ch. 4.

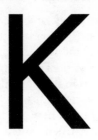

**kinship terms** The system of terms available in a given language for naming relatives. Kinship terminology varies widely among languages. English has only *uncle*, but many other languages have different words for 'father's brother' and 'mother's brother'. English distinguishes *niece* and *nephew*, but some other languages have only a single word to cover both, and this same word sometimes covers also 'grandson' and 'granddaughter'. In English, both men and women have only *sisters*, but in Basque a man has an *arreba* while a woman has an *ahizpa*, while in Seneca there are different words for 'older sister' and 'younger sister'.

The scope for variation is enormous, but anthropological linguists have found that most kinship systems can be analysed into fairly orderly combinations of a few semantic features, such as [male/female ego], [male/female referent], [older/younger], [ascending/descending generation]. Several particular systems are found to recur widely in the world's languages, such as the famous **Omaha system** found in certain North American languages and elsewhere.

*Further reading:* W.A. Foley, 1997: ch. 6.

**knowledge about language** An investigative and context-based way of teaching English to native speakers in schools. Until the 1960s, the teaching of English in schools in English-speaking countries was typically carried out within the confines of **traditional grammar**, and was characterized by a great deal of grammatical analysis of isolated sentences. This approach seemed arid, boring and irrelevant to many educators, and it was dropped from most state schools in the 1960s. At first it was replaced by nothing at all, which led to a generation of English-speakers who knew nothing whatever about the structure and functioning of their language.

In the 1980s, a group of academics and teachers, mainly in Britain, decided to try to re-introduce the teaching of English, but in a way which, it was hoped, would prove stimulating to pupils. The approach which they developed has become known as *knowledge about language*, or KAL. The chief statement of the KAL position in Britain is the *Cox Report* of 1989.

Among the several goals of KAL are the following: to ensure that all study of English is embedded within understandable *contexts*, to base the study of English upon connected texts which are relevant to the pupils, to place the study of standard English within a context of regional, social and functional varieties of English, to foster an awareness of the various purposes to which English can be put and the ways in which these purposes are reflected in the use of language (this is *language awareness*) and, above all, to make the whole thing investigative and exploratory in nature; that is, to allow pupils to examine instances of English and to draw their own conclusions, rather than merely regurgitating what has been fed to them.

Prominent in some British schools in the 1990s, KAL has been regarded as a success by some teachers and linguists, though critics complain that the pupils still end up with too little formal knowledge of English grammar. In the late 1990s, there are signs in Britain that KAL may be abandoned, or at least drastically modified, in favour of a more rigorous and traditional approach to such topics as grammar and punctuation.

*See:* **language in use**
*Further reading:* Carter, 1997: ch. 3; Carter *et al.*, 1997; McCarthy and Carter, 1993.

# L

**language** The central object of study in linguistics. Language is, of course, the central object of study in the linguistic sciences, but the term covers several rather different concepts which need to be carefully distinguished.

To begin with, of course, we need to distinguish between an individual language – such as English or Swahili – and language in general. Most linguists believe that all individual languages necessarily possess important properties in common – otherwise, **linguistics** would be a somewhat unrewarding discipline – and every individual language is therefore a combination of these **universal** properties with a number of accidental and often idiosyncratic features. For many (not all) linguists, it is these universal properties which are of greatest interest, but the only way we can get at these properties is by scrutinizing individual languages.

In this enterprise, strategies differ. The American linguist Noam Chomsky and his followers prefer to analyse a few languages in exhaustive detail, in the hope of identifying subtle abstract principles concealed deep in the data; Chomsky calls these principles **universal grammar**. Others, though, dismiss this approach as narrow and misleading, and prefer to proceed by surveying large numbers of structurally different languages and looking for both generalizations and interesting diversity.

The ultimate goal of linguistics is the elucidation of the human **language faculty** (called *langage* by Saussure).

To this end, linguists have usually found it essential to distinguish between the abstract mental system of rules, principles and constraints which are shared by speakers (called *langue* by Saussure and **competence** by Chomsky, though the terms are not quite equivalent) and the real utterances produced by individual speakers on particular occasions (Saussure's *parole*, Chomsky's **performance**). More recently Chomsky has introduced a further distinction: he suggests that an individual language may itself be viewed either as a set of rules and principles in the minds of speakers (his *I-language*), or as a set of possible sentences (his *E-language*); this latter concept is still an abstraction, distinct from actual **utterances**.

It is important to realize that only **natural languages** (mother tongues) are truly part of the subject matter of linguistics. Nevertheless, linguists are often interested in **pidgins** and even in **animal communication**, for purposes of comparison; occasionally they are even interested in **artificial languages** like Esperanto.

One way of getting at the abstract properties of natural languages, championed by Chomsky in his early days and still pursued by others (though no longer by Chomsky), is to devise *formal grammars* which can characterize *formal languages*. The idea is to compare the properties of these formal languages with the observed properties of natural languages to see which kinds of formal grammars give the best fit. This is the motivation behind the construction of **generative grammars**.

*See:* **competence**; **creole**; **language faculty**; **natural language**; **performance**
*Further reading:* Crystal, 1997a; Trask, 1995.

**language acquisition**  The process by which a child acquires its mother tongue. The acquisition of a first language is arguably the most wonderful feat we perform in our whole life, and we do it at an age when we can hardly do anything else. An explanation for this feat is now considered to be one of the central tasks of linguistics.

The serious linguistic investigation of acquisition dates mainly from the 1940s, when the Russian linguist Roman Jakobson published a pioneering study. In 1957, the American psychologist B.F. Skinner published *Verbal Behavior*, an attempt at explaining acquisition within the framework of **behaviourism**, but this book was savagely reviewed by the American linguist Noam Chomsky, who argued persuasively that Skinner's account was hopelessly inadequate to explain anything of interest.

From about the 1960s, intensive studies of children acquiring their first language became increasingly frequent; particularly influential was Roger Brown's 1973 book *A First Language*. This body of work quickly established that early acquisition proceeds through a sequence of well-defined stages, called *cooing*, *babbling*, the *one-word stage* and the *two-word stage*. After this, it becomes impossible to recognize well-defined stages, though particular constructions, such as questions and negation, are found to develop in a series of well-ordered stages which are highly consistent not only across children but across languages.

A further crucial observation is that acquisition of a first language seems to be possible only up to a certain age, the *cutoff age*, after which it is no longer possible, an observation formalized in the **critical period hypothesis** put forward by the neurologist Eric Lenneberg in the 1960s. Children deprived of exposure to language during this crucial period are *feral children*, and several such unfortunate cases have been studied.

We now know a great deal about what children can be observed to do as they acquire their first language, and attention has turned increasingly to theoretical interpretation of the raw data. Analysts have been impressed both by the speed of acquisition and by its fundamental orderliness. Many, like Chomsky, have been further impressed by the seeming observation that the data available to the child from adult utterances seem to be inadequate to account for the knowledge acquired. This *poverty-of-the-stimulus* argument led Chomsky to propose his **innateness hypothesis**, by which children are born already knowing what human languages are like, and only need to acquire the details of the language they are learning; to this end, Chomsky postulated a specific **language acquisition device** (LAD) in the human brain.

Commentators have built upon these observations by pointing to the *gavagai problem*, by which it seems to be impossible for a child to guess the meaning of a particular new utterance, and more generally to the *logical problem of language acquisition*, by which it seems to be impossible to learn anything about a language without knowing something else about it first. Not everyone is satisfied with the innateness hypothesis or with the LAD idea, but the more broadly based **genetic hypothesis of language** commands wide support, while novel proposals like the **bioprogram hypothesis** remain controversial.

However, undoubtedly the greatest single advance in the study of acquisition has been the realization that language acquisition is not merely a passive affair in which the child soaks up bits of language that come her way. Instead, it is an *active* process: children *actively construct their language*. There is now no doubt about this: children take the clues available to them and use these clues to construct their own grammatical rules, rules which grow in sophistication as acquisition proceeds. This conclusion is strongly confirmed by the observation of acquisition in unusual circumstances, such as deaf children acquiring a **sign language** or children hearing only a **pidgin** and quickly turning it into a **creole**. This determination to acquire language is very powerful and must surely be part of our biological endowment; the Canadian psycholinguist Steven Pinker has dubbed it the **language instinct**.

*See:* **bioprogram hypothesis**; **critical period hypothesis**; **genetic hypothesis of language**; **innateness hypothesis**; **language acquisition device**; **language instinct**

*Further reading:* Berko Gleason, 1997; Crystal, 1997a: section VII; Fletcher and Macwhinney, 1995; Goodluck, 1991; Ingram, 1989; Malmkjær; Owens, 1996, 1991: 239–251; Steinberg, 1993: ch. 1.

**language acquisition device**   A hypothetical mental organ dedicated to the acquisition of a first language. In the 1960s, the American linguist Noam Chomsky began developing his **innateness hypothesis**, by which we are born already knowing what human languages are like. Chomsky further elaborated his hypothesis by arguing that children must possess a *language acquisition device*, or LAD, a specific mental organ (a structure in the brain) which is dedicated to extracting from haphazard and often degenerate speech the generalizations required for the child to construct the necessary rules of phonology and grammar.

Chomsky's argument was an argument from necessity: because of the seemingly formidable obstacles to **language acquisition** explained in that entry, there simply *must* be some specialized neurological structure which can extract generalizations and construct suitable rules, even rules which are not overtly illustrated by the speech the child hears. But the LAD is purely hypothetical: no one has yet identified any areas or structures in the brain which seem to have the required characteristics, and there is no shortage of critics who see the LAD as a fantasy.

In recent years, Chomsky himself has seemingly abandoned his claims for the LAD in favour of an even stronger claim: he now believes that so much information about the nature of human language is already present in our brains at birth that all the child has to do is to 'set a few switches' to the correct values for the language being acquired. This is his *parameter-setting model*, and it too is deeply controversial.

*See:* **innateness hypothesis**; **language acquisition**; **language instinct**

*Further reading:* Aitchison, 1989: ch. 5.

**language and ethnicity**   The relation between language use and ethnic background, especially in a mixed community. In modern urban societies, it is now commonplace to find speakers of a variety of ethnic backgrounds living together and interacting in various ways. Examples include Anglos, Latinos and blacks in western American cities and speakers of Anglo-Saxon, Caribbean and Asian origin in English cities. Especially since the 1980s, some linguists have begun turning their attention to the links between language and ethnic background.

In some cases, of course, some speakers are bilingual (for example, Spanish–English bilinguals in the USA and Panjabi–English bilinguals in Britain). It is of interest to see how and in what circumstances such speakers change back and forth between their languages (this is **code-switching**), and also to find out what influence each language has on the other. More generally, linguists are interested in determining the extent to which a given language or variety serves as a badge of identity for a particular ethnic group, and how that group's variety of a language differs from varieties of the same language used by other speakers.

On the whole, the study of language and ethnicity is still in its infancy, but illuminating findings have already appeared. For example, the British sociolinguist Ben Rampton has recently discovered the phenomenon of *crossing*, in which a member of one ethnic group deliberately adopts the language or usage of another ethnic group for specific social purposes.

The study of language and ethnicity is sometimes called *ethnolinguistics*.

*See:* **Black English**; **code–switching**; **language and identity**
*Further reading:* Crystal, 1997a: ch. 9; Edwards, 1994: chs. 5, 7; Rampton, 1995; Wardhaugh, 1987: ch. 3.


**language and identity**   The role of language in providing a speaker with individuality and group membership. Every time you open your mouth, you give other people important clues about what sort of person you are: where you come from, what social class you belong to, even your sex and age (for example, on the telephone). This information says something both about your individuality and about the social, national and ethnic groups to which you consider yourself to belong.

For several decades now, sociolinguists have realized that providing each speaker with an individual and group identity is one of the most important **functions of language**.

An appreciation of this identifying function of language is crucial in understanding many types of social and linguistic behaviour. One of the most obvious of these is the seeming paradox that many people consistently describe their own speech as 'bad' or 'wrong' or 'inferior', and yet make no effort to change it towards the sort of speech they explicitly describe as 'better'. Consider the case of a plumber in east London, who speaks the 'Cockney' English typical of working-class speakers in this area. What would happen if he, dissatisfied with his speech, decided to try to abandon it in favour of something close to the middle-class English he professes to admire?

It's obvious: his family and friends would find his efforts comical for about ten seconds, and then they would become increasingly annoyed, distant, and perhaps even hostile. Soon our ambitious plumber would find himself with no friends left. But why?

Well, our plumber lives among a group of people with whom he largely shares his background, his circumstances and his values, and, like anybody, he wants to remain a valued member of this group, upon which he depends for friendship and support. But, to remain a member, he must speak the way the others do, since doing so carries the clear message 'I regard myself as a member of your group.' However, if he deliberately changes his speech, he is announcing in the clearest way possible 'I no longer regard myself as a member of your group'; if he persists, the others will quickly get the message, and he will be excluded.

The link between language and identity can involve entirely different languages. Welsh-speakers in Wales or Basque-speakers and Catalan-speakers in Spain may (and often do) regard their distinctive language as a central part of their identity, and may deeply resent pressures to abandon their ancestral language in favour of the more prestigious English or Spanish. Rather than consenting to becoming anonymous if slightly quaint speakers on the fringes of the English-speaking or Spanish-speaking world, they prefer to see themselves as part of a distinct people, with their own nation, their own history, their own traditions, their own values and their own goals; the most obvious outward sign of this distinct identity is their language. The all-too-common failure to recognize or esteem this identifying effect of language has led countless times to grief and to major social, educational and political problems.

*See:* **language and ethnicity**; **social stratification of language**
*Further reading:* Crystal, 1997a: section II.

**language and ideology** The examination of language as a political weapon. Among its many other functions, a language can be used as an instrument of political pressure, and such use is far from rare. Most obviously, language can be used either to confer validity upon a social group or political entity or to deny validity.

For example, after the French Revolution the new Republican government, finding France to be a patchwork of peoples speaking at least eight different languages, resolved to unify the country, and one of their major weapons was Parisian French. Laws were passed requiring the teaching and use of Parisian French, while the other languages were subjected to merciless condemnation and persecution; their use was presented as unpatriotic, subversive and sinister, and their speakers were condemned as reactionaries and fanatics. Much the same happened in polyglot Spain after the Fascist victory in the Spanish Civil War: the dictator General Franco declared the very speaking of any languages other than Castilian Spanish to be illegal, and Basques, Catalans and Galicians were routinely ordered to 'stop barking like dogs' and to 'speak the language of the Christians'.

It can also work the other way. In recent years, the Basques, the Catalans, the Welsh and the Irish, to name just a few, have rallied behind their traditional languages as effective public emblems of their individual identity and of their right to self-determination. They have fought for, and often obtained, the right to education, publication and broadcasting in their languages, and many people who grew up speaking only Spanish or English have learned their ancestral language and ensured that their children learn it too. It has been observed that nationalism is the principal political force of our time, and there is arguably no more powerful emblem of national identity than a distinctive language.

The political and ideological uses of language have been examined for generations, though the discussion has not always been illuminating, and it has often been dominated by avowed Marxists. Two of the most prominent figures in the debate were both Marxists: the Italian Antonio Gramsci and the Russian Mikhail Bakhtin. These two sometimes defended almost diametrically opposed positions, though it is Bakhtin whose views have probably been more influential in informing the continuing debate over the competing rights and demands of **national languages** and **minority languages**.

*See:* **language and identity**; **language and power**; **minority language**; **national language**; **official language**

*Further reading:* Bourne and Cameron, 1989; Tony Crowley, 1996; Fairclough, 1995: 70–83; Simpson, 1993.

**language and power** The relation between the type of language used by an individual and that individual's access to positions of power and influence. In almost every society of any size or complexity, there are noteable differences in the type of language used by different sectors of society, and furthermore associated differences in the access enjoyed by the different groups to powerful and well-paid positions. For example, in the English-speaking world, the contrast is primarily between standard English and the various non-standard forms of English, and it is obvious that speakers of standard English typically enjoy more power, more prestige and more money than the others, who are far more likely to be confined to positions of low prestige, with comparatively little money or influence and often with little chance for advancement. What, if anything, should we do about this state of affairs?

Broadly speaking, there have been two answers proposed to this question. Some people emphasize the importance of teaching prestige forms of language to speakers of non-prestige forms in order to empower them, while others object to the imposition of prestige forms on the ground that it effectively denies power to speakers of other varieties. In the English case, the first group are essentially arguing that it is the very command of standard English which itself confers access to power and prestige and, hence, that it is our social duty to extend this command to as many people as possible, since otherwise non-standard speakers will remain marginalized and unable to play a full part in society. The second group, in great contrast, argue that standard English is nothing more than the identifying badge of a particular and maximally powerful group, a mere sign of class membership and, hence, that stressing the imposition of standard English denies the value of non-standard forms, so that non-standard speakers are implicitly dismissed as inadequate and unworthy of power. Many members of the second group go so far as to demand that non-standard varieties of English should be formally recognized as the equal of standard English, and that non-standard English should become the vehicle of education for its speakers, a position which appals the members of the first group.

This debate continues today, and it produces deep divisions among academics, politicians and teachers. In Britain, the *Kingman Report* of 1988, which advocated the first policy, has often been at the centre of the controversy.

*See:* **language and identity**; **language and ideology**; **standard language**
*Further reading:* Tony Crowley, 1989; Honey, 1997.

**language areas**    The regions of the brain which are devoted to particular aspects of the use of language. As part of their investigations into **aphasia** in the mid-nineteenth century, the French surgeon Paul Broca and the German neurologist Carl Wernicke identified two well-defined areas in the brain which play a crucial role in the use of language. Both are located in the left hemisphere of the cerebral cortex (the wrinkly grey outer layer of the brain) in the vast majority of people, though a few people have them on the right side or even on both sides.

*Wernicke's area* is located behind and above the ear. It is responsible for comprehension and also for access to ordinary vocabulary in speaking. *Broca's area* is located close to the temple. It is responsible for providing the necessary grammatical structure, including grammatical words and affixes; in speech, it also controls intonation and the fine muscular movements of the speech organs. Originally identified by post-mortems carried out on brain-damaged patients who had suffered from aphasia, these areas can also be observed to be functioning in normal, healthy, conscious subjects by the use of modern brain scanners.

Since Wernicke's area is close to the part of the brain which processes auditory input, and since Broca's area is close to the area controlling muscular movements, we require only one further link to make sense of the whole arrangement. This link, the *arcuate fasciculus*, was found long ago. It consists of a J-shaped bundle of fibres connecting Wernicke's area to Broca's area.

Consequently, we now have a good picture of the organization of language in the brain. During listening, speech signals are passed by the ears to the auditory part of the brain, which processes the sounds and sends the result to Wernicke's area for interpretation. During speech, Wernicke's area provides the ordinary vocabulary, via the arcuate fasciculus, to Broca's area, which embeds this vocabulary into the required grammatical structure and then sends its instructions to the organs of speech. With the necessary changes for switching from a sound medium to a visual medium, essentially the same things happen during the use of **sign language**. With a high degree of reliability, damage to any of these areas produces the expected **language disability**.

*See:* **aphasia**; **language disability**; **neurolinguistics**
*Further reading:* Akmajian *et al.*, 1995: ch. 12; Crystal, 1997a: ch.
45; O'Grady *et al.*, 1996: ch. 10 [ch. 11 in the American edition];
Steinberg, 1993: ch. 9.

**language change**    Change in languages over time. One of the
fundamental facts about living languages is that they are always
changing. New words, new pronunciations, new grammatical forms and structures, and new meanings for existing
words are always coming into existence, while older ones are
always dropping out of use. It is absolutely impossible for a
living language to avoid changing.

The motivations for change are many and various, and only
some of them are reasonably well understood. New objects,
new concepts, new activities all require new names; at the
same time, old objects and activities may cease to exist, and
their names may die with them. Certain linguistic forms may
acquire social prestige and spread to the speech of those who
formerly did not use them. The physiological characteristics
of the mouth may tend to favour certain changes in pronunciation, but such changes may disrupt formerly regular
grammatical patterns, introducing irregularities which may
later be removed in one way or another. Syntactic structures
which come to be frequently used may be reduced to simpler
grammatical forms. And **language contact** may induce
speakers to import forms and usages from other languages.

Such constant change means that a language at any point
in time is always significantly different from its direct ancestor
of some centuries earlier, and often vastly different from its
ancestor of one or two millennia earlier. Moreover, a language
spoken over a sizeable area does not change everywhere in
the same way, and so, over time, it breaks up, first into regional
**dialects** and then, eventually, into several very different
languages, producing a **language family**.

The study of language change is **historical linguistics**,
and this discipline has enjoyed great success in working out
the innumerable changes which have applied in the past to

individual languages and families; it has also made progress in identifying, and sometimes explaining, principles of language change: some types of change, we now know, are more natural, more frequent and more readily explicable than others.

Not infrequently, speakers take exception to the presence in their language of certain changes, or even of *all* changes, and they campaign to 'stamp out' those innovations of which they particularly disapprove. Sometimes they even agitate to 'fix' their language into a particular form admired by them, like a dead butterfly in a specimen box, with no further changes to be tolerated except after protracted deliberation by suitable authorities. Well, it is true that certain changes may lead to a (temporary) reduction in the expressive power of a language (though most do not, and many changes actually increase its expressive power), and informed commentary on these matters may be valuable in educational contexts. On the whole, though, railing against language change is a waste of time: trying to stop languages from changing is like trying to stop the wind from blowing.

*See:* **historical linguistics**; **language contact**; **language family**; **language myths**

*Further reading:* Aitchison, 1991; Crystal, 1997a: ch. 54; McMahon, 1994; Milroy, 1992; Trask, 1994, 1995: ch. 5, 1996: chs. 1–6.

**language contact** Changes in one language resulting from the influence of another language. The speakers of any given language are almost always in some kind of contact with the speakers of one or more other languages, for any of several reasons. When two different languages are spoken in adjacent areas, speakers on both sides of the boundary will be exposed to the other language, and may often gain some fluency in that other language. Because of conquest or migration, speakers of two or more languages may be mixed together in a single community. Speakers of one language may travel and become exposed to different languages spoken elsewhere. And, of course, in modern times the mass media have brought awareness of a number of languages into regions in which these were formerly unknown.

In all such cases, speakers of one language may, deliberately or unconsciously, introduce into their language features of another language to which they have been exposed, and we therefore speak of *language contact*, or simply *contact*.

The consequences of contact may range from the trivial to the far-reaching. At the simplest level, speakers may merely take over a few words from their neighbours; this is called *borrowing*, and the words borrowed are **loan words** in the receiving language. This happens most readily because the words are the names of genuinely new things: for example, English–speakers had never seen coffee, or boomerangs, or tobacco, or chocolate, or pizzas until they encountered them being used by speakers of various other languages, and so took them over along with their foreign names. But it can also happen purely for reasons of prestige: the enormous prestige of Norman French in England after the Conquest brought thousands of Norman French words into English, where they often displaced their native equivalents, as when *army* and *face* displaced native English *here* and *andwlita*.

But contact can go much further than this, affecting grammar and pronunciation. For example, the Celtic language Breton, spoken in Brittany, has acquired a French–style uvular /r/, and it has been losing its native phoneme /h/, absent from French. The Mayan languages of Mexico and Guatemala have acquired a number of new phonemes from the local prestige language, Spanish. Some varieties of Scottish Gaelic have lost the inflected prepositions of that language and replaced them with prepositional phrases comparable to English ones. Among the Semitic languages of Ethiopia, the original Verb-Subject-Object word order of sentences has been largely changed to the Subject-Object-Verb order typical of the neighbouring Cushitic languages.

Few languages are, or have ever been, sufficiently isolated to avoid some degree of contact, and hence virtually every language shows some evidence of ancient or modern contact with other languages. On occasion, speakers of a given language may react unfavourably to such contact by embracing **purism**, with variable results. In recent years, the world dominance of English has led to massive English influence upon languages from French to Japanese.

In extreme cases, the effects of contact may be so overwhelming that one language is abandoned entirely by its speakers in favour of another, in the process called **language death**.

*See:* **language death**; **linguistic area**; **loan word**; **purism**
*Further reading:* Hock, 1986: chs. 14–16; Hock and Joseph, 1996: chs. 12–15; McMahon, 1994: ch. 8; Trask, 1996: ch. 11.

**language death**   The disappearance of a language as a mother tongue. A language, particularly a **minority language**, may come under enormous pressure from a more prestigious or more widely used language spoken nearby. Native speakers of the language under pressure may find themselves obliged, not only to learn the local prestige language, but to use it in an ever-greater number of contexts. Eventually, a time may come when many children are no longer learning the threatened language as their mother tongue, or are learning it only imperfectly. At this point we say the threatened language is *moribund* or *dying*, and the almost inevitable result is that, within a generation or two, no one will be able to speak the threatened language at all. This is *language death*, and the process which leads to it is *language shift*.

Language death is usually gradual. In any given place, at any given time, some children are still learning the dying language as their mother tongue, while others are learning it only imperfectly and still others not at all. The language may disappear completely from some areas while surviving in others.

The language spoken by the last generation or so of native speakers may be very much changed from the language spoken by an earlier generation. Irregularities may be lost; the more complex or less frequent forms and sentence patterns may drop out of use; native words may be massively replaced by words taken from the prestige language; the pronunciation may change so as to become more similar to that of the prestige language; stylistic variation may be lost, leaving only a single unvarying style. The final outcome, of course, is a **dead language**.

*See:* **dead language**; **language and power**; **language contact**; **minority language**

*Further reading:* Hock and Joseph, 1996: ch. 15; Krauss, 1992; McMahon, 1994: ch. 11.

**language disability** Any pathological condition which has adverse consequences for the sufferer's ability to use language normally. Language disabilities must be carefully distinguished from *speech defects* like stuttering, lisping and stammering; these are purely mechanical problems with the nerves and muscles controlling the organs of speech, and they have no effect upon the **language faculty** itself.

A true disability results either from a genetic defect or from damage to the **language areas** in the brain. Since the possible types of damage and defects are virtually limitless, individual sufferers naturally exhibit an enormous range of disabilities: we hardly ever find two individuals with exactly the same symptoms. Nevertheless, it has proved possible to identify a number of fairly specific disabilities and, in many case, to associate these with particular genetic defects or with damage to particular areas of the brain.

The best-known disabilities are the several types of **aphasia**, all of which result from injury to more or less identifiable areas of the brain. But other types exist. For example, the *Williams syndrome* is known to result from a genetic defect in chromosome number eleven; this defect causes both some highly specific physiological abnormalities and some rather consistent abnormalities in language use. Less well understood is *Specific Language Impairment*, or SLI, which devastates the ability to use the grammatically inflected forms of words correctly (such as *take*, *takes*, *took*, *taking*) but which has only a few non-linguistic consequences; the Canadian-based linguist Myrna Gopnik has recently uncovered evidence that this impairment too may result from a specific genetic disorder, though one which has not yet been identified.

But the known range of disabilities is positively startling. A bilingual sufferer may lose one language completely but retain the second perfectly, and then, after some time, may lose the second but regain the first. Many types of disability are characterized by greater or lesser degrees of *anomia*, the inability to remember words for things. But some sufferers exhibit astoundingly specific deficits, such as a total inability to use or understand words denoting fruits and vegetables, with *no other problems at all*. Some people lose verbs but retain nouns, and so they have no trouble with the noun *milk* (as in *a glass of milk*), but cannot handle the verb *milk* (as in *to milk a cow*). In spite of some impressive progress, we are still very far from understanding most types of language disability.

*See:* **aphasia**; **language areas**; **neurolinguistics**
*Further reading:* Caplan, 1992; Crystal, 1997a: ch. 46; Pinker, 1994: ch. 10; Steinberg, 1993: ch. 9; Trask, 1995: chs. 6–7.

**language faculty** Our biological ability to use language. Human beings are the only creatures on earth that use language, and many linguists and others have concluded that we must therefore have some kind of specific biological endowment for language, one which is totally absent, or nearly so, from all other living species: our *language faculty* (the Swiss linguist Ferdinand de Saussure used the term *langage* for this, but his label is now little used).

To be sure, this conclusion has been challenged from two directions. On the one hand, some experimenters have attempted to teach other species, usually apes, to use some simplified version of a human language (most often a version of a **sign language**) and, in spite of serious problems with their methodology and interpretations, a few observers are now prepared to accept that these creatures do indeed exhibit a (severely limited) capacity for using language – though critics of this conclusion are numerous and vigorous. On the other hand, psychologists like Jean Piaget and Jerome Bruner have argued that our language faculty, while admittedly real, is not at all an individual and distinctive part of our biological inheritance, but merely one more manifestation of our general all-purpose cognitive abilities.

Nevertheless, the majority view among linguists at present is that our language faculty is real, that it is at least largely distinct from all of our other cognitive abilities, and that it must be the biological result of some kind of distinctive evolution within the brains of our ancestors. This is the belief that underlies a number of celebrated attempts at giving an account of our language-using abilities, including the **genetic hypothesis of language**, Chomsky's **innateness hypothesis**, Bickerton's **bioprogram hypothesis**, and even the search for **universal grammar**.

A constant theme in these investigations is the issue of **modularity**. Chomsky and others have long argued that our language faculty must consist of a number of specialized and largely independent subcomponents which interact in specific ways to produce our overall linguistic behaviour. More recently, however, some people have begun to question whether our language faculty as a whole should itself be regarded as a distinctive part of our mental equipment. They suggest instead that various aspects of language use may have entirely separate evolutionary origins, and that what we call our *language faculty* is probably an epiphenomenon; that is, a purely superficial unity which in fact results from the interaction of diverse structures and processes within our brains, many of which are in no way confined to language behaviour. These debates will doubtless continue for some time.

The study of all the biological aspects of our language faculty is sometimes called *biolinguistics*.

*See:* **animal communication**; **autonomy of language**; **bioprogram hypothesis**; **genetic hypothesis of language**; **innateness hypothesis**; **modularity**; **origin and evolution of language**

*Further reading:* Jackendoff, 1993; Pinker, 1994; Sampson, 1997; Steinberg, 1993: ch. 7.

**language family**  A group of languages all of which share a common ancestor. Every living language is constantly changing, and the changes which affect the language in one place do not necessarily affect it in other places. Consequently, if the language is spoken over any significant area, then, over time, it will tend to break up into rather distinct varieties. At first these are merely the *regional dialects* of the language, but, given sufficient time, these dialects may become so different from one another that we are forced to regard them as separate languages: the *daughter languages* of that single *ancestral language* or *mother language*.

The daughter languages may in turn break up into further daughter languages, eventually producing a sizeable number of languages all of which started out as nothing more than regional varieties of that single ancestor. All the languages which share a common ancestor in this way constitute a single *language family*, and we say that all of them are *genetically related*. Around 300 such language families have been identified by linguists, some of them very large, others quite small.

English, for example, is fairly closely related to a group of other languages: Afrikaans, Danish, Dutch, Faroese, Frisian, German, Icelandic, Norwegian, Swedish, Yiddish and the extinct Gothic; we call these the *Germanic* languages, and we believe they are all descended from a single ancestor spoken perhaps around 500 BC, very likely in Scandinavia. But the Germanic languages in turn share a more remote common ancestor with a vast number of other languages, including Welsh, Spanish, Greek, Russian, Armenian, Persian and Bengali (to name just a few), and hence all of these languages belong to a single huge family called the **Indo-European** family.

*See:* **historical linguistics**; **Indo-European**; **language change**
*Further reading:* Comrie *et al.*, 1997; Crystal, 1997a: chs. 50–53; Trask, 1996: ch. 7.


**language instinct**  The powerful tendency of children to acquire language. Any physically normal child who is adequately exposed to a language will learn it perfectly, and a child exposed to two or three languages will learn all of them. A hearing child normally learns the surrounding spoken language. A deaf child exposed to a **sign language** will learn that. Children exposed only to a **pidgin** will turn that pidgin into a real language: a **creole**. A group of children exposed to no language at all will invent their own and use it.

For a long time, linguists were slow to appreciate the significance of these observations, and both creoles and sign languages were widely regarded as peripheral and even inconsequential phenomena scarcely deserving of serious study by linguists. But times have changed. Very gradually at first, and then, from about the 1970s, almost explosively, the examination of these phenomena convinced almost all working linguists that creoles and sign languages were every bit as central to the discipline as spoken languages with a long history.

We now realize that children are born with a powerful biological drive to learn language, and that only shattering disability or inhuman cruelty can prevent a child from acquiring language by one means or another. In the 1990s, the Canadian psycholinguist Steven Pinker coined the felicitous term *language instinct* to denote this remarkable aspect of our biological endowment. Our language faculty, we now strongly suspect, is built into our genes, and learning a first language may not be so different from learning to see: at birth, our visual apparatus is not working properly, and it requires some exposure to the visible world before normal vision is acquired.

Not infrequently, the term language instinct is applied more specifically to the **genetic hypothesis of language** and/or to the related **innateness hypothesis**.

*See:* **anatomy of language**; **creole**; **critical period hypothesis**; **genetic hypothesis of language**, **innateness hypothesis**; **language acquisition**; **sign language**

*Further reading:* Aitchison, 1989; Pinker, 1994.

**language in use**   An approach to the study of language which focuses upon the varied uses of language in real situations. With the decline of the traditional but often deadly dull grammar-and-parsing approach to the study of language in English-speaking schools in the 1960s, educators cast about for a new and more engaging technique to replace it. One solution which emerged in the 1970s, most notably in Britain, was the *language-in-use* approach.

The aim of this method is to present pupils with real and meaningful examples of English, both spoken and written, examples which are highly relevant to the pupils' own experience, such as news stories, advertisements, operating instructions, political speeches, poems and even cartoons; where relevant, these are often accompanied by photographs and film clips. Broadly speaking, pupils are invited to consider what the speaker or writer is trying to do and how the use of language contributes to those goals.

This approach has proved to be able to capture the interest of pupils, and it has been widely regarded as a success; in Britain, it now forms the core of most A-Level syllabuses in English language. Nevertheless, the earlier lack of attention to the purely structural aspects of language, such as verbs, direct objects and subordinate clauses, was found to be a serious defect, and today it is usual to combine the language-in-use approach with the teaching of a suitable set of terms for describing sentence structure; this is broadly the approach now known as **knowledge about language**.

University-level degree courses in linguistics have been slow to adopt language in use in the teaching of their students, with a few notable exceptions, such as Britain's Open University (a distance-learning university).

*See:* **knowledge about language**
*Further reading:* Carter *et al.*, 1997; Maybin and Mercer, 1996.

**language myths**   Widely held but false beliefs about individual languages or about language in general. For one reason or another, various absurdly false beliefs about languages have at times taken hold in the popular imagination and have often proved difficult to stamp out. Some of these misconceptions have even been maintained by knowledgeable linguists. Here are a few of these myths.

- Primitive languages. Linguists as recent and eminent as Otto Jespersen have maintained that some languages spoken today are 'primitive' or 'savage' languages, characterized by strange grammatical systems supposedly reflecting a primordial human view of the world. Non-linguists have at times gone further and supposed that some languages have little or nothing in the way of grammar, and that they have tiny vocabularies lacking abstractions or generalizations and supplemented by grunts and gestures. All this is nonsense: every human language ever discovered has a rich and complex grammar and a vocabulary of many thousands of words, and is perfectly adequate for expressing anything its speakers want to express.

- Stadialism. Many linguists formerly believed that every human language necessarily develops over time from a 'primitive' type through increasingly sophisticated types until finally (perhaps) reaching the most 'advanced' type possible. This idea was promulgated by European linguists who were inclined to see their European languages as representing the pinnacle of linguistic perfection, with significantly different languages, and especially those spoken by coloured folks, as necessarily representing some earlier stage of development. This blatantly racist idea is thankfully dead among linguists, though avowedly non-racist versions of it are still maintained in some quarters, and non-linguists sometimes still believe it is true. It is not. Languages admittedly differ markedly in their grammatical systems, and they can and do change those systems dramatically over time; however, there is no tendency for languages to change in one direction rather than another, and there is nothing special about European languages.

- Those Eskimo words for 'snow'. By a comical series of events, the legend has grown up that the Eskimo languages have vast numbers of words for different kinds of snow. In fact, the several dialects of the two Eskimo languages variously exhibit between two and four distinct words for snow. This is about the same as English, with its *snow, slush, sleet, blizzard* (not to mention skiers' terms like *hard-pack, powder* and *crust*).

- Basque. The Basque language of western Europe has no known relatives and it is noticeably different from other European languages, particularly from those (the great majority) which are related within the **Indo-European** family. Consequently, a number of myths have grown up about it: Basque is the most complex language on the planet; no outsider has ever managed to learn it; all the verbs are passive; and so on. In fact, of course, Basque is a perfectly unremarkable language. Its grammar is highly regular, and it is easy to learn: today thousands of people speak it as a second language. Its sentence structure is nearly identical to that of Japanese or Turkish. It does have a **morphology** which is somewhat unusual in Europe, but similar systems are found in hundreds of languages outside of Europe.

- The land that time forgot. Somewhere, runs the story, in the Ozarks, or in the Appalachians, or in Derbyshire in England, there's a village where the locals still speak perfect Elizabethan English, untouched by the vast changes which have transformed English everywhere else. No, there isn't: this is pure fantasy. There is no such thing as a living language which doesn't change. This myth crops up because people occasionally notice that the local English in some corner of the world preserves one or two old forms which have disappeared elsewhere. (For example, Appalachian English preserves the *a'doing* form, as in *I was a'shootin' at some squirrels*; this was once universal in English but has been lost everywhere else.) But *every* variety of English preserves a few forms lost in other varieties, and every variety also exhibits a few innovations not found elsewhere. (For example, Appalachian English has under-gone a change in its vowels such that Appalachian *think* sounds to the rest of us rather like *thank*.)

Similar myths have been maintained by speakers of other languages. Until the eighteenth century, even some linguists believed that the ancestral language of all humankind was still spoken, in its pristine state, in some favoured corner of the world; much ink was spilt over deciding which corner this might be. (For example, one such linguist argued for the Netherlands, and claimed that Dutch was the uncorrupted ancestral tongue of all humans. He was Dutch, of course.) But all languages that are spoken change incessantly, and no language anywhere is closer than any other to the remote origins of human speech.

There's a moral here: don't believe everything you read. Many journalists and authors of popular books are ignorant of the facts, and they tend to perpetuate eye-catching false-hoods in place of the more humdrum truth.

*See:* **folk linguistics**
*Further reading:* Crystal, 1997a: chs. 1–3; Pullum, 1991: ch. 19.


**language planning** Making deliberate decisions about the form of a language. Very commonly, a language 'just grows': it develops and changes in response to countless small deci-sions made more or less unconsciously by its speakers. But it is perfectly possible, and in some circumstances necessary, for the future of a language to be determined in important respects by deliberate, self-conscious decisions, often made on an official basis. This is *language planning*, sometimes also called *linguistic engineering*.

Consider the case of Finnish. For centuries, Finland had been a province of Sweden or of Russia; either Swedish or Russian had therefore been the **official language** of the country, and Finnish had remained merely the everyday language of most of the population. But, when Finland finally achieved independence in 1918, the Finns naturally chose to make Finnish their new **national language**.

161

But this decision required a great deal of work. First, there was no agreed standard form of Finnish: instead, there were only innumerable local varieties of it, differing in vocabulary, pronunciation and grammar. Second, since Finnish had never been used for such purposes as law, administration, science, technology and scholarship, there was a great dearth of technical vocabulary in all these fields: there simply *were* no Finnish equivalents for terms like *manslaughter*, *ministry*, *molecule*, *piston* and *linguistics*.

The Finns were therefore obliged to put these things right, and the task was carried out centrally, by bodies set up by the new Finnish government. Specialists in Finnish language drew up a new standard form of the language, and specialists in a huge variety of disciplines met to agree on suitable Finnish technical terms in their fields. Their decisions were official, and they were imposed upon the Finnish taught in schools, published in books and magazines, and broadcast over the radio.

The task was completed satisfactorily, and today there exists a single standard form of Finnish, known and used by everyone, together with an adequate and uniform set of technical terms. But the work is never done, since new technical terms come into use every year, in fields ranging from physics to linguistics, most of them coined in English, and the Finns are constantly obliged to keep finding Finnish equivalents.

Recently, growing awareness of **sexist language** has produced efforts directed toward language planning of a different sort.

*See:* **national language**; **official language**; **sexist language**; **standard language**
*Further reading:* Crystal, 1997a: ch. 61; Holmes, 1992: 120–129 Trask, 1996: 330–337.

**language processing** The mental activities involved in producing and comprehending language. Whenever we produce an utterance, or whenever we hear and understand one, there is a great deal of elaborate activity going on in our brains. This activity is *language processing*.

Psycholinguists have developed a battery of techniques for working out the stages involved in language processing. Subjects can be tested in a laboratory, to find out how the performance of linguistic tasks is affected by varying conditions, and evidence can be obtained from *speech errors*. The results, however, are not always easy to interpret. Nevertheless, linguists have enjoyed some success in working out the several distinct stages involved in *speech planning*, the mental processes which allow us to produce utterances. Comprehension is more difficult: a number of **perceptual strategies** have been proposed, and these are moderately successful at accounting for the understanding of simple utterances, but the comprehension of more complex utterances is still something of a mystery.

*See:* **perceptual strategy**; **psycholinguistics**
*Further reading:* Aitchison, 1989; Akmajian *et al.*, 1995: ch. 10; O'Grady *et al.*, 1996: ch. 11 [ch. 10 in the American edition].

*langue*    The abstract language system shared by the speakers of a language. The term *langue* was introduced by the Swiss linguist Ferdinand de Saussure in the early twentieth century; in Saussure's treatment, this term contrasts specifically with *parole*, actual utterances. A distinction along these lines has often been considered essential in linguistics since Saussure's day, and Noam Chomsky's more recent distinction between **competence** and **performance** is broadly analogous, but note that Saussure's *langue* is the property of a whole community of speakers, while Chomsky's *competence* is the property of a single speaker.

*See:* **competence**; **language**; *parole*
*Further reading:* Culler, 1986; Sampson, 1980: ch. 2.

**lateralization**    Specialization between the two hemispheres (halves) of the brain. By a quirk of evolution, the left side of the brain controls the right side of the body and vice-versa. But there are also notable differences in the responsibilities of the two hemispheres: the left side is chiefly responsible for analysis (breaking complex things up into smaller parts), and it handles things like doing arithmetic, solving equations and determining chronological sequences. The right hemisphere, in great contrast, is responsible for synthesis (combining pieces into integrated wholes), and hence it handles things like recognition and association, and also the enjoyment of music (though trained musicians learn to use their left hemispheres for this purpose as well).

In the vast majority of people, the **language areas** of the brain are in the left hemisphere, though a few people have them on the right or, rarely, even on both sides.

*See:* **language areas**

*Further reading:* Akmajian *et al.*, 1995: ch. 12; Crystal, 1997a: ch. 45; O'Grady *et al.*, 1996: ch. 10 [ch. 11 in the American edition]; Steinberg, 1993: ch. 9.

**Lexical–Functional Grammar** (LFG)   A particular theory of grammar. LFG was developed in the late 1970s by the American linguists Joan Bresnan and Ronald Kaplan. It differs from some other theories of grammar in holding that the syntactic structure of a sentence is something more than just the familiar **constituent structure** represented by a **tree** diagram. In LFG, the structure of a sentence consists of two distinct formal objects: *c-structure* of the familiar kind plus a *functional structure* (or *f-structure*) which displays certain additional kinds of information. Most important in the f-structure is the labelling of **grammatical relations** like *subject* and *object* (these are called *grammatical functions* in LFG).

The first part of the name reflects the fact that a great deal of work is done by the *lexical entries*, the 'dictionary' part of the framework. Lexical entries are usually rich and elaborate, and each inflected from a lexical item (such as *write*, *writes*, *wrote*, *written* and *writing*) has its own lexical entry. Lexical entries are responsible for dealing with many relations and processes handled by different machinery in other frame-works; an example is the **voice** contrast between actives and passives.

LFG was designed to be convenient for work in compu-tational linguistics and has found applications there. It was also designed in the hope that it would prove to be psycho-logically realistic, but overt psycholinguistic support has not been forthcoming.

*See:* **generative grammar**; **Government-and-Binding Theory**; **phrase-structure grammar**

*Further reading:* Horrocks, 1987: ch.4; Kaplan and Bresnan, 1982; Sells, 1985: ch. 4.

**lexicography**    The writing of dictionaries. Dictionaries of a sort have been around for a long time, but ancient and medieval efforts were mostly very different from our modern ones. To start with, the early ones were usually bilingual dictionaries, glossaries offering translations of words from one language into another. The medieval period saw the produc-tion of monoglot works, but these were not usually arranged alphabetically: instead, the words were grouped by meaning (words pertaining to farming, names of fruits, and so on). The first alphabetical dictionaries of English were not complete: instead, they were compendia of 'hard words', that is, of obscure and difficult words, often mainly of Latin origin.

By the eighteenth century, books that we can easily recog-nize as dictionaries of English were beginning to appear. By far the most prominent of these in Britain was Dr Samuel Johnson's great work published in 1755; Johnson's American counterpart, Noah Webster, published the first edition of his American dictionary in 1828. Other dictionaries followed, and lexicography became a recognized profession in the English-speaking countries.

In the second half of the nineteenth century, an enormous project was undertaken in Britain: the preparation of a huge dictionary of English recording every word, every spelling, and every sense attested in writing in English since the year

1000. Directed by the Scottish scholar James Murray, this project was carried out by methods that seem comically primitive today: an army of contributors noted down examples of words and sent them in on slips of paper, and Murray and his assistants simply built the dictionary out of these mountains of paper slips. The completed work was published in a series of volumes between 1884 and 1928, under the title *New English Dictionary on Historical Principles*. In 1933 it was republished, with a supplement, as the *Oxford English Dictionary*, or OED. Further supplements followed, and finally an expanded and updated second edition was prepared and published in 1989. Both editions are available on CD-ROM, making the OED an enormously valuable research tool. A third edition is planned for 2005.

Throughout the twentieth century, English dictionaries have been published in numbers. In the last couple of decades, lexicography has been revolutionized by the introduction of **corpus**-based techniques, and modern dictionaries are now usually based upon huge corpora of English, from which words, forms, spellings, meanings and grammatical behaviour are extracted, thus allowing lexicographers to appeal directly to the observed facts of usage. Also noteworthy are the numerous innovations introduced by the COBUILD dictionaries in Britain and by other dictionaries written especially for advanced foreign learners of English.

*See:* **corpus**
*Further reading:* Crystal, 1995: 442–445; Green, 1996; Ilson, 1986; Landau, 1984; McArthur, 1986.


**lexicon** The vocabulary of a language. Every speaker of a language possesses a certain vocabulary, and this may be divided into his (or her) *active vocabulary*, the words which he uses himself and his *passive vocabulary*, the words which he understands but doesn't normally use. In linguistics, however, we don't normally speak of the vocabulary of a particular language; instead, we speak of the *lexicon*, the total store of words available to speakers.

Very commonly, the lexicon is not regarded merely as a long list of words. Rather, we conceive of the lexicon as a set of lexical resources, including the **morphemes** of the language, plus the processes available in the language for constructing words from those resources. For example, given the existence of English verbs like *varnish* and *scratch*, and of the word-forming **affixes** *-able* and *un-*, it is perfectly possible for you to create the words *varnishable* and *unscratchable* whenever you need them, and to expect to be understood at once, even if you and the person you are speaking to have never encountered these words before.

Quite apart from the lexicon of a language as a whole, psycholinguists are interested in the *mental lexicon*, the words and lexical resources stored in an individual brain. Evidence from a variety of sources, including **language disability**, has provided a great deal of information about this. There is good evidence that words of a single grammatical class, and also words of closely related meanings, are stored in the brain 'in the same place', whatever that means exactly; and it is perfectly clear also that words are not stored in isolation, but are instead stored with innumerable links to other words which are related in function, which are related in meaning, or which merely have similar sounds.

*See:* **morphology**; **part of speech**; **word-formation**
*Further reading:* Aitchison, 1994; Bauer, 1998; Katamba, 1994.


**lingua franca**    A language which is widely used in some region for communication among people speaking a variety of languages. The original *lingua franca* (the name means 'Frankish language', though the sense is 'European language' or 'Christian language') was a variety of Italian, strongly laced with words from French, Spanish, Greek, Arabic and Turkish, used as a trade language in the eastern Mediterranean during the late Middle Ages. Since then, we have applied this label to any language which enjoys wide use among speakers of a variety of different languages in some region.

In the past, this term was applied very broadly, and many of the speech varieties called *lingue franchi* (this is the plural) were **pidgins** or **creoles**. Today, though, we more commonly use the term for a language which is the long-established mother tongue of some influential group of speakers but which is none the less widely used for inter-group communication by speakers of several other languages, such as Swahili in East Africa, Hausa in West Africa, or English in Singapore.

*See:* **creole**; **international language**; **pidgin**
*Further reading:* Crystal, 1997a: ch. 59; Holmes, 1992: 86–89.

**linguistic area**  A geographical region in which several unrelated or distantly related languages have striking characteristics in common. With only a very few exceptions, speakers of a language are always in contact with neighbours speaking different languages, and they have dealings with those neighbours. The resulting **language contact** means that words, speech sounds and even grammatical forms may pass from some languages into neighbouring languages. This is exceedingly common.

In certain cases, however, this contact may be so intense that a number of striking characteristics diffuse throughout a geographical region, becoming prominent in a number of languages which are unrelated or only distantly related. As a result, the languages in question may, in some respects, undergo *convergence*: they come to resemble one another more closely than they resemble their closest linguistic relatives in other regions. This state of affairs we call a *linguistic area* or, using the German term, a *Sprachbund*.

Several linguistic areas have been identified by linguists, among them southeast Asia and the Balkans. Southeast Asia is a particularly striking case. Many languages in this area – including Burmese, Thai and Vietnamese – are so similar in their structures that linguists believed for a while that they must all be related in a single family. But careful investigation has revealed that the three languages just named are not discoverably related at all; they all have true relatives elsewhere which are not very similar to them, and the striking resemblances result purely from convergence among neighbouring but unrelated languages.

In the Balkans, Greek and Albanian constitute distinct branches of the **Indo-European** family, while Bulgarian, Macedonian and Serbo-Croatian belong to the distinct Slavic branch of Indo-European, and Turkish is not Indo-European at all. Yet all these languages participate to varying degrees in a language area: they share a range of grammatical characteristics with one another which they do not share with their closest relatives elsewhere.

The study of language areas is called *areal linguistics*.

*See:* **language contact**
*Further reading:* Hock and Joseph, 1996: ch. 13; Trask, 1996: 315–317.


**linguistic relativity hypothesis** The hypothesis that the structure of our language to some extent determines the way we perceive the world. For centuries, scholars have speculated on possible links between language on one hand and mind, perception and culture on the other; a prominent example is the eighteenth-century German linguist and philosopher Wilhelm von Humboldt.

Around the beginning of the twentieth century, linguistics began to emerge from anthropology as a distinct discipline in the USA, and American linguists, with their anthropological background, often took a keen interest in the links just mentioned. The American linguist Edward Sapir was particularly fascinated by possible connections between language and thought; he once wrote: 'Language and our thought-grooves are . . . , in a sense, one and the same.' But it was Sapir's student, Benjamin Lee Whorf, who was to develop this idea into its most dramatic form.

Examining several native American languages, Whorf was struck by the observation that different languages appeared to divide up the world differently, and that, further, a concept that was represented as a 'thing' in one language might be represented as an 'event' or a 'process' in another. These purely linguistic differences he was inclined to see as representing genuine differences in the way that speakers of different languages perceive the world. Though he himself never made such an explicit statement, his work soon came to be interpreted as supporting a remarkable conclusion: the structure of our language in large measure determines the way we perceive the world. This dictum is known as the *linguistic relatively hypothesis*, or equally as the *Sapir-Whorf hypothesis*.

This hypothesis has been controversial from the start. In the 1960s, the anthropologists Brent Berlin and Paul Kay published a famous study of basic colour terms in a number of languages, concluding that, even though languages differ markedly in their linguistic systems for naming colours, there were important universal characteristics of colour terms, suggesting that universals of perception underlay the linguistic differences. But their conclusions were challenged on a number of grounds, most famously by the psychologists John Lucy and Richard Shweder, who in the 1970s reported some interesting differences in the behaviour of speakers of different languages.

Since then any number of linguists, anthropologists and psychologists have chipped in with fascinating data supporting one side or the other, but at present there is still no consensus on the degree of validity which can be reasonably assigned to this hypothesis. However, psycholinguists have managed to demonstrate that, in memory tests, it is easier to remember things when we have explicit names for them. So, for example, it is easier to remember colours accurately if our language provides a wide range of specific colour terms.

*See:* **anthropological linguistics**

*Further reading:* Berlin and Kay, 1969; Crystal, 1997a: ch. 5; Duranti, 1997: 60–67; Gumperz and Levinson, 1996; Lucy, 1992; Lucy and Shweder, 1979; Steinberg, 1993: ch. 8; Whorf, 1956; Wierzbicka, 1996: ch. 10.

**linguistics**  The scientific study of language. There were significant traditions of language study in ancient India, in ancient China, in ancient Greece and Rome, among the medieval Arabs and Jews, and elsewhere. Most of these investigations, though, were solely confined to studying the local prestige language. Modern linguistics does not derive from these older traditions; instead, it grew up from fresh beginnings in Europe and the USA.

By the seventeenth century, a few European scholars and philosophers were beginning to interest themselves in general questions about the nature of language, and between the seventeenth and nineteenth century, scholars like Descartes, Locke and Humboldt made a number of significant contributions. But, with a few exceptions, these men typically knew nothing about any languages other than the major languages of Europe, and their work suffered from a lack of data, with the result that much of it was speculative and *a priori*.

By the end of the eighteenth century, **historical linguistics** had begun to be firmly established, and throughout the nineteenth century the historical study of language was for many people synonymous with the scientific study of language. Towards the end of the century, though, a number of linguists began turning their attention to the serious study of the structure of language from a non-historical point of view. Prominent among them were von der Gabelentz, Kruszewski and Baudouin de Courtenay. But the most influential figure, by far, was the Swiss linguist Ferdinand de Saussure.

Though he had been trained as a historical linguist, and though he had made major contributions to historical studies, Saussure began to focus on some more general questions of language structure and to reach some profound conclusions. He failed to publish this work, but, after his death, his former students edited their lecture notes into a book, which was published under Saussure's name in 1916: this book is the famous *Cours*. So great has been the influence of the book that Saussure has been dubbed 'the father of linguistics'. The European linguistic tradition, with its heavy theoretical bias, largely derives from Saussure's work, though in Britain Bronislaw Malinowski and (especially) J.R. Firth independently developed a more strongly data-oriented descriptive approach born of anthropological fieldwork.

Meanwhile, in the USA, anthropologists were undertaking the study of the dying native American languages. This study was keenly promoted by Franz Boas, who is often regarded as the founder of the American linguistic tradition; Boas's successors, such as A.L. Kroeber and (especially) Edward Sapir, went on to develop linguistics as an independent discipline in the USA. But the single most influential figure was Leonard Bloomfield, whose 1933 textbook *Language* effectively defined the field and set the agenda for American linguists. Bloomfield's successors, the ***American structuralists*** (or ***post-Bloomfieldians***), drew their inspiration from Bloomfield, and they created a brand of linguistics which stressed hands-on experience with real data and often dismissed the contemporary European tradition as mere 'armchair theorizing'.

This is how things stood in the 1950s: a highly theoretical tradition in Europe, a highly antitheoretical tradition in the USA, and something in between in Britain. But, in 1957, the young American linguist Noam Chomsky published *Syntactic Structures*, a brief and watered-down summary of several years of original research. In that book, and in his succeeding publications, Chomsky made a number of revolutionary proposals: he introduced the idea of a **generative grammar**, developed a particular kind of generative grammar called **transformational grammar**, rejected his American predecessors' emphasis on the description of data – in favour of a highly theoretical approach based upon a search for universal principles of language (later called **universal grammar**) – proposed to turn linguistics firmly towards **mentalism**, and laid the foundations for integrating the field into the as yet unnamed new discipline of **cognitive science**.

Chomsky's ideas excited a whole generation of students; since American universities were expanding rapidly in the early 1960s, these students quickly found jobs and began preaching the new doctrines, and within a few years

Chomskyan linguistics had become the new orthodoxy in the USA. Before long, Chomsky's ideas had crossed the Atlantic and established themselves also in many parts of Europe.

Today Chomsky's influence is undimmed, and Chomskyan linguists form a large and maximally prominent cohort among the community of linguists, to such an extent that outsiders often have the impression that linguistics *is* Chomskyan linguistics, that linguistics is by definition what the Chomskyans do. But this is seriously misleading.

In fact, the majority of the world's linguists would acknowledge no more than the vaguest debt to Chomsky, if even that. Investigators of **historical linguistics**, of **socio-linguistics**, of **anthropological linguistics**, of **psycho-linguistics** and **neurolinguistics**, of **language acquisition**, of dialectology (see **dialect**), of **semantics** and **pragmatics**, of the analysis of conversation (see **conversation analysis**), **discourse** and **texts**, of **computational linguistics**, and of a dozen other areas, all have their own agendas and priorities, and they are making progress – sometimes dramatic progress – without paying any attention to Chomsky's contributions. Indeed, it can reasonably be argued that the greatest advances in our understanding of language in recent years have come from the new field of sociolinguistics, in which pioneers like William Labov, Peter Trudgill, and Jim and Lesley Milroy have transformed our whole perception of what it means to speak a language.

Linguistics today is surely as lively a discipline as any on earth. In the last forty years or so we have probably learned more about language than our ancestors managed in 2000 years, and there is no reason to believe that things are slowing down now.

*See:* **language**

*Further reading:* Akmajian *et al.*, 1995; Crystal, 1997a: ch. 65; Elgin, 1983; Fromkin and Rodman, 1998; Hudson, 1984; O'Grady *et al.*, 1996; Trask, 1995.

**linguistic sign**  A linguistic object possessing both form and meaning. The concept of the *linguistic sign* was introduced in the early twentieth century by the Swiss linguist Ferdinand de Saussure, in whose system it plays a central role. This concept is a very simple one: every linguistic object has two aspects, or facets: a linguistic form (called by Saussure the *signifiant*, or 'signifier') and a meaning (the *signifié*, or 'thing signified'). For example, the English word *dog* has a particular form (a sequence of three meaningless **phonemes**) and also a particular meaning (a specific kind of animal). The two together make up a single linguistic sign in English.

Saussure drew particular attention to the **arbitrariness** of each linguistic sign: there is no reason why any particular linguistic form should be associated with any particular meaning, and the pairing that exists in each case is an arbitrary one.

The recognition of linguistic signs lies at the heart of our view of any given language as a **symbolic system**. Saussure's idea of linguistic signs was also influential in shaping the discipline of **semiotics**.

*See:* **arbitrariness**; **semiotics**; **symbolic system**
*Further reading:* Culler, 1986.

**literacy**  The ability to read and write effectively. *Literacy* is the ability to read and write, and that sounds simple enough. But it isn't. Between the two extremes of a magisterial command of reading and writing on the one hand and total *illiteracy* on the other, we find any number of intermediate stages: literacy is a matter of degree. One person may be able to read a popular tabloid newspaper but unable to read a tax return or even the instructions on an aspirin bottle. Another may be able to read a fair range of material but be incapable of writing anything intelligible.

Attempts have been made since the 1940s at defining a level of *functional literacy* – the minimum level of reading and writing required to function effectively in a world dominated by written material – but this has proved exceedingly difficult to do.

In the English-speaking countries, the retreat since the 1960s from the explicit teaching of literacy skills in schools has aggravated the difficulties inherent in providing the population with an adequate degree of literacy. Even university graduates are now often so deficient in spelling, punctuation, vocabulary, word usage, sentence construction and text organization that they can scarcely produce a piece of writing which is intelligible to other people. This problem has been further complicated by political demands from some quarters that we should abandon all attempts at teaching standard English to speakers of non-standard varieties, and simply accept a broad range of non-standard forms and usages, even in writing.

These attitudes and policies are recent in the English-speaking world and largely confined to it. Elsewhere, the acquisition of literacy, at least in the local prestige language, is still generally regarded as a high priority, and today perhaps 75% of the world's population may be described as literate – an enormous advance, since it is not so many generations since a knowledge of reading and writing was the exclusive preserve of tiny elites.

An individual who lacks the reading and writing skills typical of his community is *illiterate*; an entire society which lacks a recognized writing system is *aliterate*, or sometimes in a historical context *preliterate*.

*See:* **oracy**; **standard language**
*Further reading:* Crystal, 1997a: ch. 44.

**loan word**   A word copied into one language from another language. The speakers of almost every language are in contact with the speakers of other languages, and very often people take a liking to some of the words used by their neighbours and take those words into their own language. This process is called *borrowing*, and the words that are taken over are *loan words* in the receiving language.

There are several motivations for borrowing a word. The simplest is that the word is the name of something totally new to those who borrow it. English, for example, has borrowed *whisky* from Scots Gaelic, *yogurt* from Turkish, *tomato* from Nahuatl, *sauna* from Finnish, *ukulele* from Hawaiian and *kangaroo* from the Guugu-Yimidhirr language of Australia. The reason for this is that English-speakers had never seen whisky or yogurt or tomatoes or saunas or ukuleles or kangaroos before encountering these things overseas, and so they simply took over the local names for them.

Another important motivation is prestige. At any given time in any given place, some languages typically enjoy more prestige than others, and speakers of less prestigious languages are often eager to show off their command of a more prestigious language by introducing some of its words into their own speech. For example, after the Norman conquest of England, Norman French enjoyed far more prestige than English, and English-speakers reacted by borrowing huge numbers of Norman French words into English, such as *picture*, *courage*, *army*, *treasure*, *language*, *female* and even *face*, *fool* and *beef*; in many cases these fashionable words simply displaced their native English equivalents, which dropped out of use, as happened with native *here* 'army' and *andwlita* 'face'.

*See:* **language contact**
*Further reading:* Crystal, 1995: ch. 10; Hock and Joseph, 1996: ch. 8; Katamba, 1994: ch. 10; Trask, 1996: 17–30.

**localization** The concentration of certain mental faculties in particular areas of the brain. We have long known that individual areas of the brain are responsible for handling specific tasks. For example, not only are there identifiable areas of the brain that process vision, there are even areas that process specific aspects of vision, such as colour vision and the perception of movement.

Language is no different: there are particular **language areas** in the brain that process specific aspects of language use. In the mid-nineteenth century, the French surgeon Paul Broca and the German neurologist Carl Wernicke identified the two most important of these: ***Broca's area*** provides the grammatical structure for utterances and sends instructions to the speech organs, while ***Wernicke's area*** handles comprehension of speech and access to vocabulary. Both of these areas are usually located on the left side of the brain.

Broca and Wernicke reached their conclusions by examining brain-damaged patients who exhibited specific disabilities of language, and then by performing post-mortem inspections to determine which parts of the brain had been damaged. In recent years, however, the development of brain-scanning devices like the ***PET scanner*** has allowed us to monitor the brain of a healthy, conscious person who is performing some linguistic task like speaking or reading; we can see directly which parts of the brain are active during each of these tasks, and as a result we now have a fairly detailed map of the language areas in the brain.

*See:* **aphasia**; **language areas**
*Further reading:* Akmajian *et al.*, 1995: ch. 12; Crystal, 1997a: ch. 45; O'Grady *et al.*, 1996: ch. 10 [ch. 11 in the American edition].

**logonomic rules**   Very high-level rules governing discourse in a particular setting. In a given setting, there are a number of high-level rules governing the conduct of discourse: rules about who is allowed to speak and when, about who is allowed to interrupt or to change the subject, about who is allowed to make jokes, about what counts as a joke, about what is considered offensive, and so on. These are the ***logonomic rules*** governing that discourse, and they are so familiar to participants (at least, to participants with experience of that type of discourse) that they are virtually subconscious.

For example, the rules governing a seminar discussion in a university are very different from those governing a performance by a stand-up comedian in a night club. What is considered acceptable, funny or offensive among a group of conservative farmers drinking in a bar in South Africa or Montana will likely be very different from the norms accepted by a lesbian or gay organization planning a political campaign against discrimination.

Every normal speaker learns the rules appropriate to each type of discourse in which he or she regularly takes part, and every normal speaker can shift effortlessly from one set of rules to another as changing settings require: this is part of that **communicative competence** which we acquire along with the acquisition of our purely linguistic knowledge. And one of the most unpleasant experiences we are likely to have is to be thrust into a setting of which we have no experience and hence don't know the rules or, still worse, in which we disapprove of the rules.

An imperfect knowledge of the logonomic rules governing a setting in which you find yourself will lead to your being regarded as, at best, lacking in charm and social graces and, at worst, ignorant, antisocial, stupid and offensive. Speaking out of turn, interrupting when you're not entitled to, using a frostily formal tone in an informal setting (or vice versa), attempting jokes which offend the others – all these are failures to observe the logonomic rules and evidence of your inadequate communicative competence.

*See:* **communicative competence**; **ethnography of speaking**

**manner of articulation** The action of the speech organs involved in producing a particular **consonant**. A *consonant* is produced by narrowing the **vocal tract** at some point along its length. The particular speech organs chosen to make the *constriction* represent the **place of articulation**, but, even at a single place, it is usually possible to make several different kinds of constriction. The type of constriction made in a particular instance is the *manner of articulation*.

There are several types of manner. In a *plosive* (like [b] or [k]), a complete closure is made, blocking off the airflow, and the closure is released suddenly. In an *affricate* (like [ʧ] or [ts]), a complete closure is made and then released gradually, with friction noise. In a *fricative* (like [f] or [z]), there is no complete closure, but air is forced through a tiny opening, producing friction noise. These three types are collectively called *obstruents*, because the airflow is strongly obstructed.

The remaining types are collectively called *sonorants*. In a *nasal* (like [m] or [n]), a complete closure is made in the mouth, but the velum is lowered, so that air flows out through the nose. In an *approximant* (like [w] or most types of English /r/), the air is allowed to flow through a relatively large opening, and no friction noise is produced. (At the phonetic level, such consonants are strictly **vowels**, but they pattern in languages like consonants.) In a *flap* (like the [ɾ] of many languages of India), an elastic organ is 'flipped' rapidly from one place to another, briefly striking something else as it moves. A *tap* (like Spanish [ɾ] in *pero* 'but') is similar except that the moving organ finishes where it started. (Some books do not distinguish between flaps and taps, but it is preferable to do so.) In a *trill* (like Spanish [r] in *perro* 'dog'), the air forced through a smallish opening forces an elastic organ to vibrate. All these are examples of *median* consonants, in which all airflow is through the centre-line of the mouth. However, it is also possible to block off the centre-line and force the air to flow through one or both sides of the mouth; such a consonant is *lateral*. We can produce a *lateral affricate* (like the [tɬ] in Nahuatl, the Aztec language of Mexico), a *lateral fricative* (like the [ɬ] of Welsh *Llanelli*), or a *lateral approximant* (commonly just called a *lateral*) (like English [l]).

*See:* **consonant**; **phonetics**; **place of articulation**
*Further reading:* Ashby, 1995: ch. 6; Ladefoged and Maddieson, 1996; Laver, 1994: part IV.

**markedness** The property which distinguishes less neutral linguistic forms from competing ones which are more neutral. Though the concept is older, the term *markedness* was introduced by the European linguists of the *Prague School* in the 1920s, and it is now regarded as linguistically central.

Markedness is a very broad notion applying at all levels of analysis. Generally speaking, a *marked form* is any linguistic form which is less usual or less neutral than some other form – the *unmarked form* – from any of a number of points of view. A marked form may be distinguished from an unmarked one by the presence of additional linguistic material, by the presence of additional nuances of meaning, by greater rarity in a particular language or in languages generally, or in several other ways.

For example, voiceless vowels and voiceless laterals are marked with respect to voiced ones, since the voiceless ones are far rarer than the voiced ones in the world's languages and since the voiceless ones are generally found only in languages that also have voiced ones, while most languages have only the voiced ones. The affricate [pf], as in German *Pflaume* 'plum', is marked with respect to both [p] and [f], since the last two are very frequent in languages, while [pf] is exceedingly rare.

English *lioness* is marked with respect to *lion*, since it contains additional morphological material and since it is of less general applicability. English *brethren* is marked with respect to *brothers*, since the first is restricted to certain special contexts, and *bunny* is marked with respect to *rabbit*, since the first carries additional emotive meaning absent from the second. A passive sentence like *Janet was arrested by the police* is marked with respect to the active *The police arrested Janet*, since the passive contains more material, has a more complex structure, and is rarer than the active.

The several criteria for markedness may not always coincide. For example, in some Pacific languages, passive sentences are far commoner than active ones; hence the passive ones, although marked from the point of view of grammar, are unmarked from the point of view of discourse. Markedness values can also change over time: the formal Latinate phrase *prior to* was once highly marked with respect to native English *before*, but for very many speakers *prior to* has now become the ordinary, and hence unmarked, form, as in *prior to the war*.

*Further reading:* P. Hawkins, 1984: 114–125.

**meaning**  The characteristic of a linguistic form which allows it to be used to pick out some aspect of the non-linguistic world. The study of meaning has a long history in a number of disciplines, notably philosophy, but the linguistic study of meaning, **semantics**, largely dates only from the late nineteenth century, and it has become generally regarded as a central part of linguistics only since the 1960s.

In contrast to other specialists, linguists are chiefly interested in the meanings of linguistic forms in everyday speech. More particularly, linguists are interested in the way some meanings relate to other meanings – that is, it is the ***system*** of meanings which is seen as important, rather than the meanings of individual items.

Like others, linguists carefully distinguish different types of meaning. The central and intrinsic meaning of a linguistic form is its **denotation** or **sense**, while the fuzzy and sometimes variable associations of that form constitute its **connotations**. The relation between a form and the non-linguistic thing it picks out in a given context is its **reference**. An extended and non-literal meaning is a **metaphor**.

*See:* **connotation**; **denotation**; **metaphor**; **reference**; **selection restriction**; **semantics**; **sense**

*Further reading:* Allan, 1986: ch. 2; Crystal, 1997a: ch. 17; Frawley, 1992: ch. 2; Hofmann, 1993; Hudson, 1995; Hurford and Heasley, 1983; Leech, 1974: chs. 1–2; F. Palmer, 1976.


**medium**  Any one of several signalling systems within which a language may be embedded. A *primary* medium for language is one which is not derived from any other medium and which may be the medium in which a child acquires its first language. The most familiar and most widely used primary medium is **speech**, in which linguistic information is encoded within sounds which are produced by the vocal tract acting upon a stream of air. Speech has been used as a medium since our remote ancestors first evolved language, and it was probably the first medium we ever used (though some scholars query this). The other primary medium is **sign language**, in which linguistic information is encoded within signs made chiefly with the hands, arms, shoulders, head and face. This is the medium used today by the majority of deaf people, at least in places in which they have a chance to learn it. Signing is of unknown antiquity; it has become steadily more prominent since the eighteenth century, but sign languages have very likely been constructed and used for a very long time, whenever circumstances permitted. It is important to realize that a true sign language is autonomous and in no way derived from a spoken language.

A *secondary* medium is one which is derived from a primary medium. The most familiar secondary medium is *writing*, which usually consists of an attempt at converting speech into permanent marks. Writing is a recent invention in human affars, being little more than 5,000 years old, and until very recently knowledge of writing (and reading) was confined to a tiny minority of the world's population. True sign languages can also be converted into writing, though systems for doing this are still in their infancy and mostly used only by specialists; most signers find it more convenient to learn to read ordinary writing. Also secondary are systems like *Signed English* (or *Manually Coded English*), in which a spoken language (like English) is transferred into the medium of hand-gestures.

A *tertiary* medium is one derived from a secondary medium. The slow and cumbersome system called *finger-spelling* is a tertiary system, since it is derived from writing, with each letter of the alphabet being rendered by a finger-sign. Early systems of *shorthand* were often tertiary, being derived from writing, but modern shorthand systems are all secondary, being derived directly from speech.

*See:* **sign language**; **speech**; **writing system**
*Further reading:* Crystal, 1997a: sections IV–VI.

**mentalism**   The doctrine that the mind can be invoked in scientific investigation and even be made the object of study itself. In the late nineteenth century, psychology had become obscurantist and almost metaphysical. The new doctrine of **behaviourism** attempted to sweep away this deadwood by focusing only on what could be directly observed and preferably measured. But the behaviourists themselves often went so far as not only to deny the possibility of appealing to unobservable things like minds, but even to reject the very existence of minds.

More recently, the pendulum has swung the other way again, and today most psychologists, philosophers and linguists are perfectly happy to invoke invisible things like minds and purposes and even to make mind itself the object of study. This approach is called **mentalism**, and it is now the dominant point of view in all three disciplines, which themselves are now partly united within the new discipline of **cognitive science**.

*See:* **behaviourism**; **cognitive linguistics**; **cognitive science**
*Further reading:* Malmkjær, 1991: 305–308; Ungerer and Schmid, 1996.

**metalanguage** A language used to talk about another language. Linguists, philosophers and many others often need to talk about particular languages, or about languages in general. Naturally, the discussion itself has to be couched in a language of some sort, and this fact can quickly lead to hopeless confusion if we are not careful. We must therefore distinguish carefully between the *object language* (the language which we are talking about) and the *metalanguage* (the language we are using to talk about the object language).

It is perfectly possible to use, say, English as a metalanguage in order to talk about English as an object language, and indeed we do this all the time, but it is precisely here that confusion can most quickly arise: if we fail to distinguish between the English we are talking about and the English we are using to talk about it, we can easily become lost.

Consider the following example. Using English as a metalanguage to talk about English, we may assert the following: a grammatical English sentence may not contain two consecutive instances of the preposition *of*. This is true. But beginning students often challenge this by pointing to examples like this one: the grammatical functions of *of* in English are numerous. Is this a counterexample?

No, it is not. It appears to be a counterexample only if we confuse the metalanguage with the object language. This last statement is a statement in the metalanguage, and the first occurrence of *of* in it is part of that statement. But the second occurrence of *of* is different: this is merely a piece of the object language, one which we happen to be talking about here. That is, the first *of* is doing what *of* normally does, while the second *of* is doing nothing at all: it is merely being talked about. If this is not obvious, observe what happens when the object language is French: the grammatical functions of *de* in French are numerous. Here it should be easy to see that the French preposition *de* is doing nothing in this English sentence except being talked about.

The two instances of *of* are an example of what philosophers call the ***use–mention distinction***: the first *of* is being used normally, while the second is merely being mentioned (talked about).

At the very least, when we use English as a metalanguage to talk about languages, we need to invoke a battery of technical terms and concepts, just as a specialist studying physics, music or psychology needs to invoke technical terms and concepts. In fact, we sometimes go further, and invent a special artificial language to use as our metalanguage. The various types of ***formal logic*** used by logicians, philosophers and linguists for describing English and other languages are just this: specially invented metalanguages.

*Further reading:* Lyons, 1995: 6–11.

**metaphor**   The non-literal use of a linguistic form, designed to draw attention to a perceived resemblance. The literary use of metaphors is ancient and well studied, and the fields of rhetoric and literary criticism have developed a formidable battery of Greek terms for naming many different kinds of metaphor. But metaphors are in fact commonplace in ordinary speech and writing: we speak of the *foot* of a mountain or the *eye* of a needle, we refer to Saussure as the *father* of linguistics, and we speak of a failing business enterprise as a *lame duck*. Like every language, English is stuffed with thousands of such metaphors, and most of them are so familiar that we no longer even regard them as metaphorical in nature. Indeed, linguists have realized for some generations now that metaphors are a commonplace way of extending the expressive resources of a language.

Since the early 1980s, however, those linguists developing the new discipline of **cognitive linguistics** have been drawing attention to the pervasive influence in languages of *cognitive metaphors*, large-scale metaphors which condition a broad range of expressions and which appear to be related to the way we perceive the world. An example is the metaphor *life is a journey*, which appears in any number of locutions: *I'll cross that bridge when I come to it* ; *She knows where she's going* ; *There were two paths open to him* ; *The baby has arrived* ; *Their paths crossed* ; *She has finally arrived* (succeeded); *He is gone* (dead); *It's been a long road* ; and many others.

*See:* **meaning**; **cognitive linguistics**

*Further reading:* Carter, 1997: ch. 7; Cruse, 1986: 41–45; Goatty, 1997; Lakoff and Johnson, 1980; Malmkjær, 1991: 308–312; Saeed, 1997: 302–308; Ungerer and Schmid, 1996: ch. 3.

**minimal pair**  A pair of words in a language which have different meanings but which have identical forms except at one single point. The English words *pet* and *bet* have different meanings, but they consist of identical sequences of sounds in all positions except one: in this case, initial position. Here the first word has [p], while the second has [b]. Consequently, the difference in meaning must derive entirely from the contrast between [p] and [b]; we must therefore assign English [p] and [b] to different **phonemes** /p/ and /b/, and *pet* and *bet* constitute a *minimal pair* for the phonemes /p/ and /b/: phonemically, these words are /pet/ and /bet/. Other minimal pairs for English /p/ and /b/ include *planned* and *bland*, *nipple* and *nibble*, and *rip* and *rib*.

Finding a minimal pair for two sounds constitutes certain proof that the two sounds in question must belong to different phonemes. Sometimes this is fairly easy, as with English [s] and [ʃ]: *sun* and *shun*, *pussy* and *pushy*, *lass* and *lash*. Sometimes it is not so easy, as with English [ʃ] and [ʒ], for which we can only find minimal pairs by invoking proper names (*Aleutian* versus *allusion*) or made-up words (*mesher* versus *measure*).

Larger minimal sets can be found. For example, the set *sum*, *sun*, *sung* constitutes a minimal triplet for the English phonemes /m/, /n/ and /ŋ/.

*See:* **distribution**; **phoneme**; **phonotactics**
*Further reading:* Carr, 1993: 88–98; Fromkin and Rodman, 1998: 254–258.


**minority language**    A long-established language spoken as a mother tongue by people in some part of a country in which the national or official language is something else. We commonly tend to assume that everybody in, say, France speaks French. In fact, virtually all adults in France *do* speak French – but not always as their first language. In various regions of the country, the first language of all or most local people is Alsatian German, Dutch, Breton, Basque, Catalan, Occitan or Corsican. Each of these is the mother tongue in its region, and people who learn one of these as their first language in early childhood may not even begin learning French until later in life, especially after beginning formal education.

Such languages are called *minority languages*, and minority languages are not confined to France. Alongside Spanish, Spain has Galician, Basque and Catalan; alongside German, Germany has Frisian and Wendish (the second is a Slavic language); alongside English, Britain has Welsh and Scots Gaelic; alongside English, the USA has Navaho, Hopi, Lakota, and dozens of other indigenous languages. Russia and China each have over a hundred minority languages, and countries with no minority languages are in fact a rarity – though Iceland and Portugal may be two cases.

In every case, a minority language has been spoken in its area for centuries, sometimes even for millennia, but its speakers have simply found themselves incorporated into a nation-state in which the principal language is something else. In some cases, most speakers of a minority language may live and die without ever acquiring an adequate command of the prestige language; in others, all speakers normally become fluent in the prestige language, or at least acquire an adequate working knowledge of it. Even in Britain, Spain and France, monoglot speakers of Welsh, Basque and Corsican were numerous only a few generations ago (and Basque, at least, still has a handful of elderly monoglot speakers today), but, because of dramatic advances in communications, transport and education, almost all European adults are today fluent in the national language of the country they find themselves living in.

This very fact, of course, places great pressure on minority languages. In the not-too-distant past, speakers of minority languages like Welsh and Basque were often openly persecuted by centralist governments, which were inclined to see the use of regional languages as unpatriotic, subversive, even dangerous. Today open persecution is less usual in Europe (though not always elsewhere, and it has not disappeared entirely in Europe: for example, Greece has recently been ferociously persecuting its Macedonian-speaking minority). However, minority languages are nevertheless often in grave danger of dying out. A good knowledge of the national language is absolutely required for living in a modern nation-state – to get an education, to find a job, to deal with tax returns and innumerable other official documents, to travel round the country, to understand newspapers, television and films. Further, knowledge of a major language like English or French opens the door to opportunities, not just throughout the country, but throughout the world. Consequently, speakers of minority languages find themselves using the prestige language ever more regularly, while the role of their mother tongue decreases correspondingly. In some cases, parents may actually strive to have their children learn the prestige language, rather than their own mother tongue, in the hope that these children will have a better life as a result.

Such pressures have already led to the disappearance of countless minority languages, including Cornish and Manx in Britain and hundreds of indigenous languages in North America and Australia. Today these pressures are greater than ever, but in many cases speakers of minority languages are waking up to the threat and becoming increasingly militant in their demands for greater official recognition and encouragement of their languages. In a few cases, as with the Swedish-speakers of Finland and the Basque-speakers of Spain, a greater or lesser degree of protection has already been achieved, but in most cases protection is limited or non-existent, and it seems inevitable that hundreds or thousands of minority languages will disappear in the next two or three generations.

*See:* **immigrant language**; **language and identity**; **language and power**; **language death**

*Further reading:* Crystal, 1997a: ch. 60; Holmes, 1992: ch. 3; Romaine, 1994: 36–43; Wardhaugh, 1987.


**modality** The **grammatical category** associated with the expression of obligation, permission, prohibition, necessity, possibility and ability. It is by no means easy to separate *modality* from the more traditional category of **mood**, which expresses degree or kind of reality. But for some decades now linguists have preferred to apply the label *modality* to the linguistic expression of the six categories named above. This term is particularly convenient in discussing a language, such as English, which contains a specific set of *modal auxiliaries* for expressing these concepts.

The English modals include *can*, *could*, *may*, *might*, *will*, *would*, *shall*, *should*, *must* and *ought (to)*, together with their negated forms. Familiar examples like *You can do it*, *You could do it*, *You may do it*, *You should do it*, *You must do it*, *You can't do it* and *You mustn't do it* all express aspects or degrees of one (or more) of the six named categories.

In practice, modality shades off imperceptibly into several other categories: *evidentiality* (the amount and nature of the evidence which you have for saying something), *modalization* (the probability or regularity of an occurrence), *modularity* (the degree of commitment or willingness involved on somebody's part), *hedging* (reducing your own commit-ment to what you are saying) and *vague language*. These extensions of modality have been particularly investigated within **Systemic Linguistics**.

*See:* **mood**
*Further reading:* Coates, 1983; Hurford, 1994: 126–129; F. Palmer, 1974: ch. 5, 1979, 1986.

**modifier** A linguistic element in a sentence which is gram-matically linked to a second element and adds information about that second element. A sentence is typically made up of smaller grammatical units called **phrases**, and a phrase typically consists of a grammatically central word, its **head**, accompanied by some *modifiers*, each of which provides some information about whatever is denoted by the head.

Consider the sentence *The little girl in the pond was shriek-ing delightedly*. Here the **noun phrase** *the little girl in the pond* has the head *girl* (the whole phrase denotes some kind of girl), and *girl* has two modifiers: *little* and *in the pond*. Each of these modifiers provides further information about the girl in question: among girls generally, this particular one is both little and in the pond. The word *the*, in contrast, is not a modifier but a *specifier*: it provides no information about the girl (it would make no sense to say that this girl is *the* compared to other girls), but rather it provides informa-tion about how the entire noun phrase fits into the whole discourse (in this case, it indicates that the girl in question has already been mentioned earlier and is familiar to the listener).

Similarly, the **verb phrase** *shrieking excitedly* consists of the head *shrieking* and the modifier *excitedly* – that is, of all the possible ways of shrieking, this particular shrieking was done in an excited manner.

Modifiers can be quite large and complex, and they need not occur immediately next to their heads. In the sentence *The women who had volunteered for the wet T-shirt contest climbed giggling onto the stage*, the head *women* is modified both by the relative clause *who had volunteered for the wet T-shirt contest* and by the adjective *giggling*, the second of which is separated from its head by the verb *climbed*.

The relation between a modifier and its head is *modification*.

*See:* **head**; **phrase**
*Further reading:* Hurford, 1994: 129–131.


**modularity** Division into several more or less independent components. A *modular* system is one which consists of several largely independent components which interact in such a way that the whole system performs some task or tasks successfully. Since the early 1980s, the concept of modularity has become prominent in linguistics and cognitive science in at least two ways.

First, the American philosopher Jerry Fodor has been arguing that the human mind is itself modular, that it consists of a number of specialized subcomponents for handling different tasks, such as speaking and seeing. (The opposing view here is *holism*, the belief that the mind is essentially a seamless whole, with no specialized subparts.) Second, the American linguist Noam Chomsky has been arguing that the human **language faculty** is modular: that it must consist of a fairly large number of semi-autonomous units, each of which is responsible for certain particular aspects of our linguistic **competence**. This belief is strongly reflected in Chomsky's theory of grammar, the **Government-and-Binding Theory**, which posits a number of specialized grammatical modules; each of these has its own requirements, and all must be satisfied for a sentence to be well formed.

*See:* **cognitive science**; **language faculty**
*Further reading:* Fodor, 1983; Pinker, 1994 *passim*.


**mood** The **grammatical category** which expresses the degree or kind of reality attached to an utterance. Mood is not well developed as a grammatical category in English, and we mostly use words and constructions to express mood distinctions. In this way, we can assign varying degrees of certainty to an utterance: *Susie smokes, I hear that Susie smokes, It appears that Susie smokes, Surely Susie smokes, Susie probably smokes, Maybe Susie smokes, I wonder if Susie smokes, It's unlikely that Susie smokes.* We can also assign different degrees of reality within conditions: *If Susie smokes, then . . .* (an open condition: maybe she smokes) is different from *If Susie smoked, then . . .* (a counterfactual condition: she doesn't smoke). American English (but not British English) makes an overt mood distinction between *I insist that Susie smokes* (I'm telling you: she definitely does) and *I insist that Susie smoke* (I demand to see her smoking – perhaps in a film role).

Questions may be regarded as expressing another kind of mood: *Does Susie smoke?* And so can commands: *Susie, smoke that cigarette!* (perhaps our tyrannical film director again, to a reluctant actress).

In some other languages, there are more or less elaborate distinctions of mood built into the grammar and frequently expressed either by variation in verb-forms or by particles.

Mood shades off imperceptibly into **modality**, and no sharp line can be drawn between them.

*See:* **modality**
*Further reading:* Hurford, 1994: 131–133 F. Palmer, 1986.


**morpheme**    The smallest identifiable grammatical unit. We sometimes think of ***words*** as the smallest units of grammar, but words in fact are not the smallest grammatical units. For example, the word *unhappiness* is clearly built up from three smaller pieces: the prefix *un-*, the stem *happy* and the suffix *-ness*. Each of these pieces is a ***morpheme*** of English, and not one of them can be broken down any further in grammatical terms: all of them are minimal units. Each of these morphemes is used to build other English words. For example, the prefix *un-* occurs also in *unhappy, unclear, unwilling, uninteresting* and *unsatisfied*; the ***stem*** *happy* occurs also in *unhappy, happiness, happier* and *happily*, and also, of course, in the word *happy* itself; and the suffix *-ness* occurs also in *quickness*, *sadness*, *lewdness*, *childishness* and *unpreparedness*.

Morphemes are of different types. We say that *happy* is a **lexical morpheme**, meaning that it has dictionary meaning: we can provide a definition for it. But the *-ly* of *happily* is different: this is a **grammatical morpheme**, which performs a strictly grammatical function – in this case, that of turning an adjective into an adverb. Quite independently, we can say that *happy* is also a **free morpheme**: it can stand alone to make a word, as it does in the word *happy*. But the prefix *un-* and the suffixes *-ness* and *-ly* are **bound morphemes**: they can never stand alone, but must always be attached to at least one other morpheme within a word.

In the ideal case, a single morpheme has a single constant form and a single constant meaning or function but, in practice, many morphemes vary in form, depending on where they occur. For example, the morpheme *sane* has one form when it occurs in the words *sane* and *insane*, but a different form when it occurs in the word *sanity* (listen to the pronunciation, since the English spelling is not very helpful here). Likewise, the negative prefix *in-* exhibits several different forms in the words *insincere*, *impossible* and *illegal*. We call these variant forms the **allomorphs** of the morpheme.

In the cases above, it is a trivial matter to divide a word into the morphemes of which it is built, but sometimes such division is not so easy. Clearly the past-tense form *loved* (as in *She loved him*) consists of two morphemes, the verb–stem *love* and a grammatical morpheme which we can call *Past*, and it's not too hard to draw a line between them. But the past-tense form *took* must likewise consist of two morphemes, the verb-stem *take* and the morpheme *Past*, yet this time we can't draw a neat line at all: the two morphemes are just wrapped up in a single bundle, and we have to appeal to a more abstract level of representation to show that *took* is really *take* plus *Past*.

The term **morpheme** was coined in the late nineteenth century by the Polish linguist Jan Baudouin de Courtenay, but it was not always used in the modern sense. That modern sense was established by the American linguist Leonard Bloomfield in the 1930s, and it was Bloomfield and his American successors who made the study of morphemes a central part of linguistics.

*See:* **affix**; **derivation**; **inflection**; **morphology**; **stem**; **word-formation**

*Further reading:* Bauer, 1988: ch. 2; Brown and Miller, 1991: chs. 12–13; Katamba, 1994: ch. 3.

**morphology**   Word structure, or the branch of linguistics which studies this. Words typically have internal structure, and in particular they consist of smaller units called **morphemes**. For example, the verb-form *taking* consists of two morphemes: the verb–stem *take* and the grammatical ending *-ing*. Similarly, the noun *textbook* consists of the morphemes *text* and *book*, and the the adverb *slowly* consists of the morphemes *slow* and *-ly*.

Morphology is conventionally divided into two main areas. These are **inflection** – the variation in form of a single word for grammatical purposes, as with *take*, *takes*, *took*, *taken*, *taking* – and **word-formation** – the construction of new words from existing words, as with *textbook* from *text* and *book* and with *slowly* from *slow* and *-ly*. A particularly important type of word-formation is **derivation**, as in *slowly*, *rewrite* and *unhappiness*.

*See:* **affix**; **derivation**; **inflection**; **morpheme**; **stem**; **word-formation**

*Further reading:* Bauer, 1988; Brown and Miller, 1991: part two; Matthews, 1991.

**movement**   Any of various processes or structures in which an element of a sentence appears in a position other than its canonical position. Grammarians have long realized that some particular sentences depart from the usual norms in the order of their elements, but it was only in the 1950s, originally within the formalism of transformational grammar, that linguists began to speak, metaphorically but conveniently, of the movement of elements out of their ordinary position.

Movement phenomena are numerous and diverse. One familiar example in English involves question-words (WH-words) like *who* and *what*: we say *Susie was talking to Mike*, but we also say *Who was Susie talking to?* and *The guy who Susie was talking to is Mike*, in both of which the question-word *who*, which is logically the object of the preposition *to*, fails to appear after *to* and instead appears earlier in the sentence. This kind of movement is called **WH-movement** or **extraction**.

A second type of movement is **extraposition**, in which a complex element is shifted to the end of its sentence. So, instead of *That Susie is drunk is obvious*, we prefer to say *It is obvious that Susie is drunk*, in which the that-clause has been extraposed. Similarly, instead of *A student who speaks Basque turned up this morning*, we can say *A student turned up this morning who speaks Basque*, in which the who-clause is extraposed.

A third type of **fronting**, in which an element is moved to the beginning of its sentence. So, instead of *She inherited her brains from her mother*, we can say *From her mother she inherited her brains*, in which the phrase *from her mother* has been fronted. Likewise, instead of *I can't cope with this* we can say *This I can't cope with*, with fronting of *this*. When, as is often the case, an element is fronted to make it an explicit topic, we speak of **topicalization**.

Finally, there is a rather unusual type of movement called **raising**; see that entry for information.

*See:* **raising**; **topic**

**name** A linguistic form which serves to pick out a unique person, place or thing. Grammatically speaking, a name is a **noun phrase**, but one with the highly distinctive function of pointing at some individual entity: *Abraham Lincoln, Paris, the Golden Gate Bridge*.

Probably every person in every society receives a *personal name*, typically shortly after birth, though in some societies an adult name is conferred later in life. In some societies, there is a conventional list of personal names, one of which is selected; in others, completely original names may be constructed and bestowed. In the first case, it may be necessary to distinguish individuals bearing the same name by adding something to the name. This can be done in several ways. A descriptive word may be used to indicate something about the individual, such as personal characteristics (size, complexion (*Little, White*), profession (*Miller, Smith*), location of dwelling (*Atwater, Woods*), place of origin (*Bristol, Welsh*), memorable incident; this is an *epithet* (or, if humorous, a *sobriquet*). Or a *patronymic* may be added, identifying the name-bearer's father (*Johnson, Prichard*).

When such a second name ceases to be the property of a particular individual, and comes to be handed down to the name-bearer's descendants, it has become a *surname* (or *family name*). As can be seen, many English surnames derive from epithets and patronymics. Surnames in Europe are mostly of medieval origin, and even today they are not in use in Iceland and are little used in Turkish Cyprus.

*Place names*, or *toponyms*, are conferred everywhere upon every kind of significant location: settlements, rivers, lakes, seas, valleys, forests, fields, mountains and hills, roads and streets, bridges, city gates, houses, places of worship, office buildings, sports stadiums. . . . The list is endless. Names are also conferred upon ships, trains, planes, railway lines, festivals, holy days, books, newspapers . . ., upon virtually everything that human beings consider important.

Name-giving practices differ considerably from society to society, and anthropological linguists are often interested in studying these practices.

Names exhibit some unusual linguistic properties, and their study is a specialist subdiscipline within linguistics. The study of names, and particularly of the origins and histories of names, is **onomastics**.

*See:* **onomastics**

*Further reading:* Crystal, 1997a: ch. 19, 1995: ch. 10; Dunkling, 1995.

**narrative**   A **text** which tells a story. A *narrative* differs from most other types of text in that it relates a connected series of events, either real or fictional, in a more or less orderly manner. In addition to familiar kinds of written narratives, such as history books and novels, there are oral narratives, that is, stories told in conversation.

Narratives are of interest to linguists from various social, anthropological and structural points of view. In the early 1970s, the American linguist William Labov examined the oral narratives of vernacular black speakers and proposed a general six-part structure for them:

● an *abstract* – indicating that a story is about to begin
● an *orientation* – setting the scene and introducing the main characters

197

- the *complicating action* – the main events
- a *resolution* – the outcome
- an *evaluation* – explaining the point of the story, and
- a *coda* – signalling that the story is over.

More recently, a number of linguists have devoted themselves to the study of narratives of various types, and some of them have attempted to develop **story grammars**, general structural outlines to which particular types of narrative tend to conform. Naturally, practitioners of **anthropological linguistics** are interested in examining the rules for constructing narratives in different languages and cultures.

*See:* **genre**; **text**

*Further reading:* Carter *et al.*, 1997: unit 5; Fabb, 1997: chs. 7–8; Labov, 1972; G. Palmer, 1996: ch. 7; Polanyi, 1985; Propp, 1968; Ryan, 1991; Toolan, 1988, 1994a, 1994b.

**national language**    The single principal language of a country. By and large, we expect citizens of France to speak French, even if their mother tongue is something else. We expect to hear French spoken in the steeets, on television and in films. We expect books and newspapers to be printed in French. We expect signs and advertisements to be in French, and we expect to be able to conduct all our business in French, from buying a loaf of bread to making a will. In other words, French is the *national language* of France – the single language that is used by pretty much everyone for pretty much everything.

In the same way, English is the national language in Britain, in Australia, in the USA and elsewhere, as German is in Germany and Dutch in the Netherlands. But not every country has a national language. Belgium is about equally divided between Dutch-speakers and French-speakers, and neither language can be used throughout the country. The same is true of Canada, divided into English-speaking and French-speaking parts, and of Switzerland, divided into regions speaking four different languages; the same was true of Czechoslovakia and Yugoslavia before they broke up, partly as a result of these very linguistic divisions.

The position of a national language may be enshrined in law (as in France) or not (as in the USA). But every country, whether it has a national language or not, is obliged to recognize one or more **official languages** in which official business may be conducted.

*See:* **minority language**; **official language**; **standard language**
*Further reading:* Holmes, 1992: ch. 5; Wardhaugh, 1987.

**natural class**   A class of linguistic objects all of which behave in much the same way in a language and which therefore often need to be referred to in a description of the language. Every language contains a large number of linguistic elements of various kinds: **phonemes**, **morphemes**, **words**, and so on. Now, if every word in a language behaved completely differently from every other word, and similarly for the other kinds of objects, then the language would be virtually chaotic, and no organized description would be possible: we would have nothing but a collection of miscellaneous observations.

But, of course, languages are not built like this at all. Instead, almost all of these linguistic objects fall rather naturally into just a few types, or classes, and all the items in one class exhibit very similar behaviour. These classes are the *natural classes* of the language.

For example, almost all the words of English (or of any other language) fall naturally into just a few classes: the **parts of speech**, such as **nouns**, **verbs** and **adjectives**. Every noun behaves in much the same way as every other noun, and so on for the other parts of speech. Consequently, when we describe English, we can make a number of important statements about the behaviour of the entire class of nouns, and we do not have to concern ourselves with every noun individually.

The same goes for morphemes, phonemes and other classes of objects. For example, the English phonemes /p t k/, as in *pip*, *tit*, *kick*, form a natural class, since what is true of one of them is nearly always true of the others as well, and so, by giving this class a suitable name, the class of **voiceless plosives**, we can make all the required statements about all of them at once.

There are two complications. First, it may be the case that, while the members of a class behave identically in some respects, they behave somewhat differently in other respects; this is the problem of **subcategorization**, which is most prominent with parts of speech. Second, our natural classes may sometimes overlap, so that a larger natural class may contain within it several smaller natural classes whose memberships are partly identical. This problem is most familiar with phonemes, and it is the reason we prefer to work with **distinctive features**.

One of the first goals in any description of a language is to identify the natural classes that it contains and to provide suitable labels for those classes, so that the description can then take advantage of these classes whenever required. Failure to do this leads inevitably to the endless unprincipled labelling of things, a feature of **traditional grammar** widely regarded as one of its failings: though the traditional grammarians certainly identified some natural classes, they failed to recognize others that were just as important. A large part of descriptive and theoretical linguistics in the twentieth century has been devoted to the development of efficient and principled ways of identifying, labelling and manipulating natural classes.

*See:* **distinctive feature**; **morpheme**; **part of speech**; **subcategorization**;
*Further reading:* O'Grady *et al.*, 1996: 96–101.


**natural language**　A language which is, or once was, somebody's mother tongue. Every physically normal young child raised in normal circumstances learns perfectly the language by which it is surrounded; that language is its mother tongue, the language which, in most (not all) cases, it will continue to use throughout its life and in which it will always be most at home. A child surrounded in early life by more than one language may acquire two mother tongues, or possibly even more. And any language which is somebody's mother tongue is, by definition, a *natural language*. A **dead language**, which was formerly somebody's mother tongue, is also a natural language.

Most linguists believe that any language which can be successfully learned and used by human beings must necessarily possess certain properties: the universal properties of human languages. In contrast, we further believe, various types of conceivable languages lack these universal properties and hence could never be successfully learned by young children as mother tongues – that is, they could not be natural languages. Consequently, it is natural languages which are, by definition, the central subject matter of **linguistics**. We want to know what the distinguishing properties of human languages are, and natural languages are our only source of information.

Not infrequently, we generalize our conception of a natural language, as follows: a natural language is any conceivable language which possesses all of the universal characteristics of human languages and which, therefore, could in principle serve as a mother tongue.

An **artificial language** like Esperanto is not, in general, a natural language. But it is reported that some children have learned Esperanto as their mother tongue, and the Esperanto that they speak is, by definition, a natural language – but note that their Esperanto is not necessarily identical to the Esperanto spoken by their parents, for whom it is not a mother tongue.

A **pidgin**, being no one's mother tongue, is not a natural language, but a **creole** which develops out of a pidgin is a mother tongue and is hence a natural language.

A natural language need not be a spoken language. Today there are very many deaf people whose first language is a **sign language**, and we now realize that a sign language used by native signers must be regarded as a natural language. Again, though, observe that the sign language used by non-native signers does not count as a natural language; it is clear that sign languages like *American Sign Language*, when used by native signers, possess important characteristics which were not built into them by the hearing people who deliberately invented them generations ago.

*See:* **artificial language**; **creole**; **language**; **pidgin**

**natural–language processing**   The use of computer programs to process large quantities of language data. ***Natural–language processing***, or NLP, began to emerge in the 1950s when high-speed computers first became available. The original goal was ***machine translation*** (MT), constructing programs that could translate a text from one language into another with a minimum of human intervention. MT is still an active area today, but most work in NLP is now concerned with a much broader range of applications.

Workers in NLP are concerned to devise computational techniques for analysing substantial bodies of material in a **natural language** in order to obtain results comparable to those a human being might obtain, but of course to do it very much faster and more accurately. The central task is the construction of efficient and robust ***parsers***. A parser is a program which can take a sentence in a natural language, work out its grammatical structure, and assign a meaning to it, so that the resulting meaning can then be manipulated by other parts of the system.

Modern NLP systems are increasingly ambitious: they try to deal not merely with single sentences but with sizeable texts, often including pragmatic and discourse factors. No system as yet comes anywhere near the vast flexibility of language processing by humans, but in particular domains NLP systems can be highly successful. A familiar if simple example is the systems used by travel agents for booking airline flights, but more elaborate systems are also in regular use; for example, for extracting information from a huge **corpus** of language data when preparing a dictionary. NLP is now a central part of the enterprise of constructing ***artificial intelligence***, computer programs which can mimic the behaviour of human beings in a range of areas.

*See:* **computational linguistics; corpus**
*Further reading:* Crystal, 1997a: 416–417; Malmkjær, 1991: 28–38.


**neurolinguistics** The study of the connections between language and brain. The study of the relation between language and brain was begun in the mid-nineteenth century by the Frenchman Paul Broca and the German Carl Wernicke. What they did was to study and characterize the **aphasia** (disturbed language) of people who had suffered brain damage, and then, after the sufferers' deaths, to conduct post-mortem examinations in order to find out which areas of the brain had been damaged.

In this way, they succeeded in identifying two specific areas of the brain, today called ***Broca's area*** and ***Wernicke's area***, each of which is responsible for specific aspects of language use. These findings confirmed the reality of the **localization** of language in the brain; moreover, since these areas are nearly always located on the left side of the brain, they also confirmed the **lateralization** of the brain.

In the mid-twentieth century, the American neurologist Norman Geschwind elaborated the view of the brain as consisting of a number of specialized components with connections between them, and he also provided the basis of our modern classification of the several **language areas** in the brain and of the types of aphasia resulting from damage to each.

More recently, the introduction of sophisticated brain scanners like the ***CAT scanner*** and the ***PET scanner*** have allowed specialists to examine the activity in the brains of healthy, conscious subjects who are performing specific linguistic tasks like reading, speaking and listening. The new data have both confirmed and extended our understanding of the location and functions of the several language areas.

*See:* **language areas; lateralization; localization**
*Further reading:* Crystal, 1997a: section VIII; Malmkjær, 1991: 261–266; O'Grady *et al.*, 1996: ch. 17; Steinberg, 1993: ch. 9.

**neutralization**   The disappearance of a phonological contrast in a particular position. It is clear that English has, among others, the two **phonemes** /p/ and /b/. These two distinguish a number of **minimal pairs**, such as *pie* and *buy*, *pike* and *bike*, *pray* and *bray*, *nipple* and *nibble*, *rip* and *rib*, and *slap* and *slab*. However, there is at least one position in which they do not contrast at all: after an /s/ in the same syllable. In English, we cannot possibly make a difference between two different words such as *spit* and *sbit*, or *spade* and *sbade*.

In this position, therefore, we say that the contrast between /p/ and /b/ is *neutralized*: it no longer exists here and, in this position, /p/ and /b/ can no longer be used to distinguish pairs of words.

The concept of neutralization was introduced and developed chiefly by the East European linguists of the *Prague School* in the 1930s, and especially by the Russian linguist Nikolai Trubetzkoy. The existence of neutralization is a powerful reminder that the **phonology** of a language is a matter of the *behaviour* and *patterning* of sounds, and not of their absolute phonetic value.

*See:* **minimal pair**; **phoneme**; **phonology**
*Further reading:* Carr, 1993: 83–88; Clark and Yallop, 1995: 142–148;
  P. Hawkins, 1984: 104–114; Lass, 1984: 40–53.

**nominalization**   Any grammatical unit which behaves like a **noun** or a **noun phrase** but which is built up from something very different. The English word *arrive* is a verb, as in *She arrived at ten o'clock*, but the word *arrival* is a noun, as in *Her sudden arrival surprised us*. Clearly the noun *arrival* is built up from the verb *arrive*, and so we say that *arrival* is a *nominalization* of *arrive*.

This is an example of the simplest kind of nominalization, but much more complex and elaborate types are possible. For example, in *Tom and Sally Perkins study volcanoes*, the sequence *study volcanoes* is a **verb phrase**, but in *Studying volcanoes is* *dangerous work*, this verb phrase has been nominalized into a noun phrase (it is the subject of the sentence).

Yet another type of nominalization can be built up from *Susie smokes*, which is a complete sentence. This entire sentence can be nominalized into a noun phrase, as in *That Susie smokes surprises me*, in which the nominalization *that Susie smokes* is again the subject of its sentence.

English allows **adjectives** to be nominalized only in limited circumstances, as in *The poor are always with us*, in which the adjective *poor* has been nominalized into a noun. But Spanish allows any adjective at all to be nominalized, as in *el rojo* 'the red one', in which the adjective *rojo* 'red' has been nominalized.

The use of nominalizations for various communicative purposes has been particularly investigated within **Systemic Linguistics**, within which nominalizations are treated as a kind of grammatical **metaphor**.


**non-verbal communication**   Any aspect of communication which does not involve words. When you talk to somebody else, you stand or sit a certain distance away, you adopt particular postures, you wear particular expressions, you make particular gestures, and your choices often communicate things that your words do not express directly: whether you are interested or bored, whether you are nervous or confident, whether you are attracted to the other person or not, and so on. All of these are aspects of non-verbal communication, and many of them are culture-bound, so that, when trying to speak a foreign language, you may inadvertently convey something you don't intend.

The various non-verbal aspects of speaking are treated chiefly under two rubrics: **paralanguage** for vocal but non-verbal behaviour and the **ethnography of speaking** for non-vocal behaviour.

(Note carefully that, in language studies, the term *verbal* means 'expressed in words, either spoken or written'; the everyday sense of this term to mean 'spoken, oral' is never used in linguistics.)

*See:* **ethnography of speaking**; **paralanguage**
*Further reading:* Crystal, 1997a: ch. 64.

**notational convention**   Any recognized shorthand for stating a linguistic **rule** briefly. Linguistics makes heavy use of notational conventions, some of them universal, others confined to particular theoretical frameworks. In **phonology**, the rule 'The consonant /n/ is lost between vowels' may be written as follows: n → Ø/V ___ V. In **syntax**, the rule VP → V NP (PP) means 'a verb phrase may consist of a verb plus a following noun phrase, with an optional prepositional phrase at the end'. Mastery of these conventions is essential for work in descriptive and theoretical linguistics; trying to do without them is a little like trying to multiply two numbers in words.

*See:* **rule**

**noun**   The **part of speech** which includes words like *girl, tree* and *happiness*. Traditional grammarians often tried to define a noun as 'the name of a person, place or thing', but this doesn't work. Clearly, for example, *red* is the name of a colour, and so, by this definition, it should be a noun – and yet it is most usually an **adjective**, as in *Susie is wearing her red skirt*.

Like any part of speech, nouns can be adequately defined only in terms of their grammatical behaviour. In English, an obvious grammatical characteristic of nouns is that most of them can appear in two different grammatical forms, called *singular* and *plural*. Most English nouns form their plural by adding *-s*, as in *girl/girls* and *tree/trees*, but some have irregular plurals, as in *child/children*, *goose/geese*, *sheep/sheep* and *radius/radii*. However, not all nouns do this: some have only a singular form (like *wheat, furniture* and *spaghetti*), while others have only a plural form (like *pants, scissors* and *police*).

A better way of identifying nouns is to use a suitable grammatical *frame*. Consider the two frames *The ___ was nice* and

*The ___ were nice.* If you can put a single word into one of these blanks to make a good sentence, then that word must be a noun, because the grammar of English allows nouns, and only nouns, to appear in these positions. The first frame accepts singular forms of nouns, like *girl*, *spaghetti* and *furniture*, while the second accepts plural forms, like *trees*, *pants* and *police*. (Of course, there is no guarantee that the result will be sensible: *The torture was nice* doesn't sound very normal, but it's clearly grammatical, and so *torture* is a noun.)

*See:* **noun phrase**; **part of speech**
*Further reading:* Crystal, 1996: units 28–32; Hurford, 1994: 139–143.


**noun phrase**   A syntactic unit which can act as a subject or an object. Consider the following unremarkable sentence: *A small party of Spanish adventurers managed to capture the Aztec capital.* A traditional view of sentence structure holds that the **subject** and the **direct object** of the sentence are the nouns *party* and *capital*, respectively. But this is not strictly correct. The true subject and object are the phrases *a small party of Spanish adventurers* and *the Aztec capital*. These are **noun phrases** (or **NPs** for short), and noun phrases are the only things that can act as subjects or objects in English sentences. A noun phrase is a syntactic unit – a constituent – and a noun phrase may be identified in two different ways. First, it must occupy one of only a few possible slots in a sentence structure. Second, it must have one of only a few possible types of internal structure.

With only a couple of exceptions, an English noun phrase is always built up around a single **noun**, and that noun is the **head** of the noun phrase, the item which is chiefly responsible for the nature of that NP. In my examples, *party* and *capital* are the heads of the two NPs. The first NP denotes a particular party, and the second a particular capital, and the other words in the NP serve only to provide further identification.

The most obvious exception is a noun phrase consisting of a **pronoun**. In the sentence *They managed to capture it*, the pronouns *they* and *it* make up complete NPs all by themselves, one serving as the subject, the other as the object. This is what a pronoun typically does: it makes up a noun phrase all by itself, and a pronominal NP is the most familiar kind of NP (in English) which is not built around a head noun (the facts are different in some other languages).

A noun phrase, then, is so called because it is (usually) built around a noun and because it constitutes a complete syntactic unit, a **phrase**. A noun phrase is one kind of **syntactic category**.

A simple but convenient way of testing whether some phrase is a noun phrase is to try inserting it into a suitable '*frame*' to see if the result is a grammatical sentence. Here's an example of a frame: ___ *am/is/are nice*. Any syntactic unit which can fit into the blank successfully must be a noun phrase, because it will have to be the subject of the sentence. (The reason we need several possible verb-forms is that an English verb shows **agreement** with its subject.) So, all of the following are NPs (or at least they *can* be NPs): *she, spaghetti, this little book, most of the other students in my class, the woman I was talking to, Rome and Paris.*

The reason for the qualification – 'or at least they *can* be NPs' – here is the following. In *Spaghetti is nice*, *spaghetti* forms an NP all by itself, but in *This spaghetti is nice*, the subject NP is *this spaghetti*, and this time *spaghetti* is not a noun phrase, but only a part of a noun phrase.

As happens with any kind of phrase, a noun phrase may contain within itself a smaller noun phrase. In my example *a small party of Spanish adventurers*, this big NP contains within it the smaller NP *Spanish adventurers* (try this in the frame). This NP is doing another typical NP job: it is serving as the object of the **preposition** *of*, and the resulting prepositional phrase has been incorporated into the bigger NP.

Among the several possible structures for an NP, by far the most frequent is a combination of a **determiner** with a certain other syntactic category; this other category is called an *N–bar* (or sometimes a *nominal group*). Examples (in each case, the first bracketed item is the determiner and the second is an N-bar): [*that*] [*girl*]; [*two*] [*little puppies*]; [*the*] [*woman in the blue skirt*]; [*a*] [*book* (*which*) *I'm reading*]. Note that *girl* in the first example is both a noun and an N-bar, and note that the other examples definitely have the structure shown; for example, the structure *[*the woman*] [*in the blue skirt*] is quite wrong for the third example, as shown by the asterisk.

Introductory textbooks often decline to recognize N-bars when drawing structures for NPs, in the hope of making life simpler for the reader: however, N-bars are essential for all serious work on English sentence structure. Note also that, within the **Government–and–Binding Theory**, noun phrases have recently been re-named *determiner phrases* (DPs), for theory-internal reasons.

*See:* **determiner**; **noun**; **phrase**; **pronoun**
*Further reading:* Crystal, 1996: units 27–47; Greenbaum and Quirk, 1990: ch. 17.

**number** The **grammatical category** which relates most directly to the number of entities. For human beings, the number of people or objects under discussion is often of some importance, and our languages typically provide us with a rich vocabulary for making limitless distinctions along this dimension: *none, one, two, three, twenty-seven, one-half, 0.42, about a hundred, some, few, many, no more than four*, and so on. So far these distinctions have nothing to do with grammar. But it is perfectly possible for a language to build some of these distinctions into its grammar – not all of them, of course – and a language which does so has the grammatical category of *number*.

English, like most European languages, has the category of number, but English has only a very simple contrast between a *singular* (representing one entity) and a *plural* (representing two or more entities). Hence **nouns** denoting things which can be counted typically have two forms: *dog/dogs, child/children, cactus/cacti*. Nouns denoting things that cannot be counted typically have only one form, most often one which is treated grammatically as a singular: *water, happiness, disgrace,* *wheat* (but note that *oats* has only a plural form). A few words, though, are idiosyncratic and exceptional, such as *furniture*, which has only a singular form, and *pants*, which has only a plural, even though both nouns appear to denote things we could reasonably count.

Observe that the English number system makes no explicit provision for zero or for fractions, and here we must arbitrarily choose either a singular or a plural form: we say *nobody is ready*, with a singular form, but we agonize in other cases: should we say *none of the students is ready* or *none of the students are ready*?

Some other languages make more elaborate distinctions of number than does English. In Arabic, for example, a noun typically has three forms: *malikun* 'king', *malikani* 'two kings', *malikuna* 'three or more kings'; the second form is called the **dual**. The Pacific language Larike has four forms for pronouns: *mane* 'he' or 'she', *matua* 'they two', *matidu* 'they three', *mati* 'they (four or more)'; the third form is the **trial**. The East African language Tigre has a different system: *färäs* 'horse', *ʔäfras* 'a few horses', *ʔäfresam* 'horses'; the second form is the **paucal**.

In still other languages, the category of number is absent altogether, at least for nouns. Mandarin Chinese is one such. The Chinese word *shū* 'book', like every noun, has only the one unvarying form, and there is nothing in Chinese corresponding to the English *book/books* distinction. When distinctions of number are important, they must be expressed in words: 'one book', 'two book', 'many book'.

Even though we give the name **number** to the grammatical category, it is important to realize that grammatical number is something quite different from real-world number: it represents no more than an (always imperfect) attempt to map certain real-world distinctions into the grammar.

*Further reading:* Hurford, 1994: 144–145.

**number of languages** A count of the total number of distinct languages spoken as mother tongues. It is by no means a simple matter to count the world's living languages. To start with, of course, we suffer from incomplete information. Until very recently, large parts of the planet were poorly investigated, and we simply had little or no information about the languages spoken there. This was particularly true of New Guinea, Australia, southeast Asia, many parts of Africa and, above all, the Amazon basin. Today, thanks to the dogged efforts of hundreds of linguists, we are much better off than we were a generation ago, but, even so, a previously unknown language still turns up occasionally: one was discovered in Brazil in 1995.

But there is a much bigger problem. Our familiar picture of Europe, in which a single language is spoken over hundreds of miles and shows rather sharp boundaries with neighbouring and quite distinct languages, is a recent development in human affairs and is still today not typical of most of the globe (and even parts of Europe are not like this). Far more typically, what we find is a *dialect continuum*. That is, as we travel across the terrain, the local speech just changes gradually, and we appear to be looking at nothing more than regional dialects of a single language. But, over a sufficient distance, we find that the differences in the local varieties are so great that speakers of these varieties cannot understand one another at all. That is, all speakers can talk easily to their near neighbours, and with more difficulty to more distant neighbours, but not at all to those still farther away.

The question then arises: how many languages are we looking at? And where should we draw the lines between them? There is no principled answer to such questions, and, in practice, linguists just have to do the best they can. Naturally, different linguists looking at the same part of the world do not always come to the same conclusions; furthermore, when better information becomes available, all of the earlier decisions may have to be revised, and linguists may not agree about what revisions to make, either. Hence, we will get different assessments of the number of languages spoken in the area depending on whose work we are reading.

211

What makes Europe different is the rise, in the last few centuries, of nation-states with central governments and well-defined boundaries. These political boundaries have largely imposed upon the dialect continua of Europe a substantial degree of order: in practice, today, what language you speak depends largely on no more than what side of a boundary you live on.

Consider Dutch and German. For centuries, a single Germanic dialect continuum has covered much of northern and central Europe. The local varieties spoken on both sides of what is now the Dutch–German frontier were not significantly different, but local varieties spoken farther apart were often very different indeed: even today, two speakers from, say, Berlin and Bonn cannot understand each other at all if they use their own local varieties. The greatest differences, in fact, have always been north–south: the Netherlands, Belgium and northern Germany on the one hand versus southern Germany, Switzerland and Austria on the other.

But the political frontiers have been drawn, and today two speakers born a kilometre apart, but finding the Dutch–German frontier separating them, consider that they speak two different languages: Dutch in one case, German in the other. And mass education, of course, reinforces this perception: one speaker learns standard Dutch in school, the other standard German, the same standard German being learned by other speakers hundreds of kilometres away whose mother tongue is incomprehensibly different. Hence the 'official' decision is that we are looking at just two languages, and the enormous regional variation is quietly ignored.

The local varieties spoken in Belgium, Luxembourg, Alsace, Switzerland and Austria are, again, all incomprehensibly different from all the other varieties and from one another. And again the decisions are political. The Swiss and the Austrians have decided that they too speak German. The Luxembourgers, after much vacillation, are now seemingly concluding that they do not, and they are making efforts to establish their **Letzebuergesch** as a distinct language. The Belgians have long insisted that they spoke a distinct language called **Flemish**, but they have now changed their minds and agreed that they speak Dutch – but note that the local speech of western Belgium is incomprehensible to speakers in Antwerp and in Amsterdam. The Alsatians, with long-standing political grievances against the Germans, also consider that they speak a separate language – though, if Germany had succeeded in her repeated attempts to annex the territory, the outcome might be very different.

Similar political decisions are important elsewhere. Varieties of Finnish, Romanian and Persian are spoken in sizeable areas of the former Soviet Union, but, for political purposes, the Soviet authorities always insisted that the varieties on their territory were entirely separate languages, called Karelian, Moldavian and Tadjik respectively. If, as most linguists do, we follow the Soviet line, then we get three additional languages that we would not have got if Soviet policy had been different.

So how many languages are there? Most estimates have ranged between 5,000 and 6,000, or occasionally as low as 4,000 or even 3,000. The most authoritative source we have at present, the *Ethnologue* volume (Grimes, 1992), currently recognizes just over 6,500 mother tongues, though a more recent study based in Wales and associated with UNESCO has reported the astounding total of just over 10,000 languages. However, because of accelerating **language death**, this total is declining rapidly, and more than half of these languages may be gone within a century.

*See:* **language death**; **national language**; **standard language**
*Further reading:* Crystal, 1997a: ch. 47; Grimes, 1992; Krauss, 1992.

**official language** A language which can be used for conducting official business in a particular country. In a modern nation-state, every one of us is constantly obliged to engage in some kind of official business with the authorities. We have to get driving licences and passports, fill in income tax returns, obtain birth certificates for our children, fill in forms both when we obtain jobs and when we become unemployed, make out wills, get our children into school, buy and sell houses, and so on. Some of us have to participate in local or national government, or to appear in court. For these purposes, every government specifies one or more languages in which such business may legally be conducted, and a language singled out in this way is an *official language* within the territory of that government. But which language or languages should be official in a given country?

In some cases the choice is easy. Since Swedish is the first language of practically all native-born Swedes, Swedish is the only reasonable choice for the official language. In other cases, the choice is more difficult. Belgium is about equally divided between Dutch-speakers and French-speakers, and the Belgian government has been obliged to draw up complicated laws about which languages can be used officially in which parts of the country. Spain has long recognized nothing but Spanish – the majority language – as official, but constant objections from the millions of Spanish citizens whose first language is Catalan,

Galician or Basque have now persuaded Madrid to set up autonomous regions with their own regional governments, several of which recognize the local language as co-official with Spanish. Nigeria is inhabited by speakers of dozens of different languages, and the government has reacted by choosing English – the language of the former colonial power – as the official language, to avoid antagonizing any part of the population. Attempts at making Hindi the sole official language in India have encountered fierce resistance from the hundreds of millions of Indians who speak other languages, and in practice English remains the official language there too.

*See:* **minority language**; **national language**
*Further reading:* Holmes, 1992: 105–110.

**onomastics**   The study of names. Onomastics is a branch of **philology**, and its pursuit requires the same painstaking scrutiny of historical documents as any other branch of philology, especially since names have a habit of changing more dramatically and more irregularly than ordinary words. For example, until the documents are consulted, it is far from obvious that the name of the English village of *Bridgwater* originally meant 'bridge [at a place owned by a man named] Walter', that the name of the American river the *Picketwire* continues an earlier French *Purgatoire* 'Purgatory', or that the district of London called *Pimlico* derives its name in a complex fashion from the North Carolina river now called the *Tar-Pamlico*.

Onomasticians study both *anthroponyms* (personal names, especially surnames, but also given names) and *toponyms* (place names); toponyms include *habitation names* (names of settlements), *hydronyms* (names of bodies of water), *oronyms* (mountain names), and the names of valleys, fields, roads, streets, houses, forests, and any other features that can be named.

*See:* **name**; **philology**
*Further reading:* Crystal, 1995: ch. 10; Trask, 1996: 350–353.

**open-endedness**    The ability to use language to say new things, without limit. A non-human species typically has no more than a handful of messages, or **calls**, available to it – perhaps one meaning 'This is my territory', another meaning 'danger in the air', and so on. Every time a non-human creature opens its mouth, it can do no more than to choose one message from this short list, and that's it. A monkey may be able to say 'Snake!', if that message is available in the system, but that same monkey cannot possibly produce an unprecedented 'Look out – two hunters with rifles!' or, still less, on spotting its first Land Rover, 'Hey, everybody – what do you suppose that is?'

Human languages are utterly different. We have not the slightest difficulty in producing and comprehending totally new utterances that we have never used or heard before, and indeed we do this almost every moment: most of the utterances you produce and hear every day have very likely never before been produced by anybody. Consider a few examples: *A large tear rolled down the little pink dragon's nose*; *Peanut butter is a poor substitute for putty*; *Luxembourg has declared war on New Zealand*; *Shakespeare wrote his plays in Swahili, and they were translated into English by his African bodyguards*. You have no difficulty in understanding these – even if you don't believe all of them.

But even your most routine utterances may never before have been uttered by anybody: *I ran into Susie's ex-husband at the match last night*; *Does anybody know what language the word 'shampoo' comes from?*; *Aunt Bea has sent us some photos of her granddaughter's christening*.

This limitless ability to produce and understand totally new utterances is called **open-endedness**, and it should be perfectly clear to you that, without it, our languages and indeed our lives would be unrecognizably different from what they are. Perhaps no other feature of language so dramatically illustrates the vast, unbridgeable gulf separating human language from the signalling systems of all other creatures.

The importance of open-endedness has been realized by linguists for decades; the term was coined by the American linguist Charles Hockett in 1960, though others have some-times preferred the labels *productivity* or *creativity*.

*See:* **design features; displacement; stimulus–freedom**

**oracy**  Skill in speaking and listening. We have long had the term *literacy* to denote skill in reading and writing, but recently a number of educationalists and academics have been drawing attention to the importance of skill in speaking and listening. To this notion the somewhat unfortunate label *oracy* has been applied, though a few people, disliking this term, use *orality* instead.

Oral skills can be deeply important, and not merely for making political speeches or selling vacuum cleaners. Sociolinguists and anthropological linguists have discovered that oral skills are highly valued in any number of societies and may confer great prestige. In American inner-city ghettos, gang members can acquire status by their ability to hurl biting insults; in small African and Asian communities, the most effective speakers are likely to be the headmen and chiefs.

In English, the evaluation of oral skills is complicated by the powerful tendency to judge speakers entirely in terms of their use of standard English: so, very often, a piece of pompous, turgid and disorganized standard English is rated more highly than a sharp and effective piece of speaking delivered in a conspicuously non-standard variety.

The academic study of oracy substantially dates only from the 1980s; prominent among its developers is the British linguist Michael Halliday.

*See:* **literacy**
*Further reading:* Halliday, 1989; Tarleton, 1988.

**origin and evolution of language**  The series of steps by which human language came into existence. Very little is known about how human language came into existence, though there is no shortage of speculation by specialists in a dozen different disciplines.

The members of most non-human species have some way of communicating with their fellows, and mammals in particular typically use a combination of **calls** (vocal signals) with postures, gestures and expressions. Proponents of the **continuity hypothesis** see language as deriving directly from such systems by simple elaboration. But most linguists and many others see these signals as more akin to such non-linguistic activities as sobbing, laughing and screaming, and they prefer to invoke **discontinuity hypotheses**, by which language has an entirely different origin, one not detectable in living non-human species.

Specialists differ in the date they assign to the rise of language. The most popular view sees language as arising with our own species, *Homo sapiens*, a little over 100,000 years ago. But some anthropologists believe they can detect evidence for language areas in the brains of our hominid ancestors of one or two million years ago, while, on the other hand, some archaeologists argue that full-blown language can only have arisen around 40–50,000 years ago, a time when they see evidence for a spectacular flowering of art, culture and material goods.

Specific proposals are almost numberless. Some see language as arising as 'vocal grooming', as a way of maintaining social bonds among the members of a group. Others see it arising primarily as 'gossip', as a way of keeping track of what one's family and neighbours have been up to. Still others see it as developing for cognitive, rather than for social, reasons, as a way of making sense of the world. Some see language as arising only very gradually, in small steps, possibly by the operation of natural selection, which might have favoured individuals with slightly superior linguistic skills. Others see it as an **emergent** phenomenon, something which burst suddenly into full-blown existence when certain critical conditions were in place.

While specialists in some other disciplines often like to portray language as something not very different from what vervet monkeys do, and hence as requiring a minimum of explanation, almost all linguists are satisfied that human language is in fact dramatically, utterly different from everything else we can see, that language, more than anything else, is what makes us human, and that the origin of language is therefore a major problem which we are not close to solving. Most linguists further believe that our language faculty is genetic in nature, that our remote ancestors simply evolved it, and hence that we are born to use language in the way that birds are born to fly.

*See:* **animal communication**; **bioprogram hypothesis**; **genetic hypothesis of language**; **innateness hypothesis**; **protolanguage hypothesis**

*Further reading:* Aitchison, 1996; Crystal, 1997a: ch. 49; W.A. Foley, 1997: ch. 2; Malmkjær, 1991: 324–329.

**orthography**   A standardized system for writing a particular language. A given orthography consists of a particular version of a particular **writing system** (in the case of English, a version of the Roman alphabet employing both small letters and capital letters), a standardized system of **spelling**, often a system of word-division (in English, by white spaces), and (in almost all cases today) a particular system of **punctuation**. Often there are additional devices, such as (in English) the use of the arabic numerals (1, 2, 3, . . . ) for writing numbers, the specialized use of certain *symbols* (such as +, =, &, %, $, @), the presence of certain *abbreviations* (such as *Dr*, *St*, *etc.*, *e.g.*), and the use of distinctive typefaces like italic and boldface; these devices may or may not be regarded as strictly a part of the orthography, but more commonly are not.

As is common, the orthography of English has developed gradually over the centuries. Quite apart from the substantial differences in the language itself, written texts from King Alfred's time to the present show numerous orthographic changes: letters have been added to or removed from the alphabet; the forms of certain letters (notably <s>) have often varied; the spellings of individual words have changed; punctuation practices have varied enormously; the use of capital letters has varied; roman numerals have mostly given way to arabic numerals; individual abbreviations have come and gone; and so on. Consequently, if you want to read texts in Old English or Middle English, you must master not only the language but the orthography as well.

*See:* **punctuation**; **spelling**; **writing system**

*Further reading:* Crystal, 1995: 66–67, 1997a: part V; Malmkjær, 1991: 497–503.

# P

**paradigm** A complete set of the inflected forms of a single word, especially as an example. In foreign-language teaching of a traditional kind, it is commonplace to present a full set of the various grammatical forms assumed by a single word, with the understanding that this set constitutes a model for the behaviour of a whole set of words belonging to a single grammatical class. Such a set of forms is a single *paradigm*. So, for example, a textbook of Latin might provide the paradigm for the noun *amicus* 'friend', as follows; the various functions of the named case-forms must be learned separately, of course:

|  | *Singular* | *Plural* |
|---|---|---|
| Nominative | *amicus* | *amici* |
| Vocative | *amice* | *amici* |
| Genitive | *amici* | *amicorum* |
| Dative | *amico* | *amicis* |
| Accusative | *amicum* | *amicos* |
| Ablative | *amico* | *amicis* |

(This is the American order; British tradition puts the accusative after the vocative.) The point of this is that all the other Latin nouns belonging to this class, the class of 'masculine second-declension nouns' or 'masculine *o*-stems',

221

behave in exactly the same way, so that, once you know the forms of *amicus*, you automatically know how to make all the forms of all these other nouns (apart from any which are irregular and must be learned separately).

Note that paradigms are not confined to nouns: verbs, adjectives and other **parts of speech** may also exhibit paradigms, sometimes very elaborate ones.

In modern language-teaching, paradigms are less prominent than formerly, but they are still routinely provided for reference. In descriptive work in linguistics, however, paradigms can still be an illuminating and economical way of presenting the morphological facts of a language in which words vary their forms substantially for grammatical purposes.

*See:* **inflection**; **morphology**; **paradigmatic relation**

**paradigmatic relation** The relation between a set of linguistic items which, in some sense, constitute choices, so that only one of them may be present at a time in a given position. The notion of a *paradigmatic relation* was introduced by the Swiss linguist Ferdinand de Saussure in the early twentieth century as a generalization of the traditional concept of a **paradigm**. If you look at the several forms of the Latin noun *amicus* listed under **paradigm**, you will realize that, in any given position in a Latin sentence in which the word *amicus* is present, one, and only one, of the several forms will occur, the choice being determined by the grammatical context.

What Saussure did was to point out that the relation among the several forms in a traditional paradigm is essentially the same as the relation among other sets of linguistic elements. So, for example, the English **determiners**, like *a(n)*, *some*, *the*, *this/these* and *that/those*, all stand in a paradigmatic relation, because, in a single **noun phrase**, there will be one and only one of them at the beginning (as a rule: there are exceptions): *a book*, *some books*, *the book*, *this book*, *those books*, and so on. It is for this reason that all these words are assigned to a single **part of speech**. In large measure, all the members of any part of speech are assigned to that part of speech because they are related in the same way: they all occur in the same positions, but only one of them can occur at a time.

The concept of a paradigmatic relation is closely related to that of a **system**, a set of competing choices and the rules for choosing among them, and the term *paradigmatic relation* contrasts most obviously with **syntagmatic relation**.

Note that, in psycholinguistics, the term *paradigmatic relation* is used in a somewhat different sense, to denote the mental associations between words which form part of a set of mutually exclusive items, as when a subject given *black* responds with *white*.

*See:* **paradigm**; **syntagmatic relation**
*Further reading:* Culler, 1986.


**paralanguage**   The non-linguistic aspects of speaking. When we speak, of course we communicate a good deal of purely linguistic information to our listeners. In addition, however, we make use of strictly non-linguistic variables like pitch, loudness, tempo, timbre and voice quality. Our use of these things conveys information about our mood and attitude: about whether we are angry, amused, nervous, excited, impatient, tired or whatever. These aspects of speaking are collectively called *paralanguage* or, informally, *tone of voice*.

Such paralinguistic features as high pitch, falsetto, creaky voice, a 'gravelly' voice, breathy or whispery voice, nasalization, and loud or soft speech are variously used in many languages to indicate respect, submission, mockery, boredom, romantic or sexual feelings, impatience and many other things; the details differ greatly from language to language.

Note that the term *paralanguage* is sometimes used more narrowly, to include only voice quality, and sometimes more broadly, to include most or even all aspects of **non-verbal communication**. The sense given here is recommended, since suitable terms are already available for the narrower and broader senses.

223

The equivalent of paralanguage can also be observed in **sign language**: signers may produce signs rapidly or slowly, more deliberately or more casually, using large movements or small ones.

*See:* **ethnography of speaking**; **non-verbal communication**

*parole*   The real utterances produced by real people in real situations. The term *parole* was introduced by the Swiss linguist Ferdinand de Saussure in the early twentieth century; in Saussure's treatment, this term contrasts specifically with **langue**, the abstract system of a language. Saussure's *parole* represents essentially the same thing as Chomsky's **performance**, though his *langue* is significantly different from Chomsky's **competence**.

*See: langue*; **performance**
*Further reading:* Culler, 1986.

**part of speech**   Any one of the grammatically characterized classes into which the **words** of a language are grouped. Every language contains many thousands of words. If all these words behaved differently for grammatical purposes, the language would be unmanageable; but they don't. Instead, they are grouped into a small number of classes, variously called *parts of speech* or *word classes* or *lexical categories*; the words in each class behave in much the same way, while words in different classes behave differently. Not all languages have the same classes: some classes, such as **noun** and **verb**, appear to be universal, while others, such as **adjective** and **preposition**, are found in some languages but not in others.

English has over a dozen parts of speech; the precise number varies according to the analysis, since some linguists prefer to draw finer distinctions than others. The meaning of a word is an unreliable guide to its part of speech. Membership is determined by grammatical criteria, and there are at least three types of criteria to which we can appeal.

The first criterion is **distribution**, the positions in which a word can occur. For example, consider the following 'frames': *This ___ is good*; *These ___ are good*. If we try to put words into the blanks to produce good sentences, we find that **nouns**, and only nouns, will work, because English grammar allows only nouns in this position. Hence *spaghetti*, *dogs* and *arrangement* are nouns, while *happy*, *from* and *deliver* are not. (The reason we need two frames is that English nouns occur in two forms: singular and plural; see **number**.)

The second criterion is **inflection**. In English, a typical noun has exactly two grammatical forms: singular and plural: *dog/dogs*, *box/boxes*, *child/children*, *radius/radii*. (A few, though, have only one or the other, such as *happiness*, *furniture*, *oats* and *police*.) An **adjective** may have three forms: *big/bigger/biggest*. A verb usually has four or more: *love/loves/loved/loving*; *take/takes/took/taken/taking*. A **preposition** has only a single form: *to*, *under*, *without*.

The third criterion is **derivation**. A noun may take the suffix *-ful* or *-ous* to form an adjective: *joy/joyful*, *power/powerful*, *glory/glorious*, *mountain/mountainous*. An adjective may take the suffix *-ness* or *-ity* to form a noun: *great/greatness*, *topical/topicality*. A verb may take the prefix *re-* or *un-* to form a different verb: *write/rewrite*, *do/undo*. In each case, only a member of the appropriate class can take that prefix or suffix successfully.

These tests are not infallible, and they must be used with care. For example, you might think that the frame *This is a ___ dress* would pick out adjectives, and it's true that adjectives will go in here: *red*, *short*, *pretty*. But nouns will equally go into this position: *cotton*, *maternity*, *cocktail*. A better frame here would be *This is a very ___ dress*, which does indeed pick out only adjectives.

A feature of English and of some other languages is that a word can belong to two or more different classes without changing its form. For example, *brown* is a noun in *a nice shade of brown*, an adjective in *a brown skirt*, and a verb in *Please brown the meat*. Likewise, *straight* is a noun in *Schumacher accelerated down the straight*, an adjective in *a straight line*, and an adverb in *She hit the ball straight*. There are many of these, but note that a word can only belong to one part of speech at a time. Some other languages do not tolerate this, and require each word to belong only to one part of speech.

As a rule, the words in a single class do not all show absolutely identical behaviour; instead, they are further divided into several subclasses, often overlapping, which show somewhat different behaviour. This is **subcategorization**.

Some word classes are large and can readily accept new members: these are called *open classes*. Others are small and accept new members only with difficulty: these are *closed classes*. In English, noun, verb and adjective are open classes, while pronoun and preposition are closed classes. Languages may differ here: in some languages, the class of adjectives is small and closed.

*See:* **adjective**; **adverb**; **conjunction**; **determiner**; **noun**; **preposition**; **pronoun**; **verb**

*Further reading:* Crystal, 1995: ch. 15; Givón, 1993: 1: 51–83; Hurford, 1994: 148–153.

**perceptual strategy**  Any of several rough principles which listeners may use in interpreting utterances. A *perceptual strategy* is essentially a kind of principled guess about how the words we are hearing fit into a syntactic structure. In the last several decades, practitioners of **psycholinguistics** have proposed a number of such strategies, and the reality of these strategies is supported by varying amounts of experimental evidence.

One of these is the *principle of late closure*, which says 'if possible, put the next word into the phrase you are currently processing'. By this principle, if you hear *Susie decided gradually to get rid of her teddy-bears*, you will associate *gradually* with *decided*, and not with *to get rid of her teddy-bears*.

Another proposed strategy is the *canonical sentoid strategy*, by which the first string of words that could possibly be a sentence is assumed to be a sentence. It is this strategy which makes *garden-path sentences* so difficult to interpret: when you hear *The horse shot from the stable fell down*, you naturally take *The horse shot from the stable* as a complete sentence and are left floundering by the continuation, even though the whole utterance has a perfectly straightforward interpretation.

Perceptual strategies have attracted a great deal of attention, and they have enjoyed some success in accounting for the comprehension of short utterances. With long and complex utterances, however, it becomes very difficult to identify any useful strategies, and some workers are now questioning the utility of perceptual strategies as a tool for investigation.

*See:* **language processing**; **performance**; **psycholinguistics**
*Further reading:* Aitchison, 1989: ch. 10.

**performance**    Real utterances produced by real people. When we speak, our utterances are frequently disturbed in various ways. We make slips of the tongue; we forget things; we pause to consider our words; we start an utterance and then break it off; we may even lose track of what we are saying altogether. Likewise, when we listen, we may fail to catch something, or we may mishear it or misunderstand it. Linguists have long realized that these disturbances to our linguistic behaviour largely result from non-linguistic causes, and hence that they should not be treated on the same footing as the linguistic behaviour itself. Consequently, we make a fundamental distinction between our (somewhat idealized) capacity to use language, called *langue* by Saussure and **competence** by Chomsky, and our actual linguistic behaviour, called *parole* by Saussure and *performance* by Chomsky.

Linguists with a theoretical orientation are usually interested in competence, and so they disregard what they see as the irrelevant 'noise' of speech errors. But there are other linguists, especially those interested in **language processing**, who are deeply interested in speech errors, and these may be fairly said to be engaged in the study of performance.

*See:* **competence**; **language processing**; *langue*
*Further reading:* Steinberg, 1993: chs. 5–6.

**performative** An utterance which is itself an act of doing something. A typical utterance, such as *I'm going to a film*, cannot readily be regarded as doing something: saying this does not constitute going to a film. But some utterances are different. Saying *I promise to buy you a teddy-bear*, all by itself, constitutes making a promise to buy a teddy-bear, and nothing further is required to complete (as opposed to fulfil) the promise. An utterance of this sort is called an (*explicit*) *performative utterance*, and a verb which can be so used, in this case *promise*, is a *performative verb*.

Further examples of performative utterances are *I now pronounce you husband and wife* and *I hereby name this ship HMS Pooty*. In these cases, clearly, the utterances will have no effect unless a number of obvious conditions are met. These are the *felicity conditions* for that utterance. If the felicity conditions are not satisfied, then the resulting utterance is not really false or wrong: it is merely infelicitous, and it has no effect (or at least not the intended effect).

The existence of explicit performative utterances was first pointed out by the British philosopher J.L. Austin in the 1960s. Austin's work has been continued by several linguists and philosophers, and it has led to the development of the theory of **speech acts**.

*See:* **speech act**
*Further reading:* Austin, 1962; Saeed, 1997: 208–211; Thomas, 1995: ch. 2; Yule, 1996: ch. 6.

**person** The **grammatical category** relating to differing roles in speech. The (personal) **pronouns** of English make a three-way distinction: the pronoun *I* means 'the speaker', *you* means 'the addressee', and *he*, *she* and *it* all mean 'somebody or something else'. We say that these forms distinguish *persons*: *first person* for *I*, *second person* for *you*, and *third person* for the others. The category represented is also called *person*, and this three-way person contrast appears to be universal in languages.

Observe that the third-person forms express further distinctions of animacy and sex, but these other distinctions have nothing to do with person. Finnish *hän* and Turkish *o* mean 'he' or 'she' indifferently; these languages lack the English sex-distinction. Other languages, though, make sex-distinctions in their word for 'you' and sometimes also for 'I'.

The plural forms of the personal pronouns are more complicated. The first-person plural *we* does not normally mean 'the speakers'; instead, it means 'the speaker and one or more others associated with the speaker', and something similar is often true when *you* is used as a plural. (Among the world's languages, English is unusual in not formally distinguishing a singular *you* from a plural *you*.)

Some North American languages distinguish two sets of third-person forms, one (the **proximate**) serving to indicate the individual who is currently the centre of attention and the other (the **obviative**) indicating all individuals who are not currently the centre of attention. The obviative has sometimes been labelled the 'fourth person', but this term is not obviously appropriate.

*Further reading:* Hurford, 1994: 165–168.

**philology** The branch of **historical linguistics** concerned with the histories of individual words and names. Historical linguists exhibit a range of interests. Some are chiefly interested in determining which languages are connected in **genetic relationships** and in working out the structures of particular **language families**; others are concerned with identifying the particular changes which have affected individual languages; still others are looking for general principles of **language change**. But some are mainly interested in identifying the origins of particular words or names and in tracing the histories of these items through time. We give the name *philology* to this pursuit, and we divide philology into **etymology** – the study of the origins of ordinary words – and **onomastics** – the study of the origins of names.

Philology has been around a long time and, until not so long ago, this term was often applied to historical linguistics generally – though no longer. Philological work is exacting, and it requires a mastery of detail perhaps greater than in any other branch of linguistics. Few other areas of the subject offer so many ways for the unwary practitioner to go astray: overlooking a single crucial datum may lead to catastrophe, and that datum may lie buried in an obscure publication or manuscript in a library hundreds of miles away. Nevertheless, philologists have achieved prodigious success in their undertakings, and the great etymological dictionaries of English, Spanish, Latin and other languages are among the treasures of linguistics – though all of them contain errors which remain to be corrected by later scholars.

*See:* **etymology**; **historical linguistics**; **language change**; **onomastics**

*Further reading:* Trask, 1996: ch. 12.

**philosophy of language**   The branch of philosophy which studies the properties of human languages. There are many aspects of language which are of equal interest to linguists and to philosophers, particularly (though not exclusively) in the domain of **semantics** (the study of meaning). Philosophers of language are often interested in such questions as how a piece of language can refer to the real or conceptual world, how the truth or falsehood of a statement can be determined, how the meaning of an utterance depends upon its context, and what the relation is between language and mind.

Though philosophers have pondered problems of language since ancient times, the subject was particularly stressed in the late nineteenth century by the German philosopher Gottlob Frege, who is consequently often regarded as the father of the discipline. Among the most prominent philosophers of language in the twentieth century are the Britons Bertrand Russell, Peter Strawson, Donald Davidson, J.L. Austin, Paul Grice and John Searle, the Pole Alfred Tarski, and the Americans Willard van Orman Quine, Richard Montague, Jerrold Katz, Jerry Fodor and Saul Kripke, but there are many others who also deserve mention.

(Special note: there is a school of philosophy called *linguistic philosophy*, so named because its proponents maintain that many philosophical problems arise from insufficient attention to language; this has nothing to do with the philosophy of language and should not be confused with it.)

*See:* **semantics**

*Further reading:* Malmkjær, 1991: 329–339; Martin, 1987; Stainton, 1996.

**phonation type**    Any one of the several different ways the vocal folds may behave in producing speech. The vocal folds (or vocal cords) are two moveable masses of tissue in the larynx between which air from the lungs must flow during speech. The vocal folds can behave in a number of different ways, sometimes with different parts of them doing different things. Most familiarly, they can be brought close enough together to vibrate along their entire length, producing **voicing**, or they can be moved far apart, preventing vibration and producing *voicelessness*, or, more precisely, *breath*. They can also be pressed tightly together, blocking all air flow and producing a different type of voicelessness.

We can also close the vocal cords except for an opening at the back through which air flows noisily; this is *whisper*. Or we can close them apart from an opening at the front which vibrates very slowly; this is *creak*. Or we can stretch them tightly along their entire length so that they vibrate very rapidly; this is *falsetto*. Various combinations of these are possible, such as *whispery voice*, *creaky voice*, *whispery falsetto* and *whispery creaky voice* ('whisky voice').

Not all of these possibilities are used for linguistic purposes, but several of them are. English contrasts only voicing and voicelessness, but many other languages have a third possibility, most often creaky voice or whispery voice.

*See:* **airstream mechanism**; **voicing**

*Further reading:* Ladefoged, 1993: ch. 6, 1971: ch. 2; Ladefoged and Maddieson, 1996: 47–77.

**phoneme**   One of the basic sound units of a language. Every spoken language, or more precisely every distinguishable **accent** of a language, possesses a smallish set of basic *abstract* sound units, both **consonants** and **vowels**, and every word in that language must consist of a permitted sequence of those basic sound units, which are called *phonemes*. The number of phonemes in particular languages varies considerably, from a known minimum of ten in the Brazilian language Pirahã to a known maximum of 141 in the African language !Xũ. The average number seems to be about 25–30.

The several accents of English vary noticeably in their set of phonemes, from as many as 45 in some accents of England to as few as 36 in some accents of North America. These differences lie mostly in the vowels, with most varieties having exactly 24 consonant phonemes, though a few varieties differ even here.

Phoneme symbols are always enclosed within slashes, and the symbol chosen for each phoneme is usually a phonetic symbol intended to suggest how that phoneme is most typically realized phonetically. So, for example, the phoneme that occurs at the beginning of *thin* is commonly realized as a voiceless dental fricative [θ], and so the phoneme is represented as /θ/. Likewise, the entire word *thin* is represented as /θɪn/, with three phoneme symbols for the three phonemes present in it, while *think* is /θɪŋk/, and *this* is /ðɪs/.

A crucial point is that a single phoneme need not always get the same phonetic realization. English /p/, for example, is phonetically an aspirated plosive [pʰ] in *pin*, but an unaspirated plosive [p] in *spin*. Phonetically, then, we have [pʰin] and [spɪn], but phonemically we have merely /pɪn/ and /spɪn/: the phonetic difference is predictable, and it 'does not count' in English. There is only one phoneme /p/ here, and English-speakers typically do not even notice the phonetic difference; we say that [pʰ] and [p] are *allophones* of the phoneme /p/. In contrast, Mandarin Chinese has pairs of words like [pʰā] 'crouch' and [pā] 'eight', and so [pʰ] and [p] clearly belong to two different phonemes, /pʰ/ and /p/, and these words are phonemically /pʰā/ and /pā/ (the diacritic is a tone mark).

English has pairs of words like [dɛn] *den* and [ðɛn] *then*, and so [d] and [ð] clearly belong to two different phonemes, /d/ and /ð/, and these two words are phonemically /den/ and /ðen/. In Spanish, however, things are different. Spanish has a single phoneme /d/, which phonetically is [d] after pause but [ð] between vowels. Thus, *dedo* 'finger' is phonemic /dedo/ but phonetic [deðo]; *dama* 'lady' is phonemic /dama/ and phonetic [dama]; but *la dama* 'the lady' is phonemic /la dama/ but phonetic [la ðama].

The phoneme concept was worked out only slowly in the nineteenth century; the two Polish linguists Jan Baudouin de Courtenay and Mikołaj Kruszewski are usually credited with being the first to understand it fully. The concept was carried to the west, where it was championed by Daniel Jones in England and by Edward Sapir in the USA; by the 1930s it was almost universally understood and used in linguistics.

In the 1960s, American linguists, led by Noam Chomsky and Morris Halle, began to develop and defend a much more abstract conception of the phoneme than had formerly been normal, within the new framework called *generative phonology*; their new conception was dubbed the *systematic phoneme*, as opposed to the traditional *autonomous* (or *classical*) *phoneme*. Moreover, the phoneme, which had previously been regarded as an indivisible minimal unit, was now decomposed into a matrix of smaller units, the **distinctive features**, which were increasingly regarded as the true fundamental units of phonology. Since the 1980s, this trend has continued to the point at which many phonologists now work exclusively with features, and ignore phonemes altogether – though an understanding of phonemes is still considered essential in most introductory linguistics courses.

*See:* **distribution**; **minimal pair**; **neutralization**; **phonology**; **phonotactics**; **transcription**

*Further reading:* Crystal, 1997a: ch. 28; Lass, 1984: ch. 2; Sommerstein, 1977: ch. 2.

**phonetics** The study of **speech sounds**. Strictly speaking, phonetics is not part of linguistics, though of course there are close connections between the two disciplines. Phoneticians (practitioners of phonetics) investigate such topics as the anatomical, physiological and neurological basis of speech (this is *physiological phonetics*), the actions of the speech organs in producing speech sounds (*articulatory phonetics*), the acoustic nature of the sound waves which transmit speech (*acoustic phonetics*), and the manner in which the ears and brain interpret speech (*auditory and perceptual phonetics*). Phoneticians have long used various mechanical devices in their investigations; today they more commonly use a battery of electronic instruments backed up by computers, and most phonetics today is therefore *instrumental phonetics*. Those phoneticians who prefer to work entirely by ear, without instruments, are said to be doing *impressionistic phonetics*.

A modern phonetician is expected to be at home in a laboratory full of instruments, but is nevertheless also expected to undergo a good deal of *ear training*, acquiring the ability to recognize and characterize speech sounds entirely by ear. Also necessary is a mastery of the **International Phonetic Alphabet**, the standard system for transcribing speech sounds.

Phoneticians may choose to investigate either the total range of speech sounds which can be produced by human beings (this is *general phonetics* or *anthropophonics*), or the manner in which speech sounds are used in real human languages (this is *linguistic phonetics*, and it overlaps with **phonology**).

Phonetics was substantially developed by the ancient Indians and by the medieval Arabs, but the modern tradition began in the sixteenth century in England, and it was in nineteenth- and twentieth-century Britain that such figures as Alexander Melville Bell, Henry Sweet and Daniel Jones chiefly created modern phonetics, though most of the instrumental techniques are far more recent.

234

*See:* **consonant**; **International Phonetic Alphabet**; **phonology**; **speech sound**; **transcription**; **vowel**
*Further reading:* Ashby, 1995; Crystal, 1997a: section IV; Ladefoged, 1993, 1971; Ladefoged and Maddieson, 1996; Laver, 1994.

**phonology**   The sound systems of languages, or the branch of linguistics which studies these. Whereas **phonetics** is chiefly concerned with the physical nature of **speech sounds**, and hence is not strictly a part of linguistics, **phonology** deals with the ways in which sounds behave in languages, and it is a central part of linguistics.

It took a long time for linguists to understand the difference between phonetics and phonology, but, by the late nineteenth century, the Polish linguists Mikołaj Kruszewski and Jan Baudouin de Courtenay had laid the foundations of phonology as a discipline. The new phonological ideas spread out gradually cross Europe in the early twentieth century; meanwhile, American linguists were making similar progress somewhat independently.

The central concept in the new phonological approach was the **phoneme** principle, an understanding of which permitted great advances in the analysis of the sound systems of languages. This principle at last allowed linguists to understand the sounds of a language as constituting an orderly *system*, instead of being a mere collection of individual sounds; this insight was one of the early successes of the general approach to language study called **structuralism**.

Important contributions to phonology were made by the European linguists of the *Prague School* in the 1930s and by the *American structuralists* in the 1940s and 1950s. In the late 1950s, phonology was transformed by the introduction of **distinctive features** (phonological units smaller than phonemes); these features were combined with certain ideas taken from Noam Chomsky's new theory of **transformational grammar** to produce a dramatically new approach named *generative phonology*, which focused on the phonological processes occurring in languages. Since the 1980s, generative phonology has broken up into a variety of more elaborate and competing approaches, the majority of which are collectively known as **non-linear phonology**; the two most prominent of these are **metrical phonology** and **autosegmental phonology**, but several others exist.

*See:* **minimal pair**; **neutralization**; **phoneme**; **phonetics**; **phonotactics**

*Further reading:* Carr, 1993; Crystal, 1997a: ch. 28; Gussenhoven and Jacobs, 1989; P. Hawkins, 1984; Lass, 1984; Sommerstein, 1977.

**phonotactics**  The rules for combining **phonemes** into words in a language. Every variety of every language possesses a larger or smaller set of phonemes, and every legitimate word in that language must consist of a permitted sequence of those phonemes. But the key word here is 'permitted': no language allows its phonemes to occur in any sequence at all. Instead, each language imposes strict limits on the sequences of phonemes which are allowed to occur in a word, and those restrictions are its **phonotactics**.

Consider English. English allows a word to begin with /b/ (as in *bed*), with /r/ (as in *red*), with /l/ (as in *led*), with /n/ (as in *net*), with the cluster /br/ (as in *bread*), and with the cluster /bl/ (as in *bled*). But it does not permit a word to begin with the cluster /bn/: no such word as \*bned is even conceivable in English (the asterisk indicates this). Moreover, if a word begins with /br/ or /bl/, then the next phoneme must be a vowel: nothing like \*blsed or \*brved is possible either (but such a combination may be possible in another language).

Phonotactic constraints may differ widely from one language to another, even when the sets of phonemes are somewhat similar. For example, Hawaiian allows no consonant clusters at all, and every syllable must end in a vowel, and so *kanaka* 'man' is a legal word, but something like \*kanak or \*kanka is not. The Caucasian language Georgian permits astounding consonant clusters, as in *mts'vrtneli* 'trainer' and *vprtskvni* 'I'm peeling it'. The Canadian language Bella Coola, unusually, permits words containing no vowels at all, like *łk'ʷtχʷ* 'make it big!'

*See:* **phoneme**; **phonology**
*Further reading:* P. Hawkins, 1984: ch. 2; Kreidler, 1989: chs. 7–8.

**phrase**   A grammatical unit which is smaller than a **clause**. The term *phrase* is an ancient one, and it has long been used to denote a grammatical unit which typically (though not invariably) consists of two or more words, but which does not contain all of the things found in a clause. For example, a *prepositional phrase* consists of a **preposition** with its object, as in *under the bed*, *with her girlfriend* and *of the wine*.

Especially since the 1940s, linguists have recognized a much larger variety of phrases than was formerly the case; among the more important are the **noun phrase** (such as *the little girl*), the **verb phrase** (such as *was singing in the bath*) and the **adjective phrase** (such as *pretty as a picture*). Each of these types of phrase represents a single *phrasal category*, and a phrasal category is one type of **syntactic category** – that is, it represents one of the basic building blocks used in constructing sentences. Generally speaking, at any point in a sentence in which, say, a noun phrase can occur, *any* noun phrase can be used, subject only to the (non-grammatical) requirement of making sense.

The precise set of phrasal categories recognized varies somewhat according to the particular grammatical framework being used; in particular, **Government-and-Binding Theory** recognizes a number of phrasal categories not recognized by most other frameworks.

Observe that a phrase may consist of only a single word; for example, the sentence *Susie smiled* consists of the noun phrase *Susie* and the verb phrase *smiled*. These units are phrases because they occupy the positions of phrases and behave like phrases; strictly speaking, therefore, we have here a verb phrase *smiled* which happens to consist only of the verb *smiled*. This double layer of structure is routinely displayed in a **tree** diagram, and failure to make it leads quickly to confusion.

Every phrase is built up from a **head**, an item (usually a single word) which itself determines what kind of phrase the whole thing is. A one-word phrase consists of a head with no other material at all.

Occasionally, in modern linguistics, the term *phrase* is generalized to denote *any* syntactic unit in a sentence (any *constituent*), of whatever size or nature; this is the sense of the term in names like **phrase–structure grammar**. So, for example, in the sentence *Susie discovered that she was pregnant*, the unit *she was pregnant* is a complete clause, and hence it is not a phrase in the narrower sense of the term, but it *is* a phrase in this extended sense.

*See:* **head**; **modifier**
*Further reading:* Hurford, 1994: 171–175.

**phrase–structure grammar**    A type of **generative grammar** which represents **constituent structure** directly. We normally regard the structure of any sentence as an instance of *constituent structure*, in which smaller syntactic units are combined into larger units, which are then combined into still larger units, and so on. This kind of structure can be readily handled by a *phrase–structure grammar* (PSG) (the full form of the name is *context-free phrase–structure grammar*, or CF-PSG).

The idea of a PSG is simple. We first note what syntactic categories appear to exist in a given language, and what different internal structures each of these can have. Then, for each such structure, we write a **rule** that displays that structure. So, for example, an English sentence typically consists of a **noun phrase** followed by a **verb phrase** (as in *My sister bought a car*), and we therefore write a *phrase–structure rule* as follows: S → NP VP. This says that a sentence may consist of a noun phrase followed by a verb phrase. Further, an English NP may consist of a **determiner** (like *the* or *my*) followed by an **N-bar** (like *little girl* or *box of chocolates*), and so we write another rule: NP → Det N'. We continue in this way until we have a rule for every structure in the language.

Now the set of rules can be used to *generate* sentences. Starting with S (for 'sentence'), we apply some suitable rule to tell us what units the sentence consists of, and then to each of those units we apply a further rule to tell us what units *it* consists of, and so on, until we reach the level of individual words, at which point we simply insert words belonging to the appropriate **parts of speech**. The result is usually displayed graphically in a **tree**.

PSGs are the most appropriate type of grammar for teaching elementary syntax, and moreover they are powerful enough to describe successfully almost every construction occurring in any language, though there exist one or two rare and unusual constructions which they cannot handle.

PSGs were introduced by the American linguist Noam Chomsky in the 1950s, but Chomsky had little interest in them, and they were not really explored seriously until the British linguist Gerald Gazdar began developing a sophisticated version around 1980; his version was dubbed *Generalized Phrase-Structure Grammar* (GPSG). More recently, the Americans Carl Pollard and Ivan Sag have constructed a very different-looking version called *Head-Driven Phrase-Structure Grammar* (HPSG), which is both linguistically interesting and convenient for computational purposes.

*See:* **constituent structure**; **generative grammar**; **tree**
*Further reading:* Bennett, 1995; Borsley, 1996; Brown and Miller, 1991: part one; Lyons, 1991: ch. 6.


**pidgin** An auxiliary language created by people with no language in common. Very many times in human history, people with no language in common have found themselves thrown together and obliged to deal with one another. Sometimes the language of just one group will be learned by the others and used as a **lingua franca**, but often something quite different happens: words from one or more of the languages of the people involved will be taken and stitched together into a kind of crude way of communicating. This is a *pidgin*. A pidgin is nobody's mother tongue, and it is not a real language at all: it has no recognizable grammar, it is very limited in what it can convey, and different people speak it differently. Still, for simple purposes, it does work, and often everybody in the area learns to handle it.

Pidgins can and do arise whenever the conditions are favourable, and very many have been created just in the last few hundred years. Several were created along the east and west coasts of Africa, to facilitate trading among Africans, Europeans and Arabs. Many others were constructed in North America and the Caribbean, particularly to enable African slaves to talk to one another and to their European masters. And still others were constructed in the far east, mainly for trading purposes. The sugar plantations of Hawaii attracted workers from a dozen countries in Asia and the Pacific, and this led to the creation of yet another pidgin.

There are several possible fates for a pidgin. First, it may eventually drop out of use. This has happened to Hawaiian pidgin, now almost entirely displaced by English, the prestige language of Hawaii. Second, it can remain in use for generations, or even centuries, as has happened with some west African pidgins. Third, and most dramatically, it can be turned into a mother tongue. This happens when the children in a community have nothing but a pidgin to use with other children, in which case the children take the pidgin and turn it into a real language, by fixing and elaborating the grammar and greatly expanding the vocabulary. The result is a **creole**, and the children who create it are the first native speakers of the creole.

*See:* **bioprogram hypothesis**; **creole**; **natural language**
*Further reading:* Crystal, 1997a: ch. 55; Holm, 1988–89; Holmes, 1992: 89–101; Romaine, 1994: ch. 6, 1988; Sebba, 1997.


**place of articulation** A label for the speech organs most directly involved in producing a **consonant**. By definition, the production of a consonant involves a *constriction* (narrowing or closure) somewhere in the vocal tract between the glottis and the lips. We have a standard terminology for labelling the particular parts of the vocal tract directly involved in making that constriction, and each such label denotes a particular *place of articulation*.

Toward the bottom end of the vocal tract, we can safely use simple labels like *glottal* and *pharyngeal*. Farther up, we need in principle to identify both the lower articulator and the upper one (in that order), and for this purpose we use a compound label with the first identifier ending in *-o* and the second in *-al* (or *-ar*). Examples:

- *dorso-velar* – back (dorsum) of tongue plus velum; e.g. [k]
- *lamino-alveolar* – blade (lamina) of tongue plus alveolar ridge; e.g. English [n] for most speakers
- *apico-dental* – tip (apex) of tongue plus upper teeth; e.g. French [t])
- *sublamino-prepalatal* – underside of tongue plus front of palate; e.g. [ɖ] in many Australian languages.

If the lower articulator is obvious or unimportant, we can omit it from the label; hence we can say *velar* instead of *dorso-velar*, or *alveolar* for any consonant involving the alveolar ridge.

A few traditional terms are unsystematic, such as *retroflex* for any consonant in which the tip of the tongue is curled up, *palato-alveolar* for a consonant involving a long constriction from the alveolar ridge to the palate, and *bilabial* in place of the expected *labio-labial*. Note also *coronal* for any consonant during which the blade of the tongue is raised, whether or not the blade is involved in the articulation.

For a consonant involving two simultaneous constrictions, we use the *-al* ending twice, so that [w], for example, is *labial-velar* (though the unsystematic *labio-velar* is also found).

*See:* **consonant**; **manner of articulation**
*Further reading:* Ashby, 1995: ch. 5; Ladefoged, 1971: ch. 5.

**politeness** The linguistic expression of courtesy and social position. While *politeness* has non-linguistic aspects, we are here concerned only with its linguistic expression. Except when we are deliberately looking for a confrontation, we normally take care to ensure that what we say (and what we don't say) is chosen appropriately so as to avoid embarrassing or offending anyone.

Sociolinguists often discuss politeness phenomena in terms of **face**. Face is what you lose when you are embarrassed or humiliated in public. We may distinguish your *positive face* (your need to maintain and demonstrate your membership in a social group) from your *negative face* (your need to be individual and independent, to get what you want without offending anyone). A *face-threatening act* is any piece of behaviour which can easily make another person lose face; a *face-saving act* is any piece of behaviour which lessens or removes the threat of losing face.

The linguistic aspects of politeness have been much studied in recent years, and a number of important variables have been identified: tone of voice, markers of status, terms of address, degrees of certainty or confidence, discourse markers (like English *please*), the choice between speaking and remaining silent, acceptability of direct questions, and others. The rules of politeness vary considerably from society to society, and it is very easy to give inadvertent offence when talking to speakers of another language.

A few examples. Speakers of Malagasy (in Madagascar) consider it impolite to give direct answers to questions or to make predictions that might turn out to be wrong. Speakers of Navaho (in the USA) consider it impolite to speak at all in the presence of a higher-ranking person, or to provide their own names. Both Javanese and Japanese have rich and complex systems for the overt linguistic marking of status among speaker, listener and person talked about, including both different vocabulary and different grammatical forms, and failing to mark status appropriately is a grave breach of decorum.

*See:* **communicative competence**; **ethnography of speaking**
*Further reading:* Bonvillain, 1993: 131–144; Brown and Levinson, 1987; Holmes, 1992: chs. 11–12.

**pragmatics**   The branch of linguistics which studies how utterances communicate meaning in context. The study of **meaning**, commonly known as **semantics**, has long been one of the most daunting and difficult areas of language study. In the 1950s and 1960s, however, linguists and philosophers slowly began to realize that part of the difficulty lay in their failure to distinguish two quite different aspects of meaning.

The first type of meaning is *intrinsic* to a linguistic expression containing it, and it cannot be separated from that expression. The study of this kind of meaning is the domain of semantics, as we now understand the term. But there is a second kind of meaning, one which is not intrinsic to the linguistic expression carrying it, but which rather results from the interaction of the linguistic expression with the *context* in which is it used. And to the study of this kind of meaning we give a new name: *pragmatics*.

Consider the sentence *Susie is a heavy smoker.* In all circumstances, this sentence carries with it its intrinsic meaning: Susie smokes a large quantity of tobacco every day. This meaning is intrinsic and inseparable. But now consider what happens when this sentence is uttered as a response to three different utterances produced by Jessica in three different contexts.

First [Jessica is trying to have smoking banned in offices]: *Can you ask Susie to sign this petition?*

Second [Jessica is trying to arrange a blind date for Dave, a non-smoker who hates cigarette smoke]: *Would Susie like to go out with Dave?*

Third [Jessica, a medical researcher, is looking for smokers to take part in some medical tests]: *Do you know of anybody I could ask?*

In each case, you will agree, something very different is being communicated. In the first case: Susie is unlikely to sign the petition, so there's no point in asking her. In the second: Dave and Susie won't get on, so there's no point in fixing them up. Third: Susie will be a suitable person for your study.

Now, it is not possible to maintain that this single unvarying sentence actually *means* all of these different things. Rather, these three meanings have been communicated as a consequence of the interaction between what was said and the *context* in which it was said. Every time the context changes, what is communicated changes as well. And it is this variable, context-bound relation between what is said and what is communicated that is the subject-matter of pragmatics.

It should be noted that, in continental Europe, the term *pragmatics* is often used in a much broader sense than in the English-speaking countries, so as to include a great number of phenomena that linguists in English-speaking countries would regard as belonging strictly to **sociolinguistics**.

*See:* **conversational implicature**; **cooperative principle**; **meaning**; **semantics**; **speech act**
*Further reading:* Crystal, 1997a: ch. 21; Grundy, 1995; Malmkjær, 1991: 354–358; Schiffrin, 1994: ch. 6; Thomas, 1995; Yule, 1996.

**predicate**    That part of a sentence other than its subject. It was the Greek philosopher Aristotle who first divided sentences into subjects and predicates. Given a fixed subject *Susie*, we can construct sentences by adding to this subject any number of different predicates: *smokes, is clever, has been promoted, wants to buy a new car, believes that astrology is garbage*. In each case (in English), the predicate role is filled by a **verb phrase**; this is typically so in languages, though some languages permit predicates belonging to other **syntactic categories**.

It is important to realize that logicians use the term *predicate* in a very different way, one which is now prominent in linguistics, especially in **semantics**. In the system of formal logic called *predicate logic*, the sentence *Bruce is bald* would typically be represented as *Bald (bruce)*. Here *Bald* is a (logical) predicate corresponding to English *is bald*, and it is a *one-place predicate* requiring only one *argument* (noun phrase) in order to be satisfied. The sentence *Bruce loves Kathy* might be similarly represented with a one-place predicate as *Love-Kathy (bruce)*, but more commonly we would represent it as with a **two-place predicate**, as follows: *Love (bruce, kathy)*. This time the predicate *Love* requires two arguments in order to be satisfied.

Since both of these conflicting usages are widespread in linguistics, you must take care that you understand which sense is intended when you encounter the term.

*See:* **verb phrase**
*Further reading:* Hurford, 1994: 185–189.


**preposition** The **part of speech** which includes words like *to, with* and *of*. Like many other languages, English possesses a smallish class of words called **prepositions**. A preposition has only one major property: it combines with a following **noun phrase** – its **object** – to form a larger syntactic unit – a **prepositional phrase**. Typical prepositions include *of, to, in, for, with, under, about, inside, after, in front of* and *in spite of*. (Note that some of these can also belong to other parts of speech.) Here are some typical prepositional phrase: *to the car, for a while, with Susie, after the war, in spite of the weather*. Some prepositions, like *under* and *after*, express identifiable meanings. Others, such as *of*, have a purely grammatical function: in the noun phrase *the end of the year*, the preposition *of* serves merely to connect the smaller noun phrase *the year* to the rest of the bigger one, but *of the year* is still a prepositional phrase.

In some languages, such as Japanese and Basque, the items that do the job of prepositions follow their object instead of preceding it, and we therefore call them **postpositions**. Japanese examples: *Tokyo ni* 'to Tokyo'; *Tokyo de* 'in Tokyo'. Prepositions and postpositions together are collectively called **adpositions**.

Some languages, such as the Australian languages, lack adpositions altogether, and use entirely different grammatical devices to do the same job.

*Further reading:* Collins Cobuild, 1990: 295–312; Hurford, 1994: 190–195.

**prescriptivism**  The imposition of arbitrary norms upon a language, often in defiance of normal usage. Every language exhibits a good deal of regional and social **variation**. If very many people want to use a language for a number of different purposes, then it is convenient and even necessary to have a single agreed form of the language – a **standard language** – known and used by everybody, or at least by all educated speakers. Otherwise, if people insist on using their own particular varieties, the result will be confusion and misunderstanding. But, since languages are always changing, there will always be doubts and disagreements over which forms and usages should be recognized as part of the standard language.

Prescriptivism consists of the attempts, by teachers and writers, to settle these disagreements by insisting upon the use of those particular forms and usages which they personally prefer and by condemning those others which they personally dislike. Of course, some degree of prescriptivism is necessary, particularly in education: people who naturally use forms which are blatantly not accepted as standard by the community as a whole must learn to use the standard forms, at least in those circumstances which call for the standard language, or else they will be severely disadvantaged.

But the problem is that many prescriptivists go too far, and try to condemn usages which are in fact perfectly normal for even educated speakers, and to insist instead upon usages which were current generations or centuries ago but which are now effectively dead, or even upon usages which have never been normal for anybody.

A famous example concerns the so-called *split infinitive*. For generations, virtually all English-speakers have spontaneously said things like *She decided to gradually get rid of the teddy-bears she had spent twenty years collecting*. Here the sequence *to gradually get rid of* is the 'split infinitive'. Many prescriptivists have condemned this usage, on the supposed ground that *to get* is a single verb-form, the 'infinitive', and therefore 'logically' cannot be split up. Such people typically insist instead on something like *She decided gradually to get rid of*. . . . But this is all wrong.

First, the proposed 'correction' is badly misleading: it suggests that it is the decision which is gradual, rather than the disposal. Second, the sequence *to get* is not an infinitive, nor is it a verb-form, nor is it even a grammatical unit at all. The true infinitive here is *get*, while *to* is nothing but a linking particle. The adverb *gradually* logically belongs next to *get rid of*, and that's where speakers normally put it. That *to get* is not a grammatical unit can be shown in a number of ways, not least of which is the observation that speakers regularly break it up. (Another test is the construction illustrated by *She has asked me to change my hairstyle, but I don't want to*, in which the understood *change* is deleted while *to* is obliged to remain – hardly possible if *to change* were really a unit.) Hence the prescriptivists' position is ignorant and wrong-headed: it represents an attempt to replace normal and elegant usage by something which is silly, unnatural and hard to understand, and which is used by nobody except some prescriptivists and those few who take them seriously.

Many prescriptivists also object to the familiar English practice of ending a sentence with a preposition, apparently on the bizarre ground that this construction is not possible in Latin. They take exception to ordinary English utterances like *Who were you talking to?*, *What's this gadget for?* and *That's something I just can't put up with*, demanding instead unnatural things like *To whom were you talking?*, *For what is this gadget?*, and I have no idea what they would do about the last one.

Prescriptivists also reject such ordinary utterances as *Who do you trust?*, demanding instead *Whom do you trust?*, a form which was current hundreds of years ago but is now dead, except in frostily formal styles of speech and writing.

There is clearly a need for informed commentary on usage. Some forms, while widely used, are unquestionably not accepted as part of the standard language, while others are ambiguous, pretentious, clumsy or hard to understand, and drawing attention to these matters is valuable: this is the good face of prescriptivism. But it is deeply unfortunate that so many commentators have seen fit to lose touch with reality and to pursue their own absurd little bugbears at such length and with such passion.

*See:* **descriptivism**; **purism**
*Further reading:* Crystal, 1997a: ch. 1; Edwards, 1994: ch. 6; Pinker, 1994: ch. 12.


**presupposition**   A particular sort of inference. Consider the sentence *John's wife runs a boutique*. Now, when we hear this, we are immediately entitled to draw the following inference: *John is married*. This is an example of a ***presupposition***: we say that the first sentence ***presupposes*** the second.

A presupposition differs from other types of inference, such as an **entailment** or a **conversational implicature**, in several ways. Most obviously, a presupposition survives negation. If I negate the original sentence, the result is *John's wife doesn't run a boutique* – and this still presupposes that *John is married*. Both the original sentence and its negation have the interesting property that they are bizarre and uncooperative things to say if John is in fact a bachelor. Very informally, then, a presupposition of statement P is something which has to be true before P can possibly be a plausible thing to say.

In a widespread view, introduced by the British philosopher Peter Strawson around 1950, we can say that P presupposes Q if and only if Q has to be true before P can be *either* true or false. That is, if Q is false, then P can be neither true nor false: it simply has no truth value at all. So, if John is a bachelor, then *John's wife runs a boutique* is not false, nor is it true; it is simply devoid of truth value. But not everyone agrees with this interpretation, and some linguists, following the British philosopher Bertrand Russell, would prefer to conclude that the statement really is false.

This disagreement is bound up in a larger controversy over whether presuppositions properly belong to the domain of **semantics** or to that of **pragmatics**. The debate continues today.

Note that questions and commands can have presuppositions. The question *Do you still drink a bottle of vodka every night?* is bizarre and unanswerable if you have never drunk vodka on that scale (this is what is informally known as a 'loaded question'), and the command *Take your hat off!* is bizarre and impossible to obey if you aren't wearing a hat.

*See:* **conversational implicature**; **entailment**
*Further reading:* Grundy, 1995: ch. 4; Levinson, 1983: ch. 4; Saeed, 1997: 93–102.

**productivity** The degree of freedom with which a particular grammatical pattern can be extended to new cases. We most often speak of productivity in connection with patterns of **word-formation**. The noun-forming suffix *-ness* is highly productive: *happiness, preparedness, salaciousness, user-friendliness*. The same is true of the verbal prefix *re-*: *rewrite, reconsider, reappoint, renegotiate, reboot* (a computer).

But the noun-forming suffix *-th* is totally unproductive: we have existing cases like *warmth* and *depth*, but we cannot form any new ones: *happyth, *bigth, *sexyth (the asterisk indicates forms that are unacceptable). The noun-forming suffix *-dom* is weakly productive: to established cases like *kingdom* and *martyrdom* we occasionally add new ones like *gangsterdom*, *tigerdom* and *stardom*, but we can't do this freely: *policedom, *universitydom, *childdom.

The adverb-forming suffix *-wise* was formerly unproductive and confined to a few cases like *clockwise* and *otherwise*, but today we freely coin new formations like *healthwise, money-wise, clotheswise* and *fitnesswise*. The noun-prefix *mini-* didn't even exist before 1960, but today it is prodigiously productive: *miniskirt, minicomputer, mini-microphone, minibus*, even *mini-war*.

*See:* **word-formation**
*Further reading:* Bauer, 1988: ch. 5; Katamba, 1994: 149–153; Matthews, 1991: 69–80.

**pronoun** The **part of speech** which includes words like *she*, *them* and *something*. Pronouns have been recognized as a distinct part of speech since ancient times. Essentially, a pronoun is a single word (or rarely a longer form), with little or no meaning of its own, which functions as a complete **noun phrase**.

Pronouns are classified into several types. A *personal pronoun* points at some participant in a speech situation: *I, you, we, she, they*. A *demonstrative pronoun* points in space or time, like the *this* in *This is a good book*. An *interrogative pronoun* asks a question, like *who* in *Who's there?* An *indefinite pronoun*, such as *somebody* or *anything*, fills a slot in a sentence without providing much specific meaning, as in *Do you need anything?* A *relative pronoun* introduces a relative clause, like the *who* in *The students who streaked the graduation ceremony are in trouble*. Finally, a *reflexive pronoun* like *herself* and a *reciprocal pronoun* like *each other* refer to other noun phrases in the sentence in specific ways, as in *She cursed herself* and *They are seeing a lot of each other*.

As a rule, a pronoun cannot take a **modifier**, but there are a few exceptions: *little me, poor you, something interesting*.

*See:* **anaphor**; **noun phrase**
*Further reading:* Collins Cobuild, 1990: 28–42; Hurford, 1994: 202–206.

**prosody**   Variations in pitch, loudness, rhythm and tempo (rate of speaking) during speech. The term *prosody* is an ancient one, but it was originally applied only to the analysis of verse structure. Linguists in the twentieth century have taken over the term and applied it specifically to the several variations in the behaviour of the voice cited above.

These prosodic features may or may not be expressly linguistic in nature. **Tone languages** and languages with *pitch* or **stress** accents make specific linguistic use of pitch and/or loudness, but utterances in all languages are characterized by noticeable variations in all four of these features. Particularly important is the use of pitch variations in **intonation**, which is universal in languages.

Prosodic phenomena are notoriously difficult to study, but some considerable progress has been made in examining at least some of them. Nevertheless, elementary textbooks of **phonetics** and of **phonology** only rarely discuss prosodic features in any detail.

It should be noted that the terms *prosody* and *prosodic* also have some rather special uses. In the theory of phonology called *prosodic phonology*, the term *prosody* is given a highly distinctive technical sense which is peculiar to that theory. In some contemporary theories of phonology and of **morphology**, the adjective *prosodic* is likewise given some rather distinctive senses for labelling things which are important in those theories. Finally, note that in some quarters *prosody* is used merely as a synonym for **suprasegmental**, a usage which is not recommended.

*See:* **intonation**; **stress**; **tone language**; **suprasegmental**
*Further reading:* Laver, 1994: section VI; Crystal, 1975.


**proto-language**  The hypothetical ancestor of a **language family**. When we find some languages which are clearly connected in a **genetic relationship**, and which therefore form a language family, it follows by definition that all are descended from a single ancestral language; that is, that they all started off long ago as no more than regional dialects of that ancestral language. Given enough data, historical linguists can apply **comparative reconstruction** to obtain substantial information about what that ancestral language was like, even though in most cases it was never itself recorded. The **reconstruction** which they obtain in this way is a reasonably accurate picture of the ancestral language, which is called the *proto-language* for the whole family.

A proto-language is named by prefixing *Proto-* to the name of the family. For example, the ancestor of the *Germanic* languages (English, German, Swedish and others) is *Proto-Germanic*; the ancestor of the *Romance* languages (Spanish, French, Italian and others) is *Proto-Romance*; and the ancestor of the vast **Indo-European** family is *Proto-Indo-European*.

*See:* **Indo-European; language family; reconstruction**
*Further reading:* Hock, 1986: 567–580; Trask, 1996: 178–181, 239–240.


**protolanguage hypothesis** The hypothesis that human language arose rather abruptly from a vastly simpler precursor. The protolanguage hypothesis was developed in the 1980s by the British-born American linguist Derek Bickerton. A keen student of **pidgins** and **creoles**, Bickerton was impressed by the rapidity with which a pidgin (which is not a language) can be converted into a creole (which is) when the conditions are right. He therefore developed the argument that some of our remote ancestors must have had only *protolanguage*, a crude and limited system somewhat resembling a pidgin, and that this must have developed, probably very suddenly, into true language when certain critical conditions were in place in the brain.

Bickerton argues that protolanguage can still be observed today in certain circumstances: in pidgins, in the speech of individuals suffering from certain kinds of disability, in the speech of very young children, and in the severely limited linguistic accomplishments of laboratory animals instructed in something resembling a human language. The hypothesis is deeply controversial.

*See:* **animal communication; origin and evolution of language**
*Further reading:* Bickerton, 1981, 1990, 1996.


**psycholinguistics** The study of the connections between language and mind. Psycholinguistics began to emerge as a distinct discipline in the 1950s. To some extent, its emergence was promoted by the insistence at the time of the linguist Noam Chomsky that **linguistics** should be regarded as a part of cognitive psychology, but there were other factors as well, notably the growing interest in the question of **language acquisition** by children.

There is no doubt that the study of acquisition has so far been the most prominent and successful area of psycholinguistics. But a number of other topics have also been explored, with varying degrees of success. Many of these are aspects of **language processing**, the steps involved in producing and comprehending speech. Others include the links between language use and memory, the linguistic examination of reading, and more recently possible links with perception and cognition.

We now possess a great deal of data in most of these areas, but progress in developing theoretical interpretations has been slow. The enthusiastic early attempts at understanding mental processing of language in terms of Chomsky's **transformational grammar** proved a failure, and contemporary theorizing tends to be less ambitious: grand schemes are out, and psycholinguists now content themselves with trying to provide accounts of specific aspects of language behaviour.

Psycholinguists would also like to link their findings to those of **neurolinguistics**, the study of language and brain, but this has not proved at all easy. Some psycholinguists are also contributing to the development of **cognitive linguistics** and of **cognitive science** generally.

*See:* **language acquisition**; **language processing**; **neurolinguistics**

*Further reading:* Aitchison, 1989, 1994; Garman, 1990; Garnham, 1985; Steinberg, 1993.

**punctuation** A conventional system of marks representing information about the structure of a written text. The earliest **writing systems** used no punctuation, and often they didn't even separate words. The Greeks introduced the earliest known punctuation during the classical period, but it was very different from ours. In those days, and for long after, silent reading was unknown, and the reader of a text spoke the words out loud, even when reading alone.

Greek orators who were preparing speeches for delivery found it helpful to add marks to their texts to remind them where to pause briefly, where to make a dramatic pause, where to raise the voice, and so on. And these marks, added purely for rhetorical purposes, were the first punctuation.

The Romans and the medieval Carolingians gradually elaborated the set of punctuation marks, and these marks began to be used to indicate structural aspects of texts, rather than breathing places. With the eventual development of silent reading, this structural function entirely displaced the old oratorical one, and today our punctuation systems express nothing but structural information.

All other widely used writing systems have also developed systems of punctuation, though it is notable that a standard punctuation system is generally the very last aspect of a writing system to become established. Even in Europe, languages like English, French and German, all written in the roman alphabet, all use slightly different punctuation and, moreover, American punctuation differs in a few respects from British. Punctuation can change: modern English punctuation is very different from that used in the eighteenth century and, at the time of writing, the three German-speaking countries have just announced some changes in German punctuation.

*See:* **writing system**; **orthography**
*Further reading:* J. Foley, 1993: 47–53; Crystal, 1995: 278–283.

**purism**   The belief that words (and other linguistic features) of foreign origin are a kind of contamination sullying the purity of a language. Almost all languages are in contact with other languages, and all languages take words (and sometimes other features) from those neighbouring languages. Sometimes speakers of the receiving language take exception to the presence in their language of these "foreign" elements, which they see as "impurities", and agitate to have them removed and replaced by native elements. This attitude is called *purism*, and it is widespread.

For example, the French authorities, dismayed by the hundreds of English words pouring into French every year, have made strenuous efforts to eradicate some of these English words from their language and to replace them with novel French creations, and their recommendations have the force of law in certain domains. Thus, *computer* has been officially replaced by *ordinateur*, *software* by *logiciel*, *light pen* by *crayon optique*, *floppy disc* by *disquette*, *pie chart* by *camembert*, *videoclip* by *bande promo*, *bookmobile* first by *bibliothèque circulante* but now by *bibliobus*, and *bulldozer* by *bouledozeur* (!) (this last was a failure and has been abandoned). The English word *debugging* was at first rendered as *débogage*, but more recently the amusing *déverminage* has been coined.

Purism has almost never been a force among speakers of English, but speakers of French, German, Icelandic, Turkish and Basque (just to name a few) have at times engaged in large-scale purges of foreign elements, with varying degrees of success.

*See:* **prescriptivism**

**qualitative approach**  A trend towards the description and explanation of language use within naturally occurring social and cultural settings. The various strands of what we now call the *qualitative approach* have been visible within sociology since the 1920s, but only since the 1980s has this approach become prominent in the study of language.

This label is applied to a particular methodology, or set of methodologies, particularly within **sociolinguistics** and **conversation analysis**, in which *authenticity* is regarded as crucial, and in which authenticity is achieved through the detailed description of the social settings and social practices which yield language data. A qualitative approach typically focuses on the study of of small numbers of speakers or texts, since an abundance of data and statistical studies are seen as less important than revealing the social meanings which speakers and writers attach to their linguistic activities. Consequently, this approach contrasts rather vividly with the **quantitative approach**.

Qualitative research employs observation, textual analysis, interviews, and the recording and transcribing of speech. While these may also be used in quantitative work, in qualitative research they are given a different status. For example, in quantitative investigations, observation is limited to the initial exploratory stages, essentially to the stages at which the topic of research is being identified, since observation

alone is here considered to be too unreliable to yield usable
data. In qualitative research, however, the observation of
participants is considered fundamental in revealing the social
and political factors which underpin language use. Thus, disciplines which regularly employ qualitative methodology, such
as ethnography, social anthropology, and cognitive anthropology, often rely solely upon observation and other
'open-ended' research procedures.

*See:* **conversation analysis**; **ethnography of speaking**; **quantitative approach**

*Further reading:* Silverman, 1993.


**quantitative approach**   A statistical approach to the study of
**variation** in language. Variation in the way people use their
language is very prominent, but for generations linguists could
see no way of making any sense of it: instead, variation was
typically seen as an irrelevant nuisance and ignored. In the
1960s, however, the American sociolinguist William Labov
pioneered a wholly new approach to language study, one
which made variation itself a prime object of examination.
The key to this approach was the introduction of statistics:
Labov collected statistical data on the frequency of competing
forms used by different speakers and then looked for correlations with non-linguistic factors. This is the *quantitative
approach*, and it has proved outstandingly successful.

What Labov and his successors found is this. If we merely
observe a speaker, or a group of speakers, all we can notice
is that speakers sometimes use this form and sometimes that
one, in a seemingly haphazard manner. However, if we tabu-
late the *frequency* of each competing form, we often find first
that one individual differs notably from another and second
that the frequency of a particular form correlates strongly
with some non-linguistic variable. Most often, the non-
linguistic variables are obvious ones like sex, age, social class
and degree of formality, but sometimes we find more unexpected correlations.

What these studies have shown is that variation is not haphazard at all. Instead, variation is highly structured: statistically speaking, each individual behaves in a highly consistent way, with some individuals behaving differently from others, depending on some of the variables just mentioned, and, moreover, the behaviour of each individual changes in a predictable way when the context of speaking becomes more or less formal.

The quantitative approach has revolutionized the study of language by demonstrating that linguistic behaviour is even more highly structured than we had previously suspected; it has contributed enormously to the study of **language change**, and it has provided a resolution of the **Saussurean paradox**.

*See:* **language change**; **social stratification of language**; **sociolinguistics**; **variation**

*Further reading:* Hudson, 1996: ch. 5; Labov, 1972; Milroy, 1992: ch. 3.

# R

**raising**  Any of various phenomena in which a linguistic element appears in a higher clause than is semantically appropriate. Consider the sentence *It appears that Susie is falling asleep*. Here *Susie* is, both logically and grammatically, the subject of the verb phrase *is falling asleep* within the lower (subordinate) clause. But the same information can be expressed differently: *Susie appears to be falling asleep*. This time *Susie*, still the logical subject of *be falling asleep*, appears as the grammatical subject of *appears*. In this case, we say that *Susie* has been **raised** out of the lower clause into the higher one, and, since the item undergoing raising is the subject of the lower clause, we call this phenomenon **subject-raising**, or sometimes more specifically subject-to-subject raising, since the raised element winds up being the subject of the higher clause.

This is not the only kind of raising. Consider the example *I believe that she is happy*. Here *she* is again the subject of the lower clause. But we can express this as *I believe her to be happy*, in which *her* is apparently now the object of the verb *believe* in the higher clause, as shown by its form. This is **subject-to-object raising**. (A note: a minority of linguists would prefer to analyse this last example as having the structure *I believe [her to be happy]*, with *her* still being the subject of *to be happy*; proponents of this unusual analysis sometimes refer to the bracketed sequence as a **small clause**.)

Now consider the example *It is difficult to please Susie*, in which *Susie* is the object of the verb *please*. This can equally be expressed as *Susie is difficult to please*, in which *Susie* has been raised to become the subject of *is difficult*. This last construction was therefore formerly called **object–to–subject raising**, though today it is more usually known by the quaint name **tough–movement**, since it is most frequent with verb phrases expressing degrees of difficulty.

Finally, consider the example *It seems that I never meet the right women*. This is more idiomatically expressed as *I never seem to meet the right women*, in which the negative item *never* has been raised out of the lower clause, where it logically belongs, into the higher clause. This is **negative raising**, and it is illustrated also by cases like *I can't seem to find my keys*, equivalent to *It seems that I can't find my keys*.

Raising phenomena are complex and intricate, and they have received a good deal of attention from syntacticians in recent years.

*See:* **control**, **movement**
*Further reading:* Borsley, 1991: ch. 10.

**reconstruction**   Working out features of dead and unrecorded languages, or of unrecorded earlier stages of single languages. In the vast majority of cases, a given language can be clearly seen to share a common ancestry with at least some other languages – that is, the languages in question all started out long ago as no more than **dialects** of a single ancestral language, which itself is almost never recorded. In such cases, practitioners of **historical linguistics** are naturally interested in trying to work out as much as they can about the nature of that unrecorded ancestral language.

Moreover, even a single language is only ever recorded since some particular point in time, often a rather recent one, and historical linguists are also interested in obtaining information about the prehistory of that language.

Since the end of the eighteenth century, historical linguists have been painstakingly constructing effective and reliable methods of performing these tasks, and we now know a great deal about how to go about them. The business of obtaining information about unrecorded languages is *reconstruction*, and there are two main types.

In **comparative reconstruction**, a linguist compares several languages which are known to be related; each of these languages normally preserves some features of their common ancestor, but has lost others. Since different languages preserve different ancestral features, it is often possible to determine in some detail what the ancestral language was like, and hence what changes have occurred in each of the daughter languages.

In **internal reconstruction**, the linguist works with only a single language, and tries to determine what an earlier unrecorded stage of that language was like, and hence what changes occurred to produce the earliest recorded form.

Both types of reconstruction are most commonly performed upon recorded languages, but, once we have managed to reconstruct some unrecorded languages in reasonable detail, it is perfectly possible to apply the same methods to these and to reconstruct even further back in time. Naturally, though, a reconstruction based upon reconstructions is generally less secure than one based upon attested languages, and in practice there are limits on how far back we can go.

*See:* **comparative reconstruction**; **historical linguistics**; **Indo-European**; **internal reconstruction**; **language change**

*Further reading:* Fox, 1995; Hock, 1986: chs. 17–19; Hock and Joseph, 1996: chs. 16–18; Trask, 1996: chs. 8–9.

**recursion**   The occurrence in a sentence of a **syntactic category** containing within it a smaller instance of the same category. Recursion is pervasive in the grammars of the languages of the world, and its presence is the chief reason we are able to produce a limitless variety of sentences of unbounded length just by combining the same few building blocks.

For example, a **noun phrase** (NP) in English may contain within it a **prepositional phrase** (PP), and a prepositional phrase always contains a noun phrase. Hence we can build up an NP containing a PP containing an NP containing a PP . . . and so on, as far as we like. In the sentence *I've bought a book about the history of the debate between defenders of different theories of education*, everything after *bought* is a single large NP beginning with *a book*; this NP contains a single large PP beginning with *about*, which in turn contains another NP beginning with *the history*, which contains a smaller PP beginning with *of*, and so on, until the final NP *education* contains no further PP. Here both the NPs and the PPs illustrate recursion.

Similarly, the well-known verse containing the line *This is the dog that chased the cat that killed the rat that ate the malt that lay in the house that Jack built* illustrates the recursion of relative clauses, with each *that* introducing a new relative clause embedded within the one already begun, so that everything after *dog* is one huge relative clause containing a series of smaller relative clauses, each one embedded within another.

*See:* **constituent structure**; **phrase**; **syntax**
*Further reading:* Brown and Miller, 1991: ch. 9; Keyser and Postal, 1976: ch. 14.


**reference** The relation between a linguistic expression and something which it picks out in the real or conceptual world. A linguistic expression which *refers* to (points at) something in the non-linguistic world is a ***referring expression***, or r. e., and the most familar such expressions are **noun phrases**.

A simple **noun** like *dog* does not itself refer to anything: it merely denotes the entire class of dogs. But, when it is embedded in a suitable noun phrase, the whole phrase may succeed in referring to something specific in the world: *this dog, the little dog with the floppy ears, that dog that Aunt Sophie used to have*, and so on. And the relation between such an expression and the thing it picks out is one of ***reference***.

*Proper names* may also refer and, indeed, they hardly do anything else: *Abraham Lincoln, the Golden Gate Bridge, Spain* – these really have no intrinsic meaning at all, and they merely point to particular entities.

Reference is entirely in the mind of the speaker, and the same linguistic expression may be an r. e. sometimes but not at other times. If I say *Janet wants to marry a Norwegian*, and I have in mind a *particular* Norwegian who Janet wants to marry – say, Olaf Thorqvist the Olympic skier – then *a Norwegian* is clearly an r. e. But, if I say the same thing, meaning only that Janet has a curious desire to acquire a Norwegian husband, *any* Norwegian husband, then *a Norwegian* is not an r. e., since I have nobody in mind for the linguistic expression to point at.

There is a further complication with expressions like *the fastest runner in Brazil*. I can use this quite happily without having the faintest idea who that fastest runner in Brazil might be. Here I am merely assuming that the expression must, in principle, pick out someone or other, even though I don't know who. Such an expression is an **attributive expression**, and it is not usually counted as a referring expression.

*See:* **deictic category**; **meaning**; **sense**
*Further reading:* Hofmann, 1993: ch. 10; Hurford and Heasley, 1983: units 4–8; Saeed, 1997: ch. 2.

**root** The minimal common form, or **morpheme**, which appears in all the different forms of a single word. In Spanish, the *root* of the verb meaning 'sing' is *cant-*, and this appears in all forms of the verb, such as *canto* 'I sing', *cantábamos* 'we were singing', *cantó* 's/he sang', *cantarás* 'you will sing', *cantarían* 'they would sing', *cantemos* 'we might sing', *cantando* 'singing', and so on. Likewise, in Arabic, the root of the verb meaning 'write' is *ktb*, which appears in all forms of the verb, including derivatives: *katab* 'he wrote', *yiktib* 'he will write', *maktuub* 'written', *kaatib* 'writer', *kitaab* 'book', *kutub* 'books', and so on.

A root must be carefully distinguished from a **stem**, which consists of a root plus some additional material. In English, though, this difference is rarely significant.

*See:* **morphology; stem**

**rule** A statement expressing a generalization about the facts of a language. Since ancient times, descriptions of languages have featured rules of one sort or another, but, before the rise of modern linguistics, these rules were usually expressed very informally, in ordinary language. Linguists, in contrast, have usually been at pains to state their rules with maximal explicitness; to this end, they have devised various **notational conventions**, which allow rules to be stated in a manner that is at once fully explicit, maximally economical and embedded within a particular theoretical framework. This drive toward explicitness was promoted by the *American structuralists* during the 1940s, but these linguists were more interested in **distribution**, and rules only became fully prominent with the rise of **generative grammar** in the 1950s.

Rules can be stated at every level of linguistic description, from phonology to pragmatics. A rule need not be exceptionless. For example, the rule of English that says that a noun forms its plural by adding <-s> is genuine, and it applies to most new nouns entering the language, but there are some well-known exceptions, like *feet, children* and *radii*.

It is important to realize that rules in linguistics are statements about actual linguistic behaviour. Earlier grammarians, with their devotion to **prescriptivism**, often stated 'rules' which were not rules at all, but only their opinions about what should be considered good usage, such as 'Don't end a sentence with a preposition'. Linguistically unsophisticated people often assume even today that this is what rules are, but such a conception has no place in serious linguistic work, which is embedded firmly within **descriptivism**.

*See:* **descriptivism; notational convention; prescriptivism**
*Further reading:* Sampson, 1975: ch. 5.

# S

**sandhi**  Any modification in pronunciation at a grammatical boundary. The term *sandhi* is taken from the ancient Sanskrit grammarians but is widely used today. In *internal sandhi*, the change applies within a single word at a boundary between two **morphemes**. For example, the word *electric* is pronounced in isolation with a final /k/, but, when the suffix *-ity* is added, the resulting *electricity* is pronounced with /s/, not with /k/. In *external sandhi*, the change applies across the boundary between two consecutive words. For example, in isolation, *don't* is pronounced with a final /t/, and *you* is pronounced with an initial /j/ (American /y/), but in the phrase *don't you?* the /t/ and the /j/ often merge into a single affricate /ʧ/: *don/ʧ/ou?*

Sandhi phenomena are very frequent in languages, and elegant accounts of them are an important goal of any description.

*See:* **alternation**
*Further reading:* Lass, 1984: 69–73; Matthews, 1991: 149–157.

**Saussurean paradox**  The following puzzle: how can speakers continue to use a language effectively when that language is constantly changing? The Swiss linguist Saussure was the first to demonstrate that a language is not just a collection of linguistic objects like speech sounds and words; instead, it is

265

a highly structured system in which each element is largely defined by the way it is related to other elements. This *structuralist* view of language has dominated linguistic thinking ever since. But it immediately leads to a puzzle.

We know that every language is constantly changing. So: how can a language continue to be a structured system of speech sounds, words, grammatical forms and sentence structures when all of these are, at any given moment, in the middle of any number of changes currently in progress?

This paradox greatly puzzled linguists for generations. Today, though, we are well on the way to resolving it at last. The key insight has come from the study of **variation** in language. Though variation was formerly dismissed as peripheral and insignificant, we now realize that variation in fact forms a large part of the very structure of any language, that speakers make use of that variation just as they make use of other aspects of language structure, and that variation is the vehicle of change, as speakers simply shift the frequencies of competing variant forms over time.

*See:* **language change**; **structuralism**; **variation**

*Further reading:* Milroy, 1992; Trask, 1996: ch. 10; Weinreich *et al.*, 1968.

**segment** Any one of the discrete units which occur in sequence in speech. In **phonetics**, a segment is a **speech sound**; in **phonology**, it is a **phoneme**. But both levels of analysis recognize that a single word or a longer piece of speech consists of a sequence of discrete units, occurring one after the other. The word *pat*, for example, may be represented at the phonetic level as [pʰæt], and at the phonological level as /pæt/, with a sequence of three segments in either case.

All those aspects of phonology which pertain to segments and their behaviour are collectively known as *segmental* phonology, in contrast to the study of **suprasegmental** phenomena, which must be described with reference to phonological units larger than a single segment.

As a general rule, a given piece of speech will contain the same number of segments at both levels, but there are exceptions. For example, in many American accents, the word *can't* contains four segments at the phonemic level, /kænt/, but only three at the phonetic level, [kʰæ̃t]. Here the phonemic segment /n/ loses its segmental nature at the phonetic level and is realized only as a feature of nasalization occurring on the vowel [æ].

Some of the more abstract theories of phonology take this possibility further. In such a theory, we might find English *sign*, phonetically [saɪn] and usually regarded phonemically as /saɪn/, represented at the abstract phonemic level as /sɪgn/, in order to account for the forms of derivatives like *signature* and *signal*. This sort of thing was very popular in the 1960s, but is less popular today.

*See:* **phoneme**; **speech sound**; **suprasegmental**
*Further reading:* Catford, 1977: 226–229.

**selection restriction**  A restriction on the combining of words in a sentence resulting from their meanings. It is easy to construct apparently grammatical sentences which are senseless because the meanings of the words in those sentences cannot be combined in a comprehensible way: *You have deceived my watermelon*; *The square root of seven is green and squishy*; *She dropped her shyness into the pond with a splash*. The restrictions which are violated here are *selection restrictions*, or *selectional restrictions*.

In the early 1960s, there was an attempt by Noam Chomsky to treat such restrictions as part of the grammar, and hence to regard my examples as ungrammatical, but this idea was quickly dropped as unworkable, and today such restrictions are universally regarded as belonging to **semantics** or (more usually) **pragmatics**. In the semantic view, we regard my examples as impossible to interpret at all; in the pragmatic view, we consider merely that it is difficult or impossible to find a context in which one of these would be a plausible thing to say.

*See:* **meaning**; **well-formedness**
*Further reading:* Allan, 1986: ch. 5; Leech, 1974: 141–146; Radford, 1988: 369–372.


**semantic role**    Any one of several ways in which a person or thing may be involved in an action or a state of affairs. The notion of *semantic roles* (also called *participant roles* or *deep cases* or *thematic roles* or *theta roles*) is important in many approaches to linguistic description, particularly in those approaches which embrace **functionalism**. The idea is that a given entity which is involved in some event must play some identifiable part in that event. For example, in the sentence *Susie tightened the nut with a spanner*, *Susie* is an Agent (she is the instigator of the action), *the nut* is a Patient (something is happening to it), and *a spanner* is an Instrument (it is being used to accomplish some purpose). In contrast, in *Susie received a letter*, *Susie* is a Recipient (something is arriving at her), while *a letter* is a Theme (nothing is happening to it except that it is being moved).

Analysis of sentences or texts in terms of semantic roles may be illuminating, but analysts often do not agree as to which semantic roles should be recognized, and it is frequently very difficult to assign roles in a principled manner. For example, in *Susie filled the bucket with water*, it is clear that *Susie* is an Agent, but what are *the bucket* and *water*? Location? Goal? Patient? Theme? Instrument? Because of the difficulty of answering such questions, many linguists have preferred to reject semantic roles altogether in constructing their descriptions, but many others are convinced that semantic roles are of fundamental importance in spite of the difficulties.

*Further reading:* Frawley, 1992: ch. 5; Hurford and Heasley, 1983: unit 20; F. Palmer, 1994: ch. 2; Radford, 1988: 372–378; Saeed, 1997: ch. 6.


**semantics**    The branch of linguistics which studies **meaning**. The study of meaning has something of a chequered history in linguistics. People have since ancient times been interested in questions of meaning, but very little progress was made before the late nineteenth century, and semantics did not really exist as a distinct field. Around that time, however, the French linguist Michel Bréal, who coined the term *semantics*, made a serious and largely successful attempt to introduce semantics into European linguistic work. And, once the Swiss linguist Ferdinand de Saussure had made the **linguistic sign** the cornerstone of his influential theories, semantics was here to stay in European linguistics.

Oddly, some of the most important work in semantics was being done from the late nineteenth century onwards by philosophers, but it was a long time before linguists became aware of this work and began to join forces with the philosophers.

American linguists were comparatively reluctant to consider semantic questions. The two principal figures in the early twentieth century, Edward Sapir and Leonard Bloomfield, did not entirely neglect the matter, but they had little to say about it, and Bloomfield's successors, the *American structuralists* of the 1940s and 1950s, were so pessimistic about the chances of applying linguistic techniques successfully to the seeming swamp of meaning that they effectively defined linguistics as a field excluding semantics.

In the 1960s, however, shortly after the Chomskyan revolution, a few American linguists began to be interested in semantic questions. They were ignorant of the vast philosophical literature, and their first attempts were fumbling, but before long they had caught up and were beginning to join forces with the philosophers. The work of the American philosopher Richard Montague had an enormous effect upon the linguists, and Montague's ideas have since become the basis of a great deal of important work in linguistic semantics.

One of the most important advances was made gradually during the 1960s, when it was realized that there were two fundamentally different types of linguistic meaning. One type of meaning is intrinsic to the linguistic form containing it, and is always present in that form, while the second type of meaning results from the interaction between the linguistic form of an utterance and the context in which it is uttered. Today we understand semantics as properly the study of the first type, while to the study of the second type we give a new name: **pragmatics** (a term actually coined by the American philosopher C.S. Peirce in the nineteenth century). Failure to make this distinction had earlier proved a severe obstacle to progress.

In recent years approaches to semantics have proliferated, and the subject is now one of the liveliest areas in linguistics. The majority of the current approaches represent versions of *formal semantics*: attempts at elucidating meaning by developing particular versions of *formal logic* that can capture aspects of meaning. Among the most influential threads of investigation have been *truth-conditional semantics*, which attempts to reduce meaning to questions of truth and falsehood, *model-theoretic semantics*, which operates in terms of miniature artificial universes called *models*, and *situation semantics*, which embeds the study of meaning within miniature contexts called *situations*.

Most of the activity just mentioned is concerned with the semantic interpretation of sentences, but the study of word-meaning, called *lexical semantics*, has also been extensively developed.

*See:* **componental analysis**; **meaning**; **selection restriction**; **sense relation**; **pragmatics**

*Further reading:* Cruse, 1986; Crystal, 1997a: ch. 17; Frawley, 1992; Hofmann, 1993; Hudson, 1995; Hurford and Heasley, 1983; Kreidler, 1998; Malmkjær, 1991: 389–398; Saeed, 1997.

**semiotics**   The study of the social production of meaning from sign systems. Semiotics, also called *semiology*, traces its origins to the work of the Swiss linguist Ferdinand de Saussure in the early twentieth century, and particularly to Saussure's idea of the **linguistic sign**. Nevertheless, semiotics has never been regarded as part of linguistics, and it has been developed almost exclusively by non-linguists, particularly in France, where it is often considered an important discipline. In the English-speaking world, it enjoys almost no institutional recognition.

Though language itself is taken to be the paradigm case of a sign system, in practice most semiotic work has concentrated upon the analysis of such varied domains as advertising, cinema and myths. The influence of the central linguistic concept of **structuralism** (another of Saussure's contributions) has led semioticists to attempt structuralist interpretations of a wide range of phenomena. An object of study, such as a film or a cycle of myths, is viewed as a **text** which communicates meaning, and that meaning is assumed to derive from the orderly interaction of meaning-bearing elements, the *signs*, which themselves are embedded in a structured system, somewhat analogously to the meaning-bearing elements in a language.

In spite of its deliberate emphasis upon the social nature of the sign systems examined, semiotics tends to be highly abstract and at times seemingly impenetrable. In recent years, however, semioticists have increasingly turned to the study of popular culture, and semiotic treatments of soap operas and pop music are now commonplace.

*See:* **linguistic sign**; **symbolic system**
*Further reading:* Eco, 1976; Leeds-Hurwitz, 1993; Sebeok, 1984, 1994; Tobin, 1990.

**sense**   The central meaning of a linguistic form, regarded from the point of view of the way it relates to other linguistic items. The central meaning of a linguistic form, such as *cat*, can be approached from at least two different points of view. One way is to consider all the things in the world and decide to which ones the form *cat* can reasonably be applied; this approach leads to what we call the **denotation** of *cat*. The other is to compare the meaning of *cat* with the meanings of other linguistic forms, such as *lion* and *dog*, and to decide what semantic characteristics the form *cat* has which allow it to be applied to some things but not to others. This leads to what we call the *sense* of the form.

A very crude interpretation of the sense of *cat* might look something like this: carnivorous mammal, has four legs and a long tail, has fangs and sharp retractable claws, has excellent eyesight even in dim light, . . . You can easily see some shortcomings here: Manx cats have no tail, cheetahs cannot retract their claws, and so on. What we are describing here is really a *stereotype* of a cat, a maximally typical (but hypothetical) cat, and a real animal qualifies as a cat if it matches the stereotype sufficiently well, even if not perfectly.

(Note: a stereotype is different from a *prototype*. A prototype of a cat would be a single real cat which was regarded as so eminently typical of cats generally that we might like to hold it up as a model of perfect cathood. But note that not everyone uses the terms *stereotype* and *prototype* in exactly the manner described here.)

In formal versions of semantics, the sense of a linguistic form is often formalized as its *intension* – that is, as the *set* (in the formal mathematical sense) of all the properties which an object must have before the form can be properly applied to it.

Sense is most commonly contrasted with **reference**, but it is essentially just a different way of looking at the same kind of meaning singled out as *denotation* in a different approach.

*See:* **denotation**; **reference**

*Further reading:* Allan, 1986: ch. 2; Hurford and Heasley, 1983: units 9–11.

**sense relation**   Any of several ways in which the meanings of words may be related. Words do not have meanings in isolation; instead, the meaning of a word is usually related in important ways to the meanings of other words. Some of the most prominent of these relations in meaning are known collectively as *sense relations*, and there are several kinds.

In *synonymy*, two words have identical or nearly identical meanings: *cat* and *feline*, *pail* and *bucket*, *violin* and *fiddle*, *fruitful* and *productive*. Such pairs of *synonyms* are not always completely interchangeable: the words may differ in degree of formality, as with *felon* and *crook*, or they may differ in their **connotations** (associations), as with *rabbit* and *bunny*. However, if both words can be applied in principle to exactly the same things, they are *cognitively synonymous*.

In *antonymy*, two words have opposite meanings. Some pairs of *antonyms* are *gradable antonyms*, representing extremes along a continuum, as with *hot* and *cold* or *big* and *small*. Other pairs are *binary antonyms*, which are mutually exclusive and which between them exhaust the possibilities, as with *alive* and *dead*.

Somewhat different are *converse pairs*, such as *wife* and *husband* or *above* and *below*: if I am your husband, then you are my wife; if the table is below the clock, then the clock is above the table.

In *meronymy*, one word denotes a part of another. For example, *hand* is a meronym of *arm*, and both words are meronyms of *body*.

In *hyponymy*, one word denotes a special case of what is denoted by the other. For example, *spaniel* is a *hyponym* of *dog*, which in turn is a hyponym of *animal*, while *dog* is a *superordinate* of *spaniel*.

These are just a few of the sense relations which have been recognized; there are others.

*See:* **meaning**; **semantics**
*Further reading:* Cruse, 1986; Hurford and Heasley, 1983: units 10–11.

**sentence**   The largest purely grammatical unit in a language. Of course, there are larger linguistic units than sentences: individual paragraphs (in writing), individual turns (in conversation) and individual discourses. But these larger units are no more than very weakly linked by purely grammatical means. The largest linguistic unit which is held together by rigid grammatical rules is the *sentence*.

We need to clarify this term a little, since it is frequently misunderstood. For most linguists, in most circumstances, a sentence is an abstract linguistic object: specifically, it is a linguistic object put together entirely in accordance with the rules for constructing sentences in a language, rules which have to be identified (in a linguistic description) by patient and painstaking investigation. More particularly, a sentence does not have to be something which somebody might reasonably say, and not everything that we might reasonably say is a sentence.

Consider this exchange. Mike: *Where's Susie?* Alice: *In the library*. Here Mike's utterance represents a sentence, but Alice's response does not: even though it is a perfectly normal and unremarkable thing to say, *★In the library* is not a sentence of English (the asterisk indicates this fact), because it is not constructed according to the rules for making English sentences. Instead, it is only a ***fragment*** of a sentence: we do not always speak in complete sentences, and we very often use fragments like this one.

Now consider Noam Chomsky's famous example sentence: *Colourless green ideas sleep furiously*. Chomsky's point is that, even though this thing makes no sense at all, it is constructed in accordance with all the rules for making sentences in English, and hence it is a grammatical (well-formed) sentence of English.

A further point is that a sentence is not just a string of words; rather, it is a string of words with a grammatical (syntactic) structure assigned to it. Consequently, an ambiguous string of words like *Visiting relatives can be a nuisance* or *I saw her duck* represents two (or more) quite different sentences, each with its own structure. We often take advantage of this possibility of assigning different structures to identical or similar strings of words for humorous effect, as in the old gag *Time flies like an arrow; fruit flies like a banana* and in the punchline of a certain cat-food commercial: *Cats like Felix like Felix*.

*See:* **ambiguity**; **clause**; **syntax**; **utterance**; **well-formedness**
*Further reading:* Brown and Miller, 1991: ch. 11; Lyons, 1968: 172–180; Matthews, 1981: ch. 2.

**sex differences in language**   Differences between the speech of men and women. In some languages, there are very conspicuous differences between men's and women's speech: men and women may use different words for the same thing, they may use different grammatical endings, they may even use different sets of consonants and vowels in their pronunciation.

English has nothing quite so dramatic as this, but several decades of research have turned up some interesting differences even in English – though not all of the early claims have been substantiated by later work. For example, it has been suggested that women use more *tag questions* than men – as in *It's nice, isn't it?* – as if to seek approval for their opinions, but this has not been borne out by investigation. It has also been suggested that men swear more than women, but this too appears not to be so, at least among younger speakers, though some of the coarser expressions are perhaps more typical of men.

On the other hand, it does appear to be true that certain words are more typical of women, including terms of approval like *cute*, *divine* and *adorable* and specific colour terms like *beige*, *burgundy* and *ecru*. Admiring one another's clothes is far more acceptable among women: a woman can say *Julia, what an absolutely divine tunic!*, but it would be decidedly unusual (in most circles, anyway) for a man to remark *Those are great jeans you're wearing, Ted*.

Far more interesting, though, is the discovery, chiefly by the British sociolinguist Jennifer Coates and the American sociolinguist Deborah Tannen, that men and women organize their conversations very differently. For one thing, men in conversation are often rather competitive: each man tries to score points and to top what the others have said. Women, in great contrast, engage in highly cooperative conversations: each women attempts to support and admire the contributions of others.

More striking still is the observation that men engage in floor-holding: one man speaks at a time, while the others remain silent and wait their turn, especially if the speaker is holding forth on a topic on which he is considered particularly knowledgeable. But women don't do this: while one woman is speaking, the others are constantly chipping in with supporting remarks, ranging from *That's true* to actually completing the speaker's sentence for her. That is, a conversation among women is a collaborative enterprise, with all the women pulling together to construct a satisfactory discourse which is the product of all of them, while a conversation among men is rather a sequence of individual efforts.

These differences can lead to serious misunderstanding in mixed conversations. While her husband or boyfriend is speaking, a woman may constantly contribute supporting remarks in the normal female fashion, but the man may well interpret these remarks as interruptions (which they are not) and become very annoyed. In fact, it is quite clear that, in mixed conversations, men interrupt women far more than the reverse.

*See:* **turn-taking**
*Further reading:* Coates, 1993, 1996; Holmes, 1992: 164–181; Romaine, 1994: ch. 4; Tannen, 1991.

**sexist language** Language which, deliberately or unconsciously, is patronizing or contemptuous towards one sex, usually women. Sexism, of course, is not specifically a linguistic issue, but it shows up in languages in various ways, some of them rather deeply embedded. Almost without exception, sexist usages are patronizing of women. Here are a few examples.

As is well known, English has only the sex-marked singular pronouns *he* and *she*, and hence a speaker addressing or talking about a mixed group has a problem: *Somebody has forgotten his umbrella* is sexist, while *Somebody has forgotten his or her umbrella* is almost unbearably clumsy. In this case, popular speech usually solves the problem by using *their*: *Somebody has forgotten their umbrella*. But some people find this distasteful, and it doesn't really work very well in cases like *Any student who considers themself adequately prepared is requested to present themself for their oral examination.*

Many pairs of sex-marked words have developed very differently. A *master* is a powerful or skilful man; a *mistress* is a woman kept for sexual purposes. A *courtier* is a polished man of high social status; a *courtesan* is just an up-market whore. There is nothing wrong with calling a man a *bachelor*, but calling a woman a *spinster* is contemptuous. Even a single word may behave differently: in American English, at least, when you call a man a *pro*, you mean that he is experienced, competent and reliable; when you call a woman a *pro*, you mean she's a prostitute.

The female suffix *-ess* causes particular problems: a man is a *poet*, while a woman is (perhaps) only a *poetess*. But there are many other such cases. Men play *golf* and *cricket*, while women play *women's golf* and *women's cricket*. A man can be a *doctor*, but a woman must often be a *woman doctor*. We are surprised when a *professor* or an *engineer* turns out to be a woman, or when a *secretary* or a *model* turns out to be a man (and *male model* is commonly used in this last case). A conference centre in Liverpool, noting that a sailors' conference and a nurses' conference were booked for the same week, put on a disco, which proved to be a disaster: all the sailors were men, and so were all the nurses.

Among the most blatant examples of all are the following, both genuine: *The assailant attacked his next-door neighbour's wife* (the woman was not his neighbour?); *The pioneers trekked across the prairies with their cattle, their seed-corn and their wives* (the wives were only there to cook, clean, sew and raise the children while their husbands were busy pioneering?).

Once rarely remarked on, sexist language has been drawing the fire of feminists for several decades now, and a number of linguists have turned their attention to the issue. Attempts at stamping out sexist usages have enjoyed some success, and terms like *fireman*, *postman* and *chairman* are now commonly replaced by *firefighter*, *letter carrier* and *chairperson* (or simply *chair*); similarly, the use of *man* or *men* to denote human beings in general is slowly giving way to *human beings* or *humans*. But cases like *manhole* and *man-eating tiger* are more refractory.

*See:* **language planning**
*Further reading:* Coates, 1993; Hofstadter, 1985.

**sign language** A language whose medium is signs made with the hands and head. **Speech** is the most familiar medium of language, but it is not the only one possible. Deaf people cannot hear speech, and many deaf people learn and use a *sign language* as their primary language, often as their first language. Many different sign languages exist, including **British Sign Language** (BSL) in the UK and **American Sign Language** (ASL) in the USA; these two are not related to each other, and neither is related in any way to English.

A true sign language is not a crude approximation to a spoken language; it is a genuine natural language with a large vocabulary and a rich and complex grammar, and it is every bit as flexible and expressive as a spoken language. The basic units are *signs* made chiefly with the hands and the head; in ASL and BSL, these signs can be modified in various ways to express shades of meaning like 'many', 'often', 'slightly', 'quickly', 'very' and 'repeatedly', notions which would require separate words in English. An example: in ASL, touching the middle finger to the forehead means 'be sick'; by modifying the distance, direction, and speed of movement, and the number of touches, the signer can explicitly express (at least) any of 'get sick', 'get sick easily', 'often sick', 'never stops being sick', 'sickly', 'slightly sick', 'very sick', and 'sick for a long time'. Indeed, it has been remarked that the grammars of ASL and BSL are more similar to the grammars of certain native American languages, such as Hopi, than to the grammar of English.

Just like **creoles**, sign languages emerge spontaneously whenever deaf children are brought together. A recent example is Nicaraguan Sign Language, created and used by the deaf children who were brought together to receive an education after the Nicaraguan revolution of 1979. ASL and

BSL, in fact, were deliberately invented by hearing people in the nineteenth century, but the modern versions are vastly more elaborate than the original ones, as native signers have expanded the vocabulary and elaborated the grammar to meet their needs. And, just like spoken languages, sign languages change over time: already ASL is showing evidence of developing regional dialects.

So strong is the **language instinct** that a deaf child will eagerly begin babbling with its hands, and it will seize upon any gestures it sees and do its best to turn them into a sign language, even without reinforcement; such a system is called *home sign*.

Linguists were at first slow to appreciate that sign languages were true languages, but, since the pioneering work of the American linguist Ursula Bellugi in the 1970s, sign languages have come to be treated on a par with spoken languages, though most introductory textbooks of linguistics provide regrettably little coverage of the topic.

*See:* **language**; **language instinct**; **natural language**
*Further reading:* Crystal, 1997a: section VI; Deuchar, 1984; Klima and Bellugi, 1979; Malmkjær, 1991: 405–414; Miles, 1988; Padden, 1988; Smith, 1990; Steinberg, 1993: ch. 4.

**slang**  Informal and often ephemeral linguistic forms. We all use our language in different ways, depending on the circumstances. Most obviously, we speak differently in formal contexts and in informal contexts. Especially when speaking informally, we often take pleasure in resorting to *slang*: informal but colourful words and expressions.

Slang expressions are usually introduced by the members of a particular social group; they may remain the property of that group and serve as a badge of group identity, or they may instead become much more widely known and used. The majority of slang forms are transient: they are used for a few months or a few years, and then they pass out of use, to be replaced by even newer slang terms.

Just in the last few years in English, something really excellent has been described at times, by certain groups of speakers at least, as *groovy, fab, brill, tremendous, wicked, ace, spiffing, cool, far out, awesome, sweet, triff, def,* and countless other terms. One or two of these are perhaps still in use, but the rest are already quaint anachronisms. We have variously said of a man who is drunk that he is *loaded, soused, fried, pickled, sozzled, pissed, blitzed, bombed, smashed* or *tired and emotional,* or that he *has had a skinful* or is *three sheets to the wind*. A few years ago, the common British slang term for 'copulate' was *bonk*; now this word has been replaced, at least among younger speakers, by *shag*; and, by the time you read this, *shag* in turn may have been replaced by yet another slang term.

An unusual case of a long-lived slang term is *booze* for alcoholic drinks; this has been in the language for centuries, but it is still used, and it is still regarded as slang. On occasion, a slang term may lose its slang status altogether; this has happened with *mob*, an old slang word which is now unquestionably standard English.

Slang has been described as 'language at play': the best slang is colourful, exuberant, witty and memorable, as when we say of a smug and intolerant person that *he has his dick up his arse,* or when we dismiss a sexually promiscuous woman as *yo-yo knickers*. Priggish critics have for generations tried to dismiss slang as a kind of disease of the language, but it is nothing of the sort: its presence is evidence of the vitality of a language.

*See:* **colloquial speech**
*Further reading:* Crystal, 1995: 182; Partridge, 1961, 1970.

**social history of language** The study of the history of language as a social institution. Traditionally, **historical linguistics**, and in particular the study of **language change**, has focused upon internal structural changes: changes in pronunciation, grammar and vocabulary. In the 1960s, however, linguists began to turn their attention to the social context of language change, to the ways in which changes are introduced and propagated by speakers, and to the social forces accompanying these changes, and this type of investigation has proved very illuminating.

More recently still, a few scholars have begun to turn their attention to broader issues in the history of language. Among these issues are the choice between languages or language varieties in particular communities at particular times, the social pressures associated with these choices, the rules governing conversation among various social groups in the past, the connections between language and both individual and national identity, and the reasons for changes in all these things over time. To this new discipline we give the name *social history of language*.

The social history of language is perhaps more obviously a branch of social history than of linguistics, but it complements the more familiar concerns of linguists by providing an overview of the circumstances in which particular languages were used in particular communities at various times in the past. It should be noted, though, that some of the most prominent writers in this area are avowed Marxists or avowed followers of the radical French thinker Michel Foucault, and hence their work is often tendentious and controversial.

*See:* **language and identity**; **language and power**; **language planning**

*Further reading:* Burke, 1993; Tony Crowley, 1989, 1996; Honey, 1997; Leith, 1997; Lodge, 1993; McCrum *et al.*, 1992.

√ **social stratification of language**   Marked differences in the speech of people belonging to different social classes in a community. In most communities of any size, there are conspicuous differences in the social status of people, and these social classes are usually hierarchically ordered in overt prestige, from highest to lowest.

It has long been realized that members of different social classes tend to speak differently, but it is only since the 1960s that sociolinguists, such as the American William Labov and the Briton Peter Trudgill, have begun to undertake systematic studies of these differences. Such studies often reveal a great deal of information about the differing linguistic behaviour of the several social classes. For example, in London, *t*-glottaling (the pronunciation of the /t/ in words like *water* as a glottal stop) is maximally prominent among working-class speakers, less prominent among lower-middle-class speakers, still less prominent among upper-middle-class speakers, and virtually absent among upper-class speakers. On the other hand, the *respectively* construction, as in *Esther and Larry drank whisky and brandy, respectively*, is maximally prominent among upper-class speakers but absent altogether in working-class speech.

These are examples of the *social stratification of language*: a steady rise or fall in the frequency of particular linguistic forms as we move through the social classes. And note that word 'frequency': only sometimes is a particular form either categorically present or totally absent in the speech of a particular class. Very often, it is present in the speech of all or nearly all classes, but it differs in frequency, and 'correct' behaviour for a member of a class involves getting the frequency right: using a form too frequently or too rarely will make an individual's speech sound anomalous to the other members of his class.

*See:* **language and identity**; **sociolinguistics**; **variation**
*Further reading:* Labov, 1972; Trudgill, 1995: ch. 2.

**sociolinguistics** The branch of linguistics which studies the relation between language and society. Though the social aspect of language attracted early attention, notably from the great Swiss linguist Ferdinand de Saussure at the beginning of the twentieth century, it was perhaps only in the 1950s that serious investigation began. Pioneers like Uriel Weinreich, Charles Ferguson and Joshua Fishman drew attention to a range of fascinating phenomena, such as **diglossia** and the effects of **language contact**. But the key figure here is arguably the American William Labov, who in the 1960s began a series of investigations of **variation** in language, investigations which have revolutionized our understanding of how speakers use their languages and which have finally resolved the **Saussurean paradox**.

Sociolinguistics may be usefully defined as the study of variation in language, or more precisely of variation within speech communities, since the purely geographical aspects of variation had been studies for generations by the students of *dialect geography*, the study of regional **dialects**. In a speech community of any size, there is considerable variation among individuals: stockbrokers do not speak like plumbers, women do not speak like men, young people do not speak like old people, and so on. Moreover, even a single individual is not confined to a single variety of the language: you do not use the language in the same way when you are chatting to friends in a bar, when you are being interviewed for a job, when you are writing an essay, and when you are being introduced to the Queen.

Earlier linguists had, of course, noticed this variation, but they were inclined to dismiss it as peripheral, as inconsequential, even as a nuisance getting in the way of good descriptions. Today, however, we recognize that variation is an integral and essential part of language, and that absence of variation is almost pathological.

*See:* **sex differences in language**; **social stratification of language**; **variation**

*Further reading:* Holmes, 1992; Hudson, 1996; Romaine, 1994; Trudgill, 1995.


**sound symbolism** An attempt at constructing a word whose sound directly conveys (some aspect of) its meaning. The most familiar type of sound symbolism is *onomatopoeia*, in which the meaning of a word is a real-world sound and the form of the word attempts to mimic the sound. Examples: *bang, boom, murmur, hiss, quack, meow, clink, ding-dong, thud*. But other types exist.

English has a group of words with initial /sl-/, all with meanings in the general area of 'slippery, slimy, gooey': *slurp, slip, slide, slink, slush, slop, slosh, sludge, slurry, slime, slug* (the creature), *slaver*, and so on. The sequence /sl-/ in these cases is a **phonaestheme**, and this kind of sound symbolism is **phonaesthesia**.

Yet another type of sound symbolism is represented by two Basque words for 'butterfly', *tximeleta* and *pinpilinpauxa* (<tx> = English <ch>, <x> = English <sh>). Here the fluttery sound of the words seems designed to mimic the fluttery appearance of the creature.

One more rather frequent type is represented by the **ideo-phones** of many languages, which attempt to mimic types of motion. Examples from the Carib language Apalai: *seky seky* 'creep up', *tɣ tɣ tɣ* 'person walking', *wɣwɣwɣwɣ* 'hammock swinging', *uroruro* 'trees falling', *tututututu* 'fast approach', and so on.

Sound symbolism constitutes a partial exception to the more usual **arbitrariness** of linguistic forms.

*See:* **arbitrariness**; **iconicity**
*Further reading:* Crystal, 1988: 122–124,1997a: ch. 30, 1995: 250–253; G. Palmer, 1996: ch. 10.

**speech**  Spoken language, either in general or in particular instances. The term *speech* is used in linguistics in three rather different ways, which sometimes need to be distinguished.

First, speech is a **medium** for language; in this sense, the term contrasts with *writing* and with **sign language**.

Second, speech is the overall linguistic behaviour of people who speak, including any patterns visible in that behaviour. This is the sense of the term in compound terms like **speech community** and **speech act**.

Third, speech is the real utterances produced by real people on real occasions. This is the sense of the term in **speech error**, and it is exactly equivalent to the terms *parole* and **performance**.

*See:* **medium**; **performance**

**speech act**   An attempt at doing something purely by speaking. There are very many things that we can do, or attempt to do, simply by speaking. We can make a promise, ask a question, order or request somebody to do something, make a threat, name a ship, pronounce somebody husband and wife, and so on. Each one of these is a particular *speech act*.

In the majority of cases, it makes no sense to ask whether an utterance constituting a speech act is true or false. Utterances like *Clean up your room!*; *Can you lend me a pen?*; *I promise to buy you a teddy bear*; and *I dub thee knight, Sir Clarence* have no truth value, but they may be more or less appropriate to the circumstances, or, as we say, more or less *felicitous*. An utterance like *Clean up your room!* is infelicitous if I have no authority over you, and *I now pronounce you husband and wife* fails unless a number of obvious conditions are met. The conditions required for a speech act to be successful are accordingly often called *felicity conditions*.

Speech acts belong to the domain of **pragmatics**, and their study, called *speech–act theory*, is a prominent part of that discipline. The study of speech acts was introduced by the British philosopher J.L. Austin in the 1960s, and it has been developed by a number of others, notably the British philosopher John Searle. Austin originally distinguished three aspects of a speech act: the *locutionary act* (saying something), the *illocutionary act* (what you're trying to do by speaking), and the *perlocutionary act* (the effect of what you say). Today, however, the term *speech act* is often used to denote specifically an illocutionary act, and the intended effect of a speech act is its *illocutionary force*.

*See:* **performative**; **pragmatics**

*Further reading:* Levinson, 1983: ch. 5; Malmkjær, 1991: 416–424; Mey, 1993: ch. 6; Saeed, 1997: ch. 8; Schiffrin, 1994: ch. 3; Thomas, 1995: ch. 2; Yule, 1996: ch. 6.

**speech community**   A group of people who regularly interact by speaking. A speech community may be large or small, and it may be highly homogeneous or decidedly heterogeneous.

What matters is that everybody in it should regularly speak to at least some of the other people in it, and that the community should not be broken up by sharp boundaries across which speaking rarely or never takes place.

Not infrequently, an individual may belong to several speech communities of different sizes. For example, a rural American in the midwest belongs to a small local community with whom he interacts intensely, a much larger surrounding community with whose members he interacts less frequently, and, less centrally, to the entire community of English-speakers in the world. In the majority of cases, though, when we speak of a speech community, we have a smaller community in mind, not a larger one.

It is not necessary for everybody in a community to speak the same variety of a language. For example, London and New York include English-speakers speaking a striking range of different varieties of English. And it is not even necessary for everybody in the community to speak the same language at all. For example, Singapore has large numbers of native speakers of Malay, Cantonese, Tamil and English; few people can speak all four, but almost everybody can speak at least two, and Singapore does not consist of several isolated communities having little to do with one another.

*See:* **bilingualism**; **diglossia**; **social stratification of language**
*Further reading:* Chambers, 1995: ch. 2; Edwards, 1994; Holmes, 1992: section I.


**speech event** A significant piece of speaking conducted according to rules. All **speech** possesses structure of some kind, but there are certain pieces of speaking which are rather special. Each one has a recognizable beginning and end and is constructed according to certain rules known to both speakers and listeners. Examples include a university lecture, a sermon, an after-dinner speech, a debate and a job interview. Such a highly structured piece of speech is a *speech event*.

A speech event involves *participants* who assume clearly defined *roles*, and it takes place in a well-defined *setting*. The *rules* governing the event are clearly defined and known to all participants; violating these rules is a serious lapse. Naturally, linguists are often interested in identifying the rules governing particular sorts of speech events.

Note: a few people apply the term *speech event* more broadly, to include ordinary conversations, brief exchanges and even *speech situations* (such as cocktail parties), but these extended usages are not usual and not recommended.

*See:* **discourse**
*Further reading:* Duranti, 1997: 284–294.

**speech sound** One of the individual sounds produced in sequence during speech. When we speak, the several speech organs are all in constant motion: the lips, the jaw, the velum, the glottis and the several parts of the tongue are all moving about at their own pace, with only the occasional moment of motionlessness. Nevertheless, we hear the result as a linear sequence of individual sounds, each following the last, and each having its own distinguishing characteristics. Each one of these perceived sounds is a *speech sound*.

For example, a typical pronunciation of the English word *cleaned* can be represented in phonetic **transcription**, with an absolute minimum of phonetic detail, as [klind]. Here the transcription shows that we hear this word as a sequence of five speech sounds, namely [k], [l], [i], [n] and [d]. In purely phonetic terms, this is an oversimplification: the voicelessness of the [k] is extended into the [l], the nasality of the [n] begins during the [i], and there are many other phonetic details not represented in this very simple transcription – and yet what we hear is something reasonably represented as [klind].

It is important to realize this perceptual nature of speech sounds. For example, a typical American pronunciation of *can't* differs from *cat* only in that the first has a nasalized vowel: [kæ̃t] versus [kæt]. Yet American speakers perceive the first as consisting of four speech sounds, [kænt], but the second as only three, [kæt]. Speakers hear the speech sounds that are 'supposed' to be there, rather than objective physical reality.

Speech sounds are classified into two types: **consonants**, which involve a significant obstruction to the flow of air, and **vowels**, which don't.

*See:* **consonant**; **phoneme**; **segment**; **vowel**
*Further reading:* Ashby, 1995; Ladefoged, 1993; Ladefoged and Maddieson, 1996.

**spelling** A conventional way of writing the words of a language using an alphabetic writing system. Most languages are not normally written at all, and a few more, like Chinese and Japanese, are usually written in non-alphabetic writing systems. The rest of the world's languages are regularly written using some alphabet or other (there are dozens in use), and, in each language, its conventional system for representing particular words in writing is its *spelling* system.

In a particular type of ideal spelling system, called *phonemic spelling* (or, informally but inaccurately, 'phonetic spelling'), each single **phoneme** is always spelled in the same way, and different phonemes are always spelled differently. Most spelling systems do not approach this ideal, though a few, such as the Finnish and Italian systems, come moderately close.

The reasons for departing from this ideal are numerous, important and often intractable. The notoriously messy and irregular spelling of English illustrates all of them.

First, once a spelling is established, it becomes part of ordinary education, and speakers are reluctant to change it, even when the pronunciation of the language changes, as it frequently does. This is the reason for such odd spellings as *knee, night, of, write, steak, iron, sugar* and *lamb*: once they represented the pronunciation perfectly, but the pronunciations of these words have changed substantially, while the spellings have not been changed.

Second, it is convenient to use similar spellings for related words even when those words are pronounced very differently. If we spelled *photograph* and *photography* just as we pronounce them, the obvious relation between them would no longer be visible.

Third, when words are taken from foreign languages, it seems natural to people who know those languages to retain the foreign spelling, even when this doesn't match the English pronunciation. This is the reason for spellings like *machine*, *Zeitgeist*, *concerto*, *lasagne* and *chic*, and, with complications, for *photograph*, *xylophone* and *psychology*.

Fourth, spellings are sometimes contaminated by the spellings of other words. So, for example, *isle* is taken from Old French and retains its Old French spelling, while the native English word *island*, which was formerly spelled *iland*, has acquired its *s* by contamination (and so has *aisle*).

Fifth, and most importantly, we do not all pronounce our words in the same way. So, for example, some people pronounce *caught* and *court* identically, while others pronounce them very differently, and so what would be a perfect spelling system for one group would be hopeless for the other – and the same is true of *caught* and *cot*, *horse* and *hoarse*, *pull* and *pool*, *marry* and *merry* (and also *Mary*), *dew* and *do*, *poor* and *pour*, *farther* and *father*, and countless other such pairs. On top of this, many individual words are pronounced in very different ways by different people: *either*, *economics*, *tomato*, *grass*, *suggest*, *library*, *sterile*, *contribute* and many, many others.

*See:* **orthography**; **writing system**
*Further reading:* Crystal, 1997a: 215–219, 1988: ch. 5.


**standard language**    That variety of a language considered by its speakers to be most appropriate in formal and educational contexts. Consider the case of English. English is spoken as a mother tongue by some 400 million people, as an everyday second language by tens of millions more, and as a fluent foreign language by further millions. Many of these people also write in English.

The English used by all these people is far from uniform: there are both regional differences and differences among social groups within a single community, and today sociolinguists often speak of ***Englishes*** to denote this whole range of varieties. But one of these varieties has a very special status: this is the variety called *standard English*.

Standard English is the form of English acquired through education; indeed, acquisition of standard English is a large part of what we understand as education in the English-speaking world. Most broadcasting, and almost all publication, is couched in standard English.

Standard English may be spoken in any of a large range of regional **accents**; no particular accent is associated with standard English, though in particular countries there are some accents often regarded as more appropriate to standard English than others. And standard English itself is not quite uniform: for example, there are detectable differences in vocabulary and grammar between standard American and standard British English, though these are not large. Further, of course, standard English is not immutable: it changes from generation to generation, and the standard English of the eighteenth century already sounds quaint and distant to us. Finally, standard spoken English is not always identical to standard written English: we write *Many students are ill*, but we don't say this; instead, we say *Lots of students are ill*.

No such thing as standard English existed 500 years ago; instead, there were only innumerable regional and social varieties. But, since then, a range of social and political pressures have combined to give rise to a single variety of English accepted as the standard everywhere.

Standard English arose largely out of a series of countless historical accidents: certain words, forms and usages happened to be accepted by educated people in positions of prestige, while others were not accepted. The single most important factor was the political, economic and cultural influence of the city of London and the surrounding region: it was largely the forms used in this area that became the basis of standard English.

In recent years, there has been a vigorous and surprising debate among academics and educators about the place of standard English in education: one group sees a command of standard English as an enormous benefit and as the right of every pupil; the other sees standard English as the elitist possession of a privileged class, and interprets attempts at teaching standard English, together with the associated dismissal of non-standard forms of English, as hostile attempts at oppressing working-class speakers and denying them power.

Almost every other language which is used in education likewise has a recognized standard form: French, German, Finnish, Basque, Arabic, and so on. A few languages even have *two* standard forms: Norway recognizes two standard forms of Norwegian, and the standard Mandarin Chinese of Taiwan is somewhat different from that of China. For many years the Dutch-speakers of Belgium attempted to maintain a different standard form of Dutch from that used in the Netherlands, but they have now abandoned this policy.

*See:* **Black English**; **dialect**; **national language**; **official language**; **vernacular**

*Further reading:* N.F. Blake, 1996: ch. 9; Crystal, 1995: 110–111; Holmes, 1992: 82–85; Honey, 1997; Leith, 1997: ch. 2.

**stem**   A linguistic form which cannot stand alone but which serves as a basis for constructing word-forms which can stand alone. In a number of European languages, the grammatical forms of a single word are constructed in a very orderly way; this is particularly noticeable with verbs.

Consider Spanish. The simplest possible form of a Spanish verb is its **root**, a form which cannot stand alone but which is always present in every form of that verb. In order to construct a verb-form, we must first add one of several possible suffixes to the root; the result, which still cannot stand alone, is one of the several *stems* of that verb. Finally, to the stem is added one of several possible *endings*, to produce a complete verb-form.

The root of the verb meaning 'sing' is *cant-*. To this we can add any of several tense or mood suffixes. The present-tense suffix happens to be *-a-*, and so the present stem is *canta-*. To this we can add any of several endings to get forms like *canta* 's/he sings', *cantamos* 'we sing' and *cantan* 'they sing'.

For the imperfect, the suffix is *-aba-*, and so the imperfect stem is *cantaba-*, leading to such forms as *cantaba* 's/he was singing', *cantábamos* 'we were singing' and *cantaban* 'they were singing'. The future suffix is *-ar-*, and so the future stem is *cantar-*, producing *cantará* 's/he will sing', *cantaremos* 'we will sing' and *cantarán* 'they will sing'. Likewise, the conditional suffix *-arí-* leads to a stem *cantarí-* and forms like *cantaría* 's/he would sing', *cantaríamos* 'we would sing' and *cantarían* 'they would sing', and present subjunctive *-e-* yields forms like *cante* 's/he might sing', *cantemos* 'we might sing' and *canten* 'they might sing'.

Not all languages exhibit this kind of structure (English doesn't), but, for those that do, recognizing roots and stems provides an elegant account of much of their **morphology**.

*See:* **root**; **morphology**

**stimulus–freedom**   Our ability to say anything at all, including nothing, in any situation. The signals used by non–human species are overwhelmingly *stimulus–bound*: each signal is produced always and only when a particular stimulus is received. For example, a vervet monkey always gives an eagle warning call upon spotting an eagle, and it never does this at any other time.

Human language is utterly different. Save only for our (non–linguistic) cries of pain and fear, we are perfectly free to choose what we are going to say in every context. In other words, our speech is *stimulus–free*. If your friend Julia asks *What do you think of my new skirt?*, you may reply *It's too short*, or *It doesn't go with your pink blouse*, or even *If that doesn't get Mike's attention, nothing will*. You can even decline to answer, and change the subject. Of course, there are all sorts of social pressures that make some replies more likely than others. If you value Julia's friendship, you probably won't reply *God, Julia – with your fat legs, you should stick to kaftans*. But there's nothing about English that prevents you from saying this, and you could say it, if you wanted to.

Though he was not the first to notice it, the American linguist Charles Hockett drew particular attention to stimulus-freedom in 1960.

*See:* **design features**; **displacement**; **open-endedness**

**stress**  Strong prominence on a particular syllable. In English, almost every word has at least one syllable which is noticeably more prominent than the other syllables; this is the *stressed* syllable, and the position of the stress is usually easy to identify. All of us agree without hesitation that the stress falls upon the first syllable of *victim* and *terrify*, on the second syllable of *linguistics* and *invention*, on the third syllable of *kangaroo* and *circulation*, and on the only syllable of *cat* and *smile*. There is some variation among speakers: some people stress the first syllable of *exquisite*, *controversy* and *vagaries*, while others stress the second.

A word of several syllables often has, in addition to its *main stress* (or *primary stress*), a *secondary stress* (a lesser degree of stress) on another syllable. For example, *education* has its main stress on the third syllable but a secondary stress on the first syllable. Even short words may bear secondary stress: the words *baseball*, *borax*, *textbook*, *croquet* and *ice cream* all bear main stress on one syllable and secondary stress on the other, though with the last two speakers vary as to which is which.

Stress differences may distinguish pairs of words otherwise identical, as with the nouns 'subject and 'record and the verbs sub'ject and re'cord. For some (not all) speakers, the same stress difference is all that distinguishes *billow* from *below*.

Stress on a syllable in English is produced by a complex interaction of several phonetic factors: a stressed syllable is louder than an unstressed one, it has a higher pitch, and it is longer.

Quite apart from the ordinary *word-stress* just described, English also allows *sentence-stress*: strong stress placed on a particular word to emphasize it within an utterance, as in *I will NEVER give in to these threats*. A sentence-stress is always placed on a syllable which bears the main stress normally.

But very different is ***contrastive stress***, in which any syllable at all, even one which is normally unstressed, may be stressed in order to highlight a contrast with something else: *I said ACcept, not EXcept.*

Many other languages also have word-stress, such as Spanish, German and Russian. Others, however, do not: French and Japanese, for example, lack word-stress.

*See:* **suprasegmental**

*Further reading:* Giegerich, 1992: ch. 7; Knowles, 1987: ch. 7; Kreidler, 1989: ch. 11; Laver, 1994: ch. 16; Lehiste, 1970: ch. 4; Roach, 1991: chs. 10–12.


**structuralism** An approach to the study of language which sees a language as a structured system. Before the twentieth century, linguists took an ***atomistic*** view of language: they saw a language as essentially a collection of individual elements, such as speech sounds, words and grammatical endings. At the beginning of the twentieth century, the Swiss linguist Ferdinand de Saussure put forward a very different view: he argued that a language is best viewed as a structured system, with each element in it defined chiefly by how it is related to other elements. In this view, which has come to be called ***structuralism***, it is the system which is the primary object of study, and not the individual elements present in that system.

Saussure's influence helped to make structuralism the dominant approach in European linguistics. In the USA, structuralist ideas were somewhat independently developed by Edward Sapir and more especially by Leonard Bloomfield. Bloomfield's successors in the 1940s and 1950s took his ideas to extremes in developing ***American structuralism***, a vigorous but excessively dogmatic approach to linguistic description which attached great importance to **distribution**. In the 1960s, Noam Chomsky and his followers rebelled against the excesses of their predecessors, and they came to use *structuralism* as a swear word to denote everything they disliked about the earlier work, but in fact Chomsky's **generative grammar** is no less structuralist than other approaches, in the original sense of the term. Indeed, virtually all serious work in linguistics in the twentieth century has been structuralist in outlook, though many contemporary linguistists continue to regard *structuralism* as a term of abuse and would not apply the term to their own work.

Structuralist ideas were eventually picked up, largely from the influential Russian linguist Roman Jakobson, by the French anthropologist Claude Lévi-Strauss, who introduced them into anthropology, from where they spread into the social sciences generally, and even into such fields as literary criticism. Quite independently, Saussure's structuralist approach was deeply influential in the development of **semiotics**.

In literary criticism, structuralism has now been largely succeeded by *post-structuralism*, which stresses the fluid nature of texts and the role of the reader in assigning content to a literary text.

*See:* **cognitive linguistics**; **generative grammar**; **linguistics**
*Further reading:* Lepschy, 1970; Malmkjær, 1991: 351–353, 436–438; Sampson, 1980: chs. 3, 5; Sturrock, 1993.

**structure**  A particular pattern which is available in a language for constructing a linguistic unit, or an instance of this. Structures can be recognized in languages at every level of analysis: phonemes combine to build morphemes, morphemes combine to build words, words combine to build phrases, phrases combine to build clauses and sentences, sentences combine to build texts, and so on. At every one of these levels, the smaller units must be combined into larger ones in particular orderly ways determined by the rules of the language, and we therefore say in each case that we are looking at an instance of a particular *structure*.

For example, the morpheme *bad* is built up from the three phonemes /b/, /æ/ and /d/, and many analysts would argue that, in fact, this is done by first combining /æ/ and /d/ into /æd/, and then adding /b/ to produce /bæd/. The adjective *happy* can take the prefix *un-* to produce the adjective *unhappy*, and this in turn can take the suffix *-ness* to produce the noun *unhappiness*. (We cannot analyse *unhappiness* as consisting instead of *un-* plus *happiness*, because *happiness* is a noun, and the rules of English word-structure do not permit *un-* to be added to a noun.) The words *little* and *girl* can be combined to construct the N-bar *little girl*, which can then take a determiner like *the* to build the noun phrase *the little girl*.

Most usually today, we apply the term **structure** both to a general pattern and to any individual instance of it, but the general pattern is sometimes called a **construction**, while an individual instance has sometimes been called a **syntagm**. The relation between the elements in a structure is a **syntagmatic relation**.

The approach to language study called **structuralism** gets its name because it emphasizes the importance of recognizing units of structure at every level, though in fact the recognition of **systems** in languages is no less important in the structuralist approach.

*See:* **structuralism**; **syntagmatic relation**; **system**

**structure–dependence**  The property of languages by which grammatical statements must be made in terms of structural units. When we describe the **syntax** of a language, we find that we never need to make any statements involving such notions as 'the second word in the sentence', 'a word ending in a vowel', 'a word of three or more syllables' or 'the first six words in the sentence'. Grammars simply do not function in terms of such notions; instead, they function in terms of purely structural units like **verb**, **noun phrase** and **auxiliary**, and we call this phenomenon *structure–dependence*.

Consider the way in which yes–no questions are constructed in English. If we mentally start with a statement, then, in order to convert it to a yes–no question, we must move the finite auxiliary out of its verb phrase and to the left of the subject noun phrase. This is so regardless of what the finite auxiliary is and regardless of whether the noun phrase and the verb phrase are small and simple or large and complex:

[*She*] [[*is*] [*dancing*]].
[*Is*] [*she*] [*dancing*]?

[*Most of our students*] [[*can*] [*do this*]].
[*Can*] [*most of our students*] [*do this*]?

[*The selection of the remaining members of the team*] [[*can't*]
    [*wait until our captain gets back*]].
[*Can't*] [*the selection of the remaining members of the team*]
    [*wait until our captain gets back*]?

In short, yes–no questions are constructed in terms of
structural units, not in terms of words, and every other
syntactic process in English and in other languages works in
the same way,

It is because of this structure-dependence that descriptions
of the syntax of a language are commonly presented in
terms of **constituent structure** and in terms of **syntactic
categories**.

*See:* **constituent structure**; **recursion**; **structure**; **syntactic
    category**
*Further reading:* Radford, 1988: 32–35.


**stylistics**    The study of the aesthetic uses of languages, particularly the use of language in literature. On the whole, the
European linguistic tradition has almost always seen the study
of the purely structural aspects of language as bound up with
the study of its aesthetic aspects; for example, in the middle
of the twentieth century, the great Russian linguist Roman
Jakobson contributed equally to theoretical linguistics and to
the critical examination of literary works.

In the English-speaking world, however, there was long a
seemingly unbridgeable gulf between linguistics and literary
criticism, and neither discipline paid any attention to the other.
In the last several decades, however, this has changed, and a
number of scholars have been applying the analytical techniques of theoretical linguistics to the elucidation of literary
works and to the examination of the aesthetic aspects of lan-

guage generally. To this discipline we now give the name **styl-istics**. A practitioner of stylistics may choose to pursue such topics as the ironic use of language in the novels of V.S. Naipaul, the sound structure of a poem by Dylan Thomas, the use of regional and social varieties of English for comic effect in Shakespeare's *Henry V*, or the use of archaisms to achieve stateliness in religious language. What sets all this apart from ordinary literary criticism is the explicit use of the concepts and analytical techniques of linguistic theory.

In the last few years the label **literary linguistics** has begun to be applied to the linguistic analysis of literature.

*See:* **structuralism**

*Further reading:* Bradford, 1997; Crystal, 1997a: ch. 12; Fabb, 1997; Fowler, 1996; Malmkjær, 1991: 438–447; Simpson, 1996; Thornborrow and Wareing, 1998; Turner, 1973.

**subcategorization** Differences in syntactic behaviour among the words in a single **part of speech**. English has a class of **verbs**, almost all of which are united by sharing certain important properties, such as being marked for **tense** and taking the ending *-ing* for certain grammatical purposes. If we didn't recognize a class of verbs, we would be unable to state a number of important generalizations. Nevertheless, not all verbs behave identically.

Consider the following frames:

(1)  *Susie will* ____ .
(2)  *Susie will* ____ *Mike.*
(3)  *Susie will* ____ *me a letter.*
(4)  *Susie will* ____ *to come.*
(5)  *Susie will* ____ *that she's ready.*
(6)  *Susie will* ____ *me that she's ready.*

Now try to fit the following verbs into each blank: *decide, tell, want, send, speak, show.* You will find that each verb fits successfully into some blanks to produce a grammatical sentence, but not into others. For example, *decide* fits only into (1), (4) and (5).

This is an instance of *subcategorization*. Even though all these words are verbs, they exhibit important differences in the structures in which they can appear, and we say that verbs are *subcategorized* accordingly. Note that the necessary subcategories all overlap considerably, and hence we cannot simply subcategorize verbs into type (1), type (2), and so on.

Subcategorization is most prominent with verbs, but other parts of speech show the same phenomenon.

*See:* **part of speech**; **syntactic category**; **syntax**
*Further reading:* Radford, 1988: 339–369.

**subordination** Any type of sentence structure in which one **clause** forms part of a larger clause. The recognition of subordination is ancient in our grammatical tradition, and any clause which is part of a larger one is a *subordinate clause*. Subordinate clauses are of several types; in the examples below, each subordinate clause is bracketed.

A *complement clause* is attached to a preceding word: *Janet suspects* [*that she is pregnant*] (a *verb-complement clause*); *Susie's announcement* [*that she was a lesbian*] *startled her parents* (a *noun-complement clause*); *Susie is happy* [*that Natalie can move in with her*] (an *adjective-complement clause*).

A *relative clause* is attached to a preceding noun, which it modifies, and always contains a **gap** somewhere inside it: *The job* [*that Susie wants e*] *involves a lot of travelling.*

An *embedded question* (or *indirect question*) is a question which is not being asked directly: *I asked them* [*if they had seen Susie*]; *Janet doesn't know* [*what she wants*].

An *adverbial clause* behaves like an **adverb** within its sentence and must be introduced by a suitable marker of subordination: [*When Susie gets here*], *we'll have dinner*; [*If you need any help*], *give me a ring*; *Susie is upset* [*because she has quarrelled with Natalie*].

Earlier grammarians took the view that a subordinate clause was not part of the clause containing it (its *matrix clause*), but today we always regard a subordinate clause as forming an integral part of its matrix clause.

*See:* **clause**; **sentence**
*Further reading:* Collins Cobuild, 1990: 342–373; Greenbaum and
  Quirk, 1990: chs. 14–15; Hurford, 1994: 232–234.

**suprasegmental**  An aspect of pronunciation whose description requires a longer sequence than a single consonant or
vowel. Though phoneticians and linguists had earlier been
aware of the importance of suprasegmental phenomena in
speech, the term *suprasegmental* was coined by the *American
structuralists* in the 1940s. It covers several rather diverse
phenomena.

A very obvious suprasegmental is **intonation**, since an intonation pattern by definition extends over a whole utterance
or a sizeable piece of an utterance. Also clearly suprasegmental is the kind of word-accent called *pitch accent*, as in Japanese
and Basque, in which an accentual pitch pattern extends over
an entire word. Less obvious is **stress**, but not only is stress a
property of a whole **syllable** but the stress level of a syllable
can only be determined by comparing it with neighbouring
syllables which have greater or lesser degrees of stress.

The tones of **tone languages** are also suprasegmental, since
not only does a tone fall on a whole syllable but tonal
differences like 'high' and 'low' can only be identified by
comparing syllables with neighbouring syllables.

The American structuralists also treated *juncture* phenomena as suprasegmental. Differences in juncture are the reason
that *night rate* does not sound like *nitrate*, or *why choose* like
*white shoes*. Since these items contain essentially the same
sequences of **segments**, the junctural differences have to be
described in terms of different juncture placement within
sequences of segments.

In most of these cases, the phonetic realization of the
suprasegmental actually extends over more than one segment,
but the key point is that, in all of them, the *description* of
the suprasegmental must involve reference to more than
one segment.

Some people use **prosody** as a synonym for *suprasegmental*,
but this is not recommended.

*See:* **intonation**; **stress**; **tone language**; **segment**
*Further reading:* Clark and Yallop, 1995: ch. 8; Crystal, 1997a: ch. 29; Ladefoged, 1993: ch. 10; Laver, 1994: part VI; Lehiste, 1970.

**surface structure**   The syntactic structure which is most obviously assignable to a particular sentence. Every sentence in every language has some kind of syntactic structure. Consider the following English example: *Susie is hard to please.* Now, while the structure assigned to this sentence may vary somewhat, depending upon the analyst and the framework used, the majority view would probably analyse it as follows: it consists of a subject noun phrase *Susie* and a predicate verb phrase *is hard to please*; the latter in turn consists of a copular verb *is* and an adjective phrase *hard to please*; the adjective phrase in turn consists of an adjective *hard* and a verb phrase *to please*. We can represent this structure schematically as follows: [*Susie*] [[*is*] [[*hard*] [*to please*]]].

Now this structure is the *surface structure* of the sentence: that is, it is the syntactic structure which we would most naturally assign to this sentence, and, in many theories of grammar, this is the *only* syntactic structure that would be assigned. However, it is obvious that the meaning of the sentence relates to this structure in a very curious way: this is really a statement about pleasing Susie, and hence, in some semantic or logical sense, *Susie* appears to be, not the subject of *is*, but rather the object of *please*.

Most frameworks would treat this fact in a strictly semantic way, but **transformational grammar** and its various descendants take a different line: they assign a **deep structure** to the sentence, a structure which is very different from the surface structure and much closer to the meaning – something along the following lines: [[NP] [[*please*] [*Susie*]]] [[*is*] [*hard*]], where 'NP' represents an unidentified subject for *please*. A good deal of grammatical machinery is then required to convert this deep structure into the required surface structure.

*See:* **deep structure**
*Further reading:* Lyons, 1991: ch. 7.

**syllable**   A fundamental but elusive unit in **phonology**. Every word consists of a sequence of some number of *syllables*, and even speakers with no knowledge of phonetics or of linguistics usually find it easy to agree on how many syllables a word contains. For example, we all agree that *girl* and *salt* contain one syllable, that *butter* and *behind* contain two, that *linguistics* and *kangaroo* contain three, that *education* and *development* contain four, and so on.

Differences in judgement usually reflect genuine differences in pronunciation. For example, *police* and *collapse* are pronounced as one syllable by some speakers but as two by others, and *library* and *medicine* are pronounced as two syllables by some but as three by others. And *temporarily* has five syllables for most Americans but only three for many Britons.

In spite of the conspicuous prominence of syllables, however, it has proved exceedingly difficult to provide an objective definition of the syllable. Attempts have been made at defining the syllable in terms of everything from muscular contractions to perceived peaks of loudness, but so far no definition has proved satisfactory.

Nevertheless, the syllable appears to be a genuinely fundamental unit in **phonology**, and many important generalizations about the sound systems of languages can be stated in terms of syllables more readily than in any other way. As a consequence, the most influential theories of phonology developed since the 1980s have generally attached great importance to syllables, and in some of them the syllable is taken as the most fundamental unit of all, in terms of which everything else is defined. (In contrast, earlier theories of phonology generally took either **phonemes** or **distinctive features** as the fundamental units.)

*See:* **phonology**; **segment**
*Further reading:* Hogg and McCully, 1987: ch. 2; Katamba, 1989: ch. 9; Lass, 1984: 248–268.

**symbolic system** An integrated set of signs, each with a conventional meaning. The notion of a *symbolic system* lies at the heart of the discipline called **semiotics**. A very simple symbolic system is the set of colours exhibited by a traffic light, each of which has a conventional but agreed significance. Only slightly more complex is the set of signals used by a cricket umpire or an American football referee to announce what has happened on the field. Yet another example is the system of stripes, bars, stars and other items worn on a military uniform to indicate rank and affiliation.

**Language** is often viewed as a paradigm case of a symbolic system, though one that is vastly more complex than these simple examples. Much of the driving force of semiotics is the belief that such socially constructed objects as myths and films can also be usefully viewed as symbolic systems, and interpreted as such in illuminating ways.

*See:* **semiotics, linguistic sign**

**synchrony** The absence of a time element in linguistic description. In the early twentieth century, the Swiss linguist Ferdinand de Saussure introduced his celebrated distinction between *synchrony* and **diachrony**. In a synchronic approach to describing a language, we focus on that language at one moment in time and describe it as we find it at that moment. This need not be the present moment: we can equally construct a description of present-day English or of Shakespeare's English. In either case, we take no interest in how the language of that moment differs from the same language at any earlier or later moment; as soon as we start paying attention to that, we are taking a diachronic approach.

*See:* **diachrony; descriptivism**

**syntactic category** Any one of the several types of grammatical unit from which the sentences of a language are constructed. The structure of a sentence is **constituent structure**, and a constituent structure is built up by combining smaller units into larger ones. These units, the ***syntactic categories***, are of several types, and they are also of different sizes.

The smallest syntactic categories are the ***lexical categories***, commonly called the **parts of speech**, such as **noun**, **verb**, **preposition** and **determiner**; there are about fifteen of these in English. Each member of a lexical category is a single word.

Much larger are ***phrasal categories***, representing the several different types of **phrase** existing in the languages, such as **noun phrase** and **verb phrase**. A typical instance of a phrasal category consists of several words, but a particular phrase may contain only one word or dozens. Most grammarians recognize only five different phrasal categories in English, though some prefer to acknowledge a larger number.

In between these two sizes are the ***intermediate categories***. The need for these is debated among grammarians, but one kind is essential: the ***N-bar***. A noun phrase like *the little girl* unquestionably consists of a determiner *the* and an N-bar *little girl*, which itself consists of the adjective *little* and the noun *girl*.

Of course, we also need the unique syntactic category **sentence**. Subordinate clauses present a few difficulties. In the sentence *Susie decided that she would go home*, the complement clause *that she would go home* is often assigned to another special syntactic category called ***S-bar***; an S-bar consists of a ***complementizer*** (here *that*; ***complementizer*** is another part of speech) plus the sentence *she would go home*.

The recognition of a suitable set of syntactic categories allows us to analyse all the sentences of a language as being built up, by means of a fairly small set of rules allowing **recursion**, from just these few categories.

*See:* **head**; **part of speech**; **phrase**; **recursion**; **subcategorization**

*Further reading:* Brown and Miller, 1991: part one.

**syntagmatic relation** The relation between any linguistic elements which are simultaneously present in a **structure**.

The concept of a ***syntagmatic relation*** was introduced in the early twentieth century by the Swiss linguist Ferdinand de Saussure. In Saussure's terminology, any kind of structural unit in a language at any level is a ***syntagm*** or ***syntagma***, a word constructed on the analogy of **paradigm**, and a syntagm consists of some set of smaller structural units, all combined according to the appropriate rules and all standing in syntagmatic relation to one another.

For example, the English phonemes /t/, /k/ and /æ/ are syntagmatically related in one way in the word /tæk/ *tack*, in a second way in /kæt/ *cat*, in a third way in /ækt/ *act*, and in a fourth way in /tækt/ *tact*. Similarly, the morphemes {*un-*}, {*happy*} and {*-ness*} are syntagmatically related in a particular way in the word *unhappiness*, and the words *the*, *little* and *girl* are syntagmatically related in the noun phrase *the little girl*. In every case, the larger unit which is composed of smaller ones is a syntagm.

A particular pattern into which a large number of individual syntagms fit is a **structure**. So, for example, the structure illustrated by *the little girl* recurs in other, similar, syntagms like *these old clothes*, *my new car* and *some dirty books*. (Today, however, we more usually apply the term ***structure*** to each particular instance of a general pattern, and avoid the word ***syntagm***.)

Syntagmatic relations contrast most obviously with **paradigmatic relations**, and this pair of terms constitutes one of Saussure's famous dichotomies.

Note that, in psycholinguistics, the term ***syntagmatic relation*** is used in a somewhat different sense, to denote the mental association between words which frequently occur together, as when a subject given *black* responds with *magic*, *tie* or *sheep*.

*See:* **distribution**; **paradigmatic relation**; **structure**

**syntax**  Sentence structure, or the branch of linguistics which studies this. The first European steps in the examination of syntax were taken by the ancient Greeks, beginning with

Aristotle, who first divided sentences into **subjects** and **predicates**. Thereafter, progress was slow, and toward the middle of the twentieth century syntax was lagging far behind **phonology** and **morphology**.

In the 1940s, the idiosyncratic American linguist Zellig Harris began developing an interesting new way of looking at syntax. A decade later, his student Noam Chomsky presented a greatly modified version of Harris's ideas, involving the introduction of **generative grammar** and of the particular variety of generative grammar called **transformational grammar**. Chomsky argued that syntax was not only tractable but the very heart of serious linguistic investigation, and he persuaded a generation of linguists that he was correct. As a result, the study of syntax became vastly more prominent than formerly; still today, many linguists of a Chomskyan persuasion see syntax as the very core of language structure, though non-Chomskyan linguists, thanks to the dramatic advances in other areas of investigation, would now see syntax as only one important area among many.

In the 1960s, the American linguist Joseph Greenberg published his pioneering work in syntactic **typology**, as a result of which another tradition of syntactic investigation, independent of Chomsky's, has grown up and flourished. Often closely linked to this typological work, but partly independent of it, is the kind of syntactic work favoured by the proponents of **functionalism**.

This recent concentration of effort upon syntactic problems has uncovered a wealth of fascinating data and led to innumerable theoretical interpretations. Here are just two examples of the many striking phenomena discovered in English.

First, consider the following four virtually identical-looking sentences:

(1) *After Lisa got up, she had a shower.*
(2) *After she got up, Lisa had a shower.*
(3) *Lisa had a shower after she got up.*
(4) *She had a shower after Lisa got up.*

In the first three of these, *she* can possibly refer to *Lisa*, but, in the fourth, it cannot.

Second, the sentence *It is easy to annoy Janet* can be readily recast as *Janet is easy to annoy*, but the similar-looking *It is inadvisable to annoy Janet* cannot be recast as *Janet is inadvisable to annoy* (*indicates ungrammaticality).

Facts like these, previously unnoticed and largely unsuspected, have provided the grist for decades of syntactic investigation and theorizing, and quite a number of different *theories of grammar* have been put forward and developed.

*See:* **recursion**; **structure–dependence grammar**; **syntactic category**

*Further reading:* Brown and Miller, 1991; Hudson, 1998; Lyons, 1968: chs. 4–6; Matthews, 1981; O'Grady *et al.*, 1996: ch. 5.


**system**   A set of competing possibilities in a language, together with the rules for choosing among them. The single greatest insight of the approach to language study called **structuralism** was the recognition that a language is best viewed as a *system* of elements, with each element being chiefly defined by its place within the system, by the way it is related to other elements. Further, the overall system of a language consists of a number of subsystems and sub-subsystems, all of which overlap in various ways.

A simple example of a system in English is our (personal) pronoun system, which consists of the items *I/me*, *we/us*, *you*, *he/him*, *she/her*, *it* and *they/them*. Whenever we need to use a pronoun, we must choose exactly one item from this system, and in many cases we must choose one of the two forms that exist. Naturally, the choice is not free: it is dependent upon other choices which are being made at the same time. This whole set of forms, together with the rules determining which one is appropriate in a given instance, constitutes our pronoun system.

Among the other systems present in English are the consonant system, the verb system, and the system of word-forming prefixes. All the items forming part of a single system stand in a **paradigmatic relation** to one another, meaning that they represent mutually exclusive choices.

*See:* **paradigmatic relation**; **structuralism**; **structure**

**systematic correspondence**    A certain type of pattern linking words in different languages. The members of a **language family** share a common ancestor – that is, they all started off long ago as nothing more than regional dialects of that ancestral language, but have diverged over time into distinct languages. One type of change is change in pronunciation, and it is characteristic of change in pronunciation that it is often highly regular: a particular sound in a particular environment tends strongly to change in the same way in a given language in every word containing it.

As a result of this, the words of related languages often exhibit a set of conspicuous patterns, each of the following general form: if word W1 in language L1 contains a sound S1 in a particular position, then word W2 of the same meaning in language L2 will contain the sound S2 in the same position. Such a pattern is a *systematic correspondence*.

Here is a simple example, from the two New Guinean languages Sinaugoro and Motu (data from Terry Crowley 1992: 107); these data are only a sample of some patterns which in fact apply to a much larger set of words:

| Sinaugoro | Motu | |
|-----------|------|------|
| tama | tama | 'father' |
| tina | sina | 'mother' |
| taŋi | tai | 'cry' |
| tui | tui | 'elbow, knee' |
| ɣita | ita | 'see' |
| ɣate | ase | 'liver' |
| mate | mase | 'die' |
| natu | natu | 'child' |
| toi | toi | 'three' |

We can easily see several systematic correspondences here which apply in all positions: Sin /m/ : Motu /m/; Sin /n/: Motu /n/; Sin /a/ : Motu /a/; Sin /ɣ/ : Motu zero; and so on. Whenever a Sinaugoro word contains one of the sounds in a correspondence, the Motu word of the same meaning contains the other one in the same position.

But Sinaugoro /t/ is more complicated: some words show the correspondence Sin /t/ : Motu /t/, while others show Sin /t/ : Motu /s/. Further examination, though, reveals that there is a clear basis for the difference: the second correspondence applies always and only when the consonant is followed by a front vowel /i/ or /e/, while the first applies in all other circumstances.

The existence of such correspondences demonstrates that the languages in question share a common ancestor (in this case, of course, a rather recent one), and these correspondences are the material to which we apply **comparative reconstruction** in order to work out the properties of the unrecorded ancestral language.

*See:* **comparative reconstruction**; **historical linguistics**; **language family**
*Further reading:* Terry Crowley, 1992: ch. 5; Trask, 1996: 202–216.


**Systemic Linguistics**   An important version of **functionalism**. In the 1930s and 1940s, the British linguist J.R. Firth began laying the groundwork for a somewhat novel social approach to language. His student Michael Halliday greatly developed Firth's ideas in distinctive directions of his own. Beginning in the 1960s with a new approach to grammatical analysis which he called *Scale-and-Category Grammar*, Halliday went on to construct an elaborate and ambitious framework which eventually came to be called *Systemic Linguistics*, or SL.

SL is an avowedly *functionalist* approach to language, and it is arguably the functionalist approach which has been most highly developed. In contrast to most other approaches, SL explicitly attempts to combine purely structural information with overtly social factors in a single integrated description. Like other functionalist frameworks, SL is deeply concerned with the *purposes* of language use. Systemicists constantly ask the following questions: What is this writer (or speaker) trying to do? What linguistic devices are available to help her (or him) to do it, and on what basis does she make her choices?

Halliday distinguishes among three rather distinctive **functions of language** (or *metafunctions*). The *ideational* (or *experiential*) *function* is the conveying of semantic content representing information about our experience of the external world (including our own minds). The *textual function* is the linking of linguistic elements to other linguistic elements, so that the various parts of a **text** can be integrated into a coherent and cohesive whole and related to the wider context of our speech or writing. The *interpersonal function* is the establishment and maintenance of social relations, including persuading other people to do things or to believe things. Systemicists stress the utility of their framework in the analysis of **texts**, an area beyond the scope of many other approaches, and they accordingly devote more attention to the treatment of texts than to the analysis of isolated sentences. Because of this preoccupation with texts, the concepts of **coherence** and **cohesion** play a central role in the framework. SL has developed an elaborate and highly distinctive system of terminology which often seems to owe little to what we can call 'mainstream' linguistics.

Halliday and his followers have recently been applying the name **Functional Grammar** to the more explicitly grammatical aspects of SL.

*See:* **coherence**; **cohesion**; **functionalism**; **text**
*Further reading:* Butler, 1985; Halliday, 1994; Thompson, 1996.

# T

**tense** The **grammatical category** which relates to time. Every language is capable of expressing limitless distinctions of time: *soon, tomorrow, next Wednesday at 2.00, 137 years ago, 138 years ago.* It is possible for a language to build a few of these time distinctions into its grammar, and a language which does so has the category of *tense*. Tense is thus the grammaticalization of time. In most tense languages, tense is marked on **verbs**, but there are exceptions.

Some languages lack tense entirely; an example is Chinese, which has nothing corresponding to the *I go/I went* contrast of English. Some tense languages distinguish only two tenses, while others have three, four, five or more; the African language Bamileke-Dschang distinguishes eleven tenses.

English has only two tenses: a *non-past* ('present') tense, mostly used for talking about present and future time, and a *past* tense, mostly used for talking about past time. English verb-forms therefore generally come in pairs, one for each tense:

*She lives in London/She lived in London.*
*She is living in London/She was living in London.*
*She has lived in London/She had lived in London.*
*She has been living in London/She had been living in London.*
*She is going to live in London/She was going to live in London.*

*She will live in London/She would live in London.*
*She can live in London/She could live in London.*

Unlike some other languages, English has no distinct future tense. Instead, we use a variety of non-past ('present') forms for expressing a range of attitudes toward future events: *I go to London tomorrow; I'm going to London tomorrow; I'm going to go to London tomorrow; I'll go to London tomorrow; I'll be going to London tomorrow; I must go to London tomorrow; I may go to London tomorrow.*

Observe that all these examples illustrate some further distinctions of importance in English grammar, but these others are not distinctions of tense. Instead, they are distinctions of **aspect** or of **modality**.

*See:* **aspect**, **modality**
*Further reading:* Comrie, 1985; Hurford, 1994: 239–242.

**text** A continuous piece of spoken or written language, especially one with a recognizable beginning and ending. Linguists have long used the word *text* very informally to denote any stretch of language they happened to be interested in. Especially since the 1960s, however, the notion of a text has acquired a theoretical status in several quarters, and the analysis of texts is now seen as a major goal of linguistic investigation. However, the conception of what constitutes a text is not everywhere the same.

For some linguists, a text is no different from a **discourse**. For others, a text is a more or less physical product, the *result* of a discourse, which itself is then seen as a process leading to the construction of a text. For still others, a text is primarily defined by its possession of an identifiable purpose, an approach which leads quickly to the classification of texts into a number of kinds differing in purpose – and, consequently, often also in their linguistic characteristics. Yet others see a text as an abstraction, with a discourse being the physical realization of a text. Finally, some linguists merely consider that a text is written while a discourse is spoken.

The analysis of texts is a prominent feature of several types of **functionalism**, and above all of **Systemic Linguistics**, in which the analysis of texts is often seen as the primary goal of linguistic investigation, with the analysis of smaller units like sentences being interpreted largely in terms of their contribution to a text. Quite independently, the approach to teaching English called **language in use** focuses strongly upon the analysis of texts, particularly those which are familiar and meaningful to students. In Europe, a particular approach called **text linguistics** has become prominent in recent decades; this lays particular emphasis on **textuality**, the defining characteristics of different types of texts.

Particularly associated with Systemic Linguistics, but also prominent in other approaches, are the two concepts of **coherence** and **cohesion**. Some linguistic approaches have recently incorporated the originally literary concept of **intertextuality**.

It should be noted that, in educational contexts, the study of texts has acquired political value. Some academics and educators reject the traditional concentration of language studies (especially English) upon the received canon of great literary works, and argue that students are better employed in examining the widest possible variety of texts, from West Indian oral poetry to television commercials, which are to be treated on much the same footing as the works of Shakespeare. Not everyone agrees.

*See:* **coherence**; **cohesion**; **intertextuality**; **Systemic Linguistics**; **text linguistics**; **textuality**
*Further reading:* Crystal, 1997a: ch. 20; Gramley and Pätzold, 1992: ch. 5; Schiffrin, 1994: ch. 10; van Peer, 1994.

**text linguistics**    A particular approach to the analysis of **texts**. *Text linguistics* is primarily a European creation, and it is especially prominent in Germany and the Netherlands. This approach focuses upon the varying purposes of different texts and upon the explicit identification of the formal linguistic properties which distinguish one type of text from another;

these properties are taken to define the **textuality** of a text. In the 1970s, a pioneering project at the University of Konstanz in Germany attempted to construct an explicit text grammar; the project was not seen as a success, and more recent investigations have been characterized by greater elaboration and sophistication.

Text linguistics makes heavy use of familiar linguistic concepts and terminology, and much work in the field consists of attempts at extending familiar types of linguistic analysis to units larger than a single sentence. Consequently, it has a great deal in common with the approach called **discourse analysis** in the English-speaking world, and some outsiders see little difference between the two. The functionalist approach called **Systemic Linguistics** shares important ideas with text linguistics, but is rather distinct in nature.

*See:* **discourse analysis**; **Systemic Linguistics**; **text**; **textuality**
*Further reading:* de Beaugrande, 1994; de Beaugrande and Dressler, 1981; Malmkjær, 1991: 461–471.

**textuality** The characteristics of a **text** which make clear what sort of text it is intended to be. A newspaper story does not resemble a scholarly monograph, and a poem is quite dissimilar to a television commercial. Each particular type of text has its own typical characteristics; when we encounter a text, we expect to see the appropriate characteristics, and recognizing those characteristics allows us to recognize quickly what sort of text we are looking at.

The identifying properties of each type of text constitute its *textuality*, or *texture*. One of the principal goals of **text linguistics** is to identify, as explicitly as possible, the distinguishing features of each type of text.

*See:* **genre**; **intertextuality**

**tone language** A language in which words can be distinguished purely by the pitch of the voice used on individual syllables. In a tone language, words consisting of identical sequences of consonants and vowels can be distinguished in pronunciation (and meaning) by the differing ways in which the pitch of the voice behaves on each syllable; these different pitch patterns are called **tones**. A tone language may have between two and eight (or, rarely, more) different tones.

Mandarin Chinese is a tone language with four tones. In Mandarin, a syllable like *shu* means nothing until it receives a tone. We thus have *shū* 'write' (with a high level tone), *shú* 'sorghum' (with a rising tone), *shù* 'technique' (with a falling tone), and *shǔ* 'category' (with a falling–rising tone).

Most Chinese words are one syllable long, but not all tone languages are like this. Margi (spoken in Nigeria) has contrasts like these: *yíná* 'to dye' (two high tones), *yìnà* 'to rinse' (two low tones), *ámà* 'husband's mother' (high–low), *àmá* 'but' (low–high).

Tones can be used for grammatical purposes. Many African languages use tones to inflect verbs, as does Kanuri (spoken in Nigeria): *lezê* 'he goes' (falling tone), *lezé* 'he is to go' (high tone), *tussê* 'he rests', *tussé* 'he is to rest'.

In a true tone language, every syllable has its own tone, which is independent of the tones on other syllables. Rather different is a language with a **pitch accent**, in which a single pitch contour is superimposed upon an entire word, and the pitch of one syllable is not independent of the pitch of other syllables. In Japanese, for example, which has two possible pitches, high (H) and low (L), all that can ever happen in a word is that the pitch may go up once and then (later) go down once. Examples: *hana* (LL) 'nose', *hana* (LH) 'flower'; *shiro* (LH) 'castle', *shiro* (HL) 'white'; *sakura* (LHH) 'cherry', *zakuro* (HLL) 'pomegranate', *kokoro* (LHL) 'heart'. Patterns like HLH, HLLH and LHLH are prohibited, and so also are HH and HHH.

*See:* **intonation**; **suprasegmental**

*Further reading:* Hyman, 1975: 212–230; Katamba, 1989: 186–208; Ladefoged, 1971: 84–88; Lehiste, 1970: ch. 3; Malmkjær, 1991: 471–477.

**topic**  That part of a sentence or utterance which the whole thing is 'about'. The division of a sentence, from the point of view of its information content, into a *topic* and a *comment* is essentially the same as the **given/new** distinction, but the notion of a *topic* has some further linguistic uses.

The topic of a sentence is that part of it which the whole sentence is about. For example, if I am advising my students as to which books they should read to learn about a particular subject, I might hold up a particular book and say *I can't recommend this book*. Here the topic is clearly *this book*: this noun phrase identifies what I'm talking about, and the rest of my utterance constitutes the comment, what I'm saying about it.

English provides us with some more explicit ways of marking something as a topic. One is *topicalization*, in which the topic is simply moved to the front of the sentence: *This book I can't recommend*. Here *this book* has been explicitly topicalized. Another device is the *as for* construction: *As for this book, I can't recommend it.*

The notion of a *topic* must be clearly distinguished from that of **focus**; even some professional linguists confuse these two.

*See:* **focus**; **given/new**
*Further reading:* Brown and Miller, 1991: ch. 20; Greenbaum and Quirk, 1990: ch. 18; Thompson, 1996: ch. 6.

**traditional grammar**  The entire body of grammatical work done in Europe and America before the rise of modern **linguistics** in the twentieth century. The European grammatical tradition began with the Greeks and was continued by the Romans, both of whom were chiefly interested in describing their own languages. The descriptive procedures and terminology they developed eventually came to be applied to modern languages like French and English, and the resulting Latin-based descriptions of English were taught in schools until at least the 1960s, since when many schools in

English-speaking countries have ceased teaching any English grammar at all.

The work of the traditional grammarians still forms the foundation of modern grammatical work, but we have introduced very many changes and extensions. We reject their insistence on **prescriptivism** as the basis of description; we recognize many more **parts of speech** than they did; we assign **constituent structure** to sentences; we have identified a large number of grammatical phenomena which they overlooked; we try to construct **generative grammars**; and we deny that there is anything special about the grammar of Latin, which is now seen as just one possible grammatical system among many.

Some contemporary work, such as the series of English grammars prepared by Randolph Quirk and his colleagues, is still noticeably traditional in orientation, but it is nonetheless strongly influenced by the advances in grammatical study achieved during the twentieth century.

*See:* **descriptivism**; **linguistics**; **prescriptivism**
*Further reading:* Lepschy, 1994; Malmkjær, 1991: 477–482; F. Palmer, 1971: ch. 2; Robins, 1997.

**transcription** A representation on paper of speech, using conventional symbols. Since conventional writing systems are almost never adequate for representing pronunciation in a fully explicit and consistent manner, phoneticians and linguists have found it necessary to invent their own systems of symbols for transcribing speech sounds, individual words and connected speech.

There are two types of transcription, and the difference is very important, though both types commonly use the **International Phonetic Alphabet**. In a *phonetic transcription*, the object is to record the physical and objectively real speech sounds in as much detail as is required for the current purpose, and two transcriptions of the same utterance may differ in the amount of detail they include. A phonetic transcription is always enclosed in square brackets. So, for example, if we take a typical pronunciation of the English word *please*, the phonetic transcription [pliz] presents only the bare minimum of phonetic information. For many purposes, we would prefer the more detailed transcription [pʰliːz], which explicitly records both the aspiration (puff of breath) following the [p] and the length of the vowel [iː]. A still more detailed version would be [pʰl̥iːz], which notes that the [l] is voiceless, because of the presence of the aspiration. If the speaker is American, we might write [pʰɫiːz], where the symbol [ɫ] explicitly indicates the typical American 'dark *l*' (an [l] pronounced with the back of the tongue raised). The amount of phonetic detail that might be included in a phonetic transcription is almost unlimited, but we normally content ourselves with recording only the information that seems relevant to our purpose. The more detail we include, the **narrower** is the transcription; the less detail we include, the **broader** is the transcription.

It is important to note that a phonetic transcription records physical reality. Hence a trained phonetician can successfully transcribe *any* piece of speech, even one in a language unknown to her (or him). She does not need to know anything about the language she is listening to; she only needs to be able to hear the speech sounds being produced and to identify them.

A *phonemic transcription* is very different. In a phonemic transcription, we do not transcribe any physical speech sounds at all. Instead, we transcribe the **phonemes** of the language we are listening to, the basic sound units of that language. But this is only possible after we have first carried out a complete phonological analysis of the language and decided what phonemes exist, which speech sounds belong to which phonemes, and what symbols we will use to represent the phonemes. It is therefore not possible to produce a phonemic transcription of a totally unfamiliar language.

A phonemic transcription is always enclosed in phoneme slashes. Since we already have a complete phonemic analysis of English, we are therefore able to provide a phonemic transcription of *please*, as soon as we agree on the phoneme symbols to be used. Naturally enough, we all prefer /p/ for the first consonant phoneme, /l/ for the second consonant phoneme, and /z/ for the last one, but there is some disagreement about the vowel: some linguists prefer to represent the vowel phoneme as /i/, but others prefer /iː/, and so *please* is phonemically either /pliz/ or /pliːz/, depending on which symbol we prefer for the vowel phoneme. (We must be consistent, of course.)

*See:* **International Phonetic Alphabet**; **phonetics**; **phonology**
*Further reading:* Ladefoged, 1993: ch. 2.

**transformational grammar**   A particular type of **generative grammar**. In the 1950s, Noam Chomsky introduced into linguistics the notion of a **generative grammar**, which has proved to be very influential. Now there are very many different types of generative grammar which can be conceived of, and Chomsky himself defined and discussed several quite different types in his early work. But, from the beginning, he himself favoured a particular type, to which he gave the name *transformational grammar*, or TG; TG has sometimes also been called *transformational generative grammar*, or TGG.

Most types of generative grammar in which anybody has ever been interested can be usefully viewed as working like this: starting with nothing, the rules of the grammar build up the structure of a sentence piece by piece, adding something at each step, until the sentence structure is complete. Crucially, once something has been added to a sentence structure, it must remain: it cannot be changed, deleted or moved to a different location.

TG is hugely different. In TG, the structure of a sentence is first built up in the manner just described, using only *context-free rules*, which are a simple type of rule widely used in other types of generative grammar. The structure which results is called the **deep structure** of the sentence. But, after this, some further rules apply. These rules are called *transformations*, and they are different in nature. Transformations have the power to change the structure which is already present in a number of ways: not only can they add new material to the structure (though only in the early versions), but they can also change material which is already present in various ways, they can move material to a different location, and they can even delete material from the structure altogether. When all the relevant transformations have finished applying, the resulting structure is the **surface structure** of the sentence. Because of the vast power of transformations, the surface structure may look extremely different from the deep structure.

TG is thus a theory of grammar which holds that a sentence typically has more than one level of structure. Apart from the structure which it obviously has on the surface, it also has an abstract underlying structure (the deep structure) which may be substantially different. The point of all this, in Chomsky's view, is that certain important generalizations about the structures of the sentences in a language may be stated far more easily in terms of abstract deep structures than otherwise; in addition, the meaning of a sentence can often be determined much more straightforwardly from its deep structure.

TG has developed through a number of versions, each succeeding the other. In his 1957 book *Syntactic Structures*, Chomsky provided only a partial sketch of a very simple type of transformational grammar. This proved to be inadequate, and, in his 1965 book *Aspects of the Theory of Syntax*, Chomsky proposed a very different, and much more complete, version. This version is variously known as the ***Aspects model*** or as the ***Standard Theory***. All textbooks of TG published before 1980 (and a few of those published more recently) present what is essentially the Standard Theory, sometimes with a few additions from later work.

Around 1968 the Standard Theory came under attack from a group of younger linguists who hoped to equate deep structure, previously a purely syntactic level of representation, with the semantic structure of a sentence (its meaning). This programme, called ***Generative Semantics***, led to the positing of ever more abstract underlying structures for sentences; it proved unworkable, and it finally collapsed. Around the same time, two mathematical linguists demonstrated that standard TG was so enormously powerful that it could, in principle, describe anything which could be described at all – a potentially catastrophic result, since the whole point of a theory of grammar is to tell us what is possible in languages and what is not possible. Yet these **Peters–Ritchie results** suggested that TG was placing no constraints at all on what the grammar of a human language could be like.

Chomsky responded to all this in the early 1970s by introducing a number of changes to his framework; the result became known as the **Extended Standard Theory**, or EST. By the late 1970s further changes had led to a radically different version dubbed the **Revised Extended Standard Theory**, or REST. Among the major innovations of the REST were the introduction of **traces**, invisible flags marking the former positions of elements which had been moved, a reduction in the number of distinct transformations from dozens to just two, and a switch of attention away from the transformations themselves to the **constraints** which applied to them.

But Chomsky continued to develop his ideas, and in 1981 he published *Lectures on Government and Binding*; this book swept away much of the apparatus of the earlier transformational theories in favour of a dramatically different, and far more complex, approach called **Government–and–Binding Theory**, or GB. GB retains exactly one transformation, and, in spite of the obvious continuity between the new framework and its predecessors, the name 'transformational grammar' is not usually applied to GB or to its even more recent successor, the **Minimalist Programme**. Hence, for purposes of linguistic research, transformational grammar may now be regarded as dead, though its influence has been enormous, and its successors are maximally prominent.

*See:* **derivation** (sense 2); **generative grammar**; **Government-and-Binding Theory**

*Further reading:* Grinder and Elgin, 1973; Lyons, 1991: chs. 7–8; Malmkjær, 1991: 482–497.

**transitivity** The manner in which a **verb** is related to the **noun phrases** in its clause. Grammarians have been aware of differences in transitivity since ancient times, though in the twentieth century we have become aware that transitivity is a more complex matter than had previously been thought.

We may begin by noting a fundamental difference between two types of clause (or sentence). In a prototypical *intransitive* construction, the (intransitive) verb has a subject but no object: *Susie smiled*; *Susie is vacationing in Bermuda*. Here it would make no sense to ask 'What did Susie smile?' or 'What is Susie vacationing?' In a prototypical *transitive* construction, the (transitive) verb has both a subject and an object; the subject represents an agent instigating the action, and the object represents a patient affected by the action: *Susie slapped Dave*; *Susie is ironing a skirt*.

However, in English and in other languages, these two constructions are also used to express states of affairs which are less than prototypical. For example, *Susie smokes* and *Susie is eating* are clearly intransitive, and yet here it *does* make sense to ask 'What does Susie smoke?' or 'What is Susie eating?' In some sense, the verbs *smoke* and *eat* are really transitive, but we do not bother here to identify the object (what is smoked or eaten), because it is obvious or unimportant. Such an intransitive construction is sometimes called an *absolute transitive* construction.

Consider the following sentences, all of which are transitive in form: *Susie bought a car*; *Susie speaks French*; *Susie understands our problem*; *Susie weighs 110 pounds*. These illustrate steadily decreasing levels of prototypical transitivity: *Susie* is less and less of an agent, and the object is less and less affected by the action – indeed, the last two don't really involve any action at all.

In short, the world provides a very wide range of possible relations between entities, but English, like many other languages, provides only two grammatical constructions, and every possibility must be squeezed into one or the other of the two constructions.

Unlike some other languages, English exhibits a special type of transitive construction in which the verb takes *two* objects. Examples of this *ditransitive* construction are *Susie gave Natalie a kiss* and *Susie showed me her new skirt*. And, like many other languages, English also has a special type of intransitive construction in which the verb is followed by a noun phrase which does not behave like an object, as in *Susie is our regional manager* and *Susie has become a mother*.

Within **Systemic Linguistics**, the notion of transitivity has been greatly extended and generalized; here the term is understood as denoting the kind of activity or process expressed by a sentence, the number of participants involved and the manner in which they are involved.

*See:* **verb**

*Further reading:* Collins Cobuild, 1990: 137–171; Halliday, 1994, ch. 5; Kilby, 1984: ch. 2; Thompson, 1996.

**tree**  A particular type of graphical representation of the structure of a sentence. Most linguists believe that the structure of any sentence is typically a **constituent structure**, in which the sentence consists of some pieces, and each piece consists of some smaller pieces, and so on, down to the smallest pieces; moreover, each piece belongs to some particular **syntactic category**. This kind of structure can be vividly illustrated by a graphical device called a *tree*.

Consider the sentence *The little girl washed her doll*. The tree overleaf illustrates its structure.

Every *branch* of the tree represents a single *constituent* of the sentence, and every constituent, or *node*, is labelled with a *node label* explaining to which syntactic category it belongs. These standard abbreviations have the following meanings: S = Sentence; NP = Noun Phrase; VP = Verb Phrase; Det = Determiner; N' = N-bar; V = Verb; AP = Adjective Phrase; A = Adjective; N = Noun. A tree of this sort may also be called a *tree structure*, a *tree diagram* or a *phrase marker*.

The precise nature of the tree drawn depends to some extent on the particular grammatical framework being used.

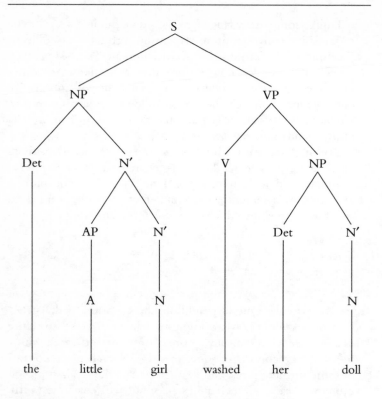

The tree shown above would be more or less the tree preferred by most linguists, but the proponents of certain frameworks, most notably the Chomskyan framework called **Government-and-Binding Theory**, would draw a much more elaborate tree involving a number of abstract nodes containing no overt material; the Chomskyans would also regard the tree as strictly representing only the **surface structure** of the sentence, which might have a significantly different **deep structure**, also representable as a tree.

*See:* **constituent structure; phrase-structure grammar; surface structure**

**turn-taking**   That aspect of conversational structure by which the identity of the speaker changes from time to time. In our conventional idea of a conversation, we expect the floor to pass from one individual to another in an orderly manner: one person speaks while the others remain silent, and then the speaker falls silent and another person takes the floor. What is interesting about this is that there appear to be clear rules determining when and how the floor is handed over from one person to another: if there were not, a conversation would be merely a noisy jumble of several people trying to speak at once.

It was the American sociologist Harvey Sacks and his colleagues who first drew attention, in the 1970s, to the importance of turn-taking and the rules governing it. However, these rules are by no means easy to discover, and sociolinguists have in recent years devoted a good deal of study to trying to elucidate them. Moreover, it seems clear that very young children do not understand the concept of turn-taking, and specialists in **language acquisition** are therefore curious to find out how an understanding of turn-taking is acquired.

An interesting point is that explicit turn-taking is perhaps more typical of conversations between men. Because of the more cooperative nature of conversations between women, overt turn-taking is less prominent among women; for example, it is more usual for a woman to finish someone else's utterance for her than it is for a man to do the same.

*See:* **communicative competence**; **ethnography of speaking**; **sex differences in language**
*Further reading:* Coates, 1996; Duranti, 1997: 247–263.

**typology**   The classification of languages according to their structural features. One way of classifying languages is according to the **genetic relationships** among them; that is, according to their historical origin. However, we can also classify languages according to the kinds of structures they exhibit. Such a classification is *typological*, and a typological classification is, in principle, entirely independent of the histories of the languages involved – though languages which are genetically rather closely related, naturally, are often also very similar typologically.

In principle, we might pick on virtually any structural feature and use it as the basis of a classification. For example, we could divide languages into those in which the word for a canine animal is [dɔg] and those in which it isn't. (The first group here would contain exactly two known languages: English and the Australian language Mbabaram.) But such a classification would be pointless, since it wouldn't lead anywhere.

The only typological classifications which are of interest are those which are *fruitful*. By this we mean that the languages in each category should turn out to have other features in common, features which were not used to set up the classification in the first place.

For example, we might classify languages into those which have **tones** (like Chinese and Yoruba) and those which don't (like English and Japanese). But this isn't very fruitful, since neither the tone languages nor the non-tone languages turn out to have much of anything else in common, apart perhaps from an interesting geographical distribution, with tone languages concentrated in east Asia and west Africa.

Another possibility is to classify languages according to their **morphology**, or word-structure. In the early nineteenth century, Wilhelm von Humboldt tried this. He classified languages into three types: *isolating* (a word typically consists only of a single morpheme, as in Vietnamese or classical Chinese), *agglutinating* (a word typically consists of a neat linear sequence of morphemes, all clearly recognizable, as in Turkish or Swahili), and *inflecting* (a word typically consists of several morphemes which are tangled up together in a messy way and cannot easily be separated, as in Latin or Russian). While famous, and possibly descriptively useful, this classification too has failed to be very fruitful, though it was later developed further by Edward Sapir, who proposed several numerical indices for characterizing word structure in some detail.

But the most celebrated and fruitful of all typological classifications has proved to be one in terms of **basic word order**. Proposed by Joseph Greenberg in 1963 and more recently developed by John Hawkins and others, word-order typology has revealed a number of striking and previously unsuspected correlations. For example, a language with SOV order is highly likely to have modifiers that precede their head nouns, auxiliaries that follow their main verbs, postpositions instead of prepositions, and a rich case system for nouns. A VSO language, in contrast, usually has modifiers that follows their nouns, auxiliaries that precede their verbs, prepositions, and no cases.

*See:* **basic word order**; **morphology**; **universal**
*Further reading:* Comrie, 1989; Croft, 1990; Crystal, 1997a: ch. 14;
  J. Hawkins, 1983; Horne, 1966; Whaley, 1997.

**universal** A statement which is true of all languages. Investigators of the past, such as the eighteenth-century German
philosopher Wilhelm von Humboldt, were sometimes interested in searching for universal properties of language. But
the modern interest in the subject was really touched off
by the American linguist Joseph Greenberg in the 1960s.
Since Greenberg's pioneering work, which led to a major
project based at Stanford University, a number of other
linguists have thrown themselves into the search for universals of language.

A separate strand of investigation was opened up around
the same time by the American linguist Noam Chomsky,
who proposed a search for **universal grammar**. As a result,
we now distinguish between *formal universals* – universal
constraints upon the form the grammar of any language can
take, and usually stated at a high level of abstraction within
some particular theory of grammar – and *substantive universals* – statements about the linguistic objects which can or
cannot be present in languages and about their behaviour.

Here are a few substantive universals which have so
far stood up well: every language distinguishes nouns and
verbs; every language distinguishes three persons; every
language has at least three vowels (the Caucasian language
Kabardian is a possible exception to this last one, with perhaps
only two vowels).

A *near-universal* is a statement which has only a very few exceptions. Here is an example: every language has at least one nasal consonant. This is almost true, but there are a couple of exceptions, which therefore become intriguing.

A particularly rewarding approach has been the identification of *implicational universals*, which have the form 'if a language has property P, then it must also have property Q'. Pioneered by Greenberg, this approach has been particularly developed by John Hawkins. An example: if a language has front rounded vowels, then it also has back rounded vowels.

The search for universals may sometimes lead to a **typology**. If we contemplate a conceivably universal property P, and we then find that a number of languages lack P, we may be able to set up a typological classification of P-languages versus non-P-languages. Of course, like any typology, this one will only be interesting if it turns out that the languages in each group fairly consistently have *other* properties in common besides P or not-P.

*See:* **typology**; **universal grammar**

*Further reading:* Comrie, 1989; Croft, 1990; Crystal, 1997a: ch. 14; Greenberg, 1963; J. Hawkins, 1983.


**universal grammar**  The grammatical properties shared by all human languages. When the American linguist Noam Chomsky introduced his **innateness hypothesis** in the 1960s, he was arguing that important parts of the structure of human languages are built into our brains at birth. Since about 1980, Chomsky has been elaborating his position and arguing that certain fundamental principles for constructing sentences can be found in all languages and must be part of our genetic endowment, present from birth. These principles he collectively terms *universal grammar*.

Naturally, Chomsky attempts to formulate these principles within his own theoretical framework, although that framework has changed dramatically over the years. The principles are necessarily rather abstract, having to do with things like how far apart two linguistic elements can be within a sentence when they are linked in some way.

Chomsky and his followers are convinced that such principles genuinely exist, and much of their work has been devoted to uncovering them. But this has proved to be difficult: proposed principles are endlessly re-formulated to cope with recalcitrant data, and a number of apparent counterexamples are dealt with by appealing to various theoretical gadgets which allow the principles to be violated in certain circumstances. Critics are often deeply suspicious of these seemingly *ad hoc* manoeuvres, and some of them doubt whether the principles of universal grammar are really there at all: are they perhaps no more than an article of faith?

*See:* **Government–and–Binding Theory**
*Further reading:* Cook, 1996: ch. 1.

**usage**   The collective speaking and writing habits of a particular group of people, or a particular one of these habits. English, like any language, is far from being completely uniform. In particular, certain words, spellings, pronunciations, meanings and grammatical forms are not commonly found everywhere, but are typical only of certain places, certain professions or certain styles. Consequently, a careful description of English must provide this information, and good dictionaries of English regularly do this. Dictionaries routinely label certain forms with annotations such as (for geography) *Australian, Scots, chiefly American,* (for technical terms in various professions) *mathematics, botany, nautical, grammar,* and (for style) *slang, taboo, archaic, informal.* Such **usage labels** indicate that a particular usage is only appropriate in some particular context, and would be unexpected or out of place elsewhere.

It should be stressed that most items marked with such usage labels are no less a part of English than other items, and it is a misunderstanding to conclude that, say, slang terms or four-letter words are not 'real English'. But archaic words are something of a special case. These are words which have dropped out of use and no longer form a part of the modern language, except perhaps in deliberately archaic contexts like religious language, and dictionaries sometimes include them purely as a convenience to users who are trying to read texts written centuries ago. For example, because of the importance we attach to the works of Shakespeare, some dictionaries make a point of including every single word and word-meaning found in Shakespeare, even if these are found nowhere else at all.

The application of usage labels is a natural part of the approach we call **descriptivism**: describing the facts of a language as they appear to exist.

*See:* **descriptivism**
*Further reading:* Crystal, 1995: ch. 12.


**utterance**   A particular piece of **speech** produced by a particular individual on a particular occasion. In linguistics, a **sentence** is an abstract linguistic object forming one part of the total expressive resources of a given language. When we speak, therefore, we do not strictly produce sentences: instead, we produce *utterances*. An utterance is a single piece of speech marked off as a unit in some way; for example, by pauses and **intonation**.

There is only one English sentence of the form *What's for dinner?* But, every time you say *What's for dinner?*, you are producing a different utterance. Each one of these utterances may differ noticeably from others: it may be faster or slower, louder or softer; one may be cheerful or eager, while another may be bored or suspicious. But every one of these utterances corresponds to the same English sentence.

Moreover, an utterance need not correspond to a sentence at all. Consider the following exchange. Mike: *Where's Susie?* Sarah: *In the library*. Here Mike's utterance corresponds to an English sentence, but Sarah's response does not: there is no English sentence of the form *In the library (as the asterisk indicates). Of course, Sarah's response is perfectly normal: it's just that not all of our utterances correspond to sentences.

Instead, some of them correspond only to *fragments* of sentences.

Even more dramatically, we frequently produce utterances which are interrupted or broken off. Examples: *Mike, would you get me . . . oh, never mind; I'll get it myself; I was just looking for the . . . um . . .* [tails off into silence]. These are still utterances, but obviously they do not correspond to any sentences.

*See:* **sentence**, **speech**

**variation** The existence of observable differences in the way a language is used in a speech community. It is a commonplace observation that a single language is not used in a totally homogeneous manner within a single community. Stockbrokers do not speak like plumbers; men do not speak like women; older people do not speak like younger people. Moreover, even the speech of a single person is not homogeneous: you don't speak in the same way when you're chatting to friends in a bar and when you're being interviewed for a job, and even in a single context you might say *telephone* or *I got cheated* one moment but *phone* or *I got ripped off* the next.

This *variation* was long regarded by most linguists as no more than a collection of tiresome details getting in the way of good descriptions, as something to be swept under the carpet and forgotten about. But times have changed.

In the 1960s, the sociolinguists, led by the American William Labov, began to make variation a central object of investigation, and the result has been a revolution in linguistics: we now realize that variation, far from being peripheral and inconsequential, is a vital part of ordinary linguistic behaviour.

To begin with, variation often shows strong correlations with social variables like social class and sex, and the **social stratification of language** is now a prominent feature of sociolinguistic investigations. Further, the introduction of the **quantitative approach** to language description has revealed important patterns of linguistic behaviour which were previously invisible. The concept of a sociolinguistic *variable* has become central to the description of speech. A variable is some point of usage for which two or more competing forms are available in a community, with speakers showing interesting and significant differences in the frequency with which they use one or another of these competing forms.

Furthermore, it has been discovered that variation is typically the vehicle of **language change**, and as a result a satisfactory resolution has finally been obtained for the **Saussurean paradox**.

*See:* **quantitative method**; **Saussurean paradox**; **social stratification of language**; **sociolinguistics**

*Further reading:* Chambers, 1995; Holmes, 1992: chs. 6–14; Hudson, 1996: ch. 5.


**verb** The **part of speech** which includes words like *go*, *see*, *understand* and *seem*. The class of *verbs* is universal: no language has ever been discovered which lacked a distinct class of verbs. The most prototypical verbs denote actions performed by an agent, such as *run*, *sing*, *throw*, *hit* and *give*. But many other items are verbs even though they have less typical meanings, such as *die*, *sleep*, *believe*, *understand*, *elapse*, *ensue*, *become*, *seem*, *have* and *be*. The English **auxiliaries**, like *must* and *should*, are also usually classed as verbs, though a few linguists disagree here.

What unites the class of verbs is their grammatical behaviour. For example, verbs in English and in many other languages are marked for **tense**: *Susie drinks brandy* versus *Susie drank brandy*. Verbs also frequently exhibit **agreement**, though English has only a tiny amount of this, as in *Susie smokes* versus *Susie and Janet smoke*.

But the most central characteristic of a verb is the requirement that it must be accompanied by one or more **noun phrases**, its *arguments*, in a grammatical sentence. For example, *smile* and *smoke* take only one argument (*Susie smiled*; *Susie smokes*); *buy* and *kiss* require two (*Susie bought a car*; *Susie kissed Natalie*); and *give* and *show* require three (*Susie gave me this book*; *Susie showed Mike her new car*). A very few verbs, though, are unusual, such as *rain* and *seem*: *It's raining*; *It seems that Susie is away*.

These differences in grammatical behaviour illustrate **sub-categorization**, and they involve differences in **transitivity**.

*See:* **subcategorization**; **tense**; **transitivity**
*Further reading:* Greenbaum and Quirk, 1990: ch. 3; Hurford, 1994: 244–246.


**verb phrase**   A unit of sentence structure consisting of a **verb** and the other elements closely linked to it. Traditional grammarians divided a typical sentence into two parts: a *subject* and a *predicate*. In our modern elaboration of this, the **syntactic category** which acts as a subject is a **noun phrase**, while the category acting as a predicate is a **verb phrase**. A verb phrase always contains a verb, and it usually contains some other material closely linked to that verb.

Here are some examples, with the verb phrases serving as predicates bracketed: *Susie [smokes]*; *Susie's sister [has a new girlfriend]*; *The rest of us [strolled down to the pub for a drink]*.

A verb phrase need not serve as a predicate. In the following examples, the bracketed verb phrases are doing something different: *[Smoking forty cigarettes a day] is bad for your health*; *[Needing some legal advice], Susie rang her lawyer*; *Susie has decided [to buy a new car]*.

When a sentence contains an **auxiliary**, linguists differ in their analyses. For most linguists, the sentence *Susie has finished her dinner* contains two verb phrases, a smaller one inside a larger one, as follows: *Susie [has [finished her dinner]]*. Others, though, would recognize only one verb phrase: either *Susie [has finished her dinner]* or *Susie has [finished her dinner]*, with the auxiliary excluded from the verb phrase in this last analysis.

With multiple auxiliaries, things become more complicated. Most linguists would analyse *Susie [has [been [smoking a lot]]]* as containing three verb phrases, as shown. The first dissenting view would again recognize only one, as in *Susie [has been smoking a lot]*, while the other has a serious problem, possibly to be resolved as *Susie [has been] [smoking a lot]*.

*See:* **syntactic category**; **predicate, verb**
*Further reading:* Gramley and Pätzold, 1992: 139–161; Greenbaum and Quirk, 1990: ch. 4.


**vernacular** The ordinary, everyday speech of a particular community. The term *vernacular* is most commonly contrasted with **standard language**. The vernacular speech of a particular community is the ordinary speech used by the people in a particular community, such as Chicago, Liverpool or Sydney, when this is noticeably different from the standard form of the language.

Especially where European languages were concerned, the linguists of the past normally concentrated on the standard forms of languages. Non-standard vernacular forms were silently ignored, excepting only in the study of regional **dialects**, for which the speech of elderly rural speakers was considered most appropriate; at the same time, the speech of younger speakers or of urban speakers was similarly ignored.

Interest in vernacular forms developed only slowly during the twentieth century, but it became increasingly prominent with the rise of **sociolinguistics** in the 1960s. Today, there is intense interest in vernacular forms of speech, which are now seen as every bit as worthy of study as standard varieties of languages. Most prominent so far is the study of vernacular forms of English, for which the British sociolinguists Jim and Lesley Milroy have recently coined the slightly facetious term *real English*, partly in recognition of the observation that certain forms and usages absent from standard English, such as *he don't*, are extremely widespread in vernacular forms of English almost everywhere.

*See:* **standard language**
*Further reading:* Cheshire and Stein, 1997; Milroy and Milroy, 1993.

**vocal tract**  The part of our body through which air passes during speech. The vocal tract runs from the lungs up through the trachea (or windpipe), through the pharynx (the space at the back of the mouth), and there it divides into the oral cavity (the space inside the mouth) and the nasal cavity; it reaches the outside world at the lips and at the nostrils. As a general rule, during speech air flows upwards and outwards through the vocal tract, though in certain less usual **airstream mechanisms** something different happens.

In the throat, the vocal tract passes through a complex structure called the *larynx*; within the larynx is an opening called the *glottis*, which can be opened wide to allow air to pass through freely, closed tight to block the flow of air, or closed loosely. In this last case, two bands of tissue called the *vocal folds* – between which the glottis is located – undergo vibration, and this produces **voicing**.

Between the oral cavity and the nasal cavity is a hinged flap of tissue called the *velum* (or 'soft palate'); when the velum is raised, the nasal cavity is closed off, and no air can flow through it, but, when the velum is lowered, air can flow out through the nose.

Within the oral cavity, the size and shape of the vocal tract can be greatly varied, by raising or lowering the jaw, by moving the tongue around, and by altering the position of the lips. Whenever these movements are such as to greatly obstruct the flow of air, the resulting sound is a **consonant**; when the obstruction is minimal, the result is a **vowel**.

*See:* **airstream mechanism**; **phonetics**; **voicing**
*Further reading:* Ashby, 1995; Clark and Yallop, 1995: ch. 2; Crystal, 1997a: ch. 22; Denes and Pinson, 1993: ch. 4.


**voice**  The **grammatical category** governing the way the subject of a sentence is related to the action of the verb. English has only a two-way distinction of voice. In the *active voice*, the subject of the sentence is typically the entity performing the action, as in *Tamerlane imprisoned Sultan Bayezit*. In the *passive voice*, the subject is instead the entity undergoing the action, as in *Sultan Bayezit was imprisoned by Tamerlane*, or in *Sultan Bayezit was imprisoned*. The first is called the **long passive**, or **passive-with-agent**; the second is the **short passive**.

In English, the active voice is **unmarked** (see **markedness**): it is grammatically simpler and far more frequent in speech. The passive voice is **marked**, and it is most typically used either to make the entity undergoing the action the centre of attention, or to remove the entity performing the action (the **agent**) from the centre of attention, and possibly to remove it from the sentence altogether. For example, we write *Uranium was discovered in 1789, but its importance was not recognized before the middle of the twentieth century.* Here the dates are far more important than the name of the discoverer, and identifying the people who failed to recognize the importance of uranium would be pointless, since these people included everybody.

Not all languages have a contrast between active and passive voices. But some other languages have additional voices, allowing the subject of the sentence to be not only the performer of the action or the recipient of the action, but also the instrument with which the action is performed, or the place in which the action is done.

*See:* **verb**

*Further reading:* Greenbaum and Quirk, 1990: 44–46; Hurford, 1994: 6–8, 154–157; Klaiman, 1991; F. Palmer, 1971: section 2.5.

**voicing** Vibration of the vocal folds. The vocal folds (or vocal cords) are two movable masses of tissue in the larynx (the voice box). They can be brought close together so that they vibrate all along their length as air flows up from the lungs and into the pharynx, mouth and nose. This vibration is **voicing**, and any speech sound which is produced with such vibration is **voiced**. Examples of voiced sounds are [a], [w], [n], [l], [z], [b] and [dʒ]. If you put your fingers to your throat while pronouncing one of these, you can feel the vibration.

If the vocal folds are moved farther apart, they cannot vibrate. A speech sound produced without vibration is **voiceless**. Examples of voiceless sounds are [f], [s], [p], [k], [h] and [ʧ]. The glottal stop, [ʔ], is also voiceless, but for a different reason: here the vocal folds are pressed so tightly together that no air can flow through them and hence no vibration occurs.

The vocal folds can also behave in more complicated ways, producing several complex **phonation types** in addition to voicing and voicelessness.

Note that the term *voicing* is also applied to something else: to a change in pronunciation in which a formerly voiceless sound becomes voiced. For example, the Spanish phoneme /s/ is normally a voiceless sound [s], but in certain circumstances it becomes a voiced sound [z], as in *mismo* 'same' (in standard European pronunciation, however, not all speakers do this).

*See:* **consonant**; **phonation type**
*Further reading:* Catford, 1988: ch. 3; Laver, 1994: ch. 7.


**vowel**  A **speech sound** produced with no obstruction of the airstream. From the point of view of **phonetics**, speech sounds may be conveniently divided into two types: those which are produced with a substantial obstruction of the airstream and those which are not. The first are **consonants**, the second *vowels*.

If you pronounce a few vowels, such as [a], [i] and [u], you will find that the flow of air through your **vocal tract** is nowhere impeded. What makes one vowel sound different from another is the size and shape of the space within your mouth: the jaw is higher or lower, the tongue is higher or lower, either the front or the back of the tongue may be raised, and the lips may be rounded or spread. These variations affect the way in which the air in the mouth resonates, and they are responsible for the different qualities of the vowels.

Certain speech sounds which are strictly vowels are commonly treated as consonants, for a reason to be explained below. For example, the English *y*-sound, as in *yes* and *yard*, whose phonetic symbol is [j], is really nothing but a very brief version of the vowel [i], as in *see*, and the [w] of *weed* and *war* is likewise only a brief version of the vowel [u], as in *moon*. Moreover, for most (not all) English-speakers, the /r/ at the beginning of *red* is really only a slightly odd vowel pronounced with some part of the tongue raised. Yet all of these are generally classed as consonants.

The reason for this is that there is a second way of defining vowels and consonants, one which gives different results from the first. This second approach is the one preferred in **phonology**, in which we are more concerned with the way sounds behave than with their phonetic nature. And the point is that the sounds just mentioned, even though they are phonetically vowels, *behave* like consonants in English.

A **syllable** always contains a ***peak of sonority***, a part which is louder and more sonorous than the rest, and in most languages (including English), this peak must be a vowel. In the majority of syllables, this vowel is preceded and/or followed by some number of consonants. Usually these consonants are consonants by any definition, as in *key* /kiː/, *eat* /iːt/, *sat* /sæt/, *slap* /slæp/ and *fleeced* /fliːst/. However, the sounds /j/, /w/ and /r/ pattern like consonants, not like vowels, as in *yes* /jes/, *wet* /wet/ and *red* /red/, and consequently they are classed as consonants, in spite of their phonetic nature.

When you come across the word ***vowel***, therefore, you must check to see if it is being used in the phonetic sense or in the phonological sense.

*See:* **consonant**; **speech sound**; **syllable**
*Further reading:* Ladefoged, 1993: ch. 4; Ladefoged and Maddieson, 1996: ch. 9; Laver, 1994: ch. 10.

**well-formedness**  The status of a linguistic form in a language which conforms to the rules of that language. Well-formedness is a central concept in the analytical study of language, and it can be recognized at several different levels of analysis.

At the level of **phonology**, it is clear that *brick* is a well-formed English word, consisting of a permissible sequence of English consonants and vowels. So is *blick*, even though no such word happens to exist: this word *could* exist, since it obeys all the rules. But *bnick* is not well-formed, since the rules of English do not permit a word to begin with the sequence /bn-/. Even a real word may be ill-formed: the French word **genre** is well-formed in French, but not in English, and English-speakers must either struggle to give it a French-style pronunciation, or simply change the pronunciation to conform to the rules of English, producing something that sounds like *jonra* or *jonner*. Even *sphere* is arguably not well-formed, since English does not normally allow a word to begin with the sequence /sf-/: nobody would name a new detergent *Sfizz*.

At the level of **morphology**, words like *unhappiness* and *existentialism* are well-formed, since they obey all the rules for combining **morphemes** into words, but things like *happy-un-ness* and *exist-al-ism-ence* are not, since they violate these same rules. Even though they follow the regular rules for making plurals, the forms *womans* and *childs* are not well-formed, since *woman* and *child* happen to be subject to special rules that require their plurals to be *women* and *children*.

At the level of **syntax**, *There's a spider on the bed* is well-formed, but *Bed the on spider a there's* is anything but well-formed, since it violates the rules of English word–order. Similarly, *Susie has written a letter* is well-formed, but *Susie has writing a letter* is not, since it violates a rule of English syntax. Syntactic well-formedness is often called *grammaticality*.

At the level of **semantics**, there are also rules for combining meanings. For example, the phrase *a tall woman* is semantically well-formed, while *a female woman* is somewhat anomalous, since the meaning of *female* is already present in the meaning of *woman*, and *a valid woman* is virtually impossible to interpret sensibly. *Jezebel killed Ahab, but Ahab didn't die* is semantically anomalous, assuming only one Ahab is involved, since *Ahab died* is an integral part of the meaning of *killed Ahab*.

At the level of **pragmatics** and **discourse**, some utterances and exchanges are well-formed while others are not. In reply to the question *Is Susie coming to Mike's party on Saturday?*, the response *I don't think so* is obviously well-formed, and the response *Natalie wants to go to a concert* might be well-formed in certain circumstances (for example, if Natalie is Susie's girlfriend), but the response *Susie used to be that little girl in the pizza commercial* would probably not be well-formed in any circumstances.

Anything which is not well-formed is *ill-formed*, or sometimes *anomalous*. A very great deal of work in linguistics consists of identifying the rules governing well-formedness at all levels of analysis.

*See:* **rule**; **structure**

**word**   A linguistic unit typically larger than a **morpheme** but smaller than a **phrase**. The term *word* might seem familiar and straightforward enough, but in fact words can be defined in at least four different ways, and these ways are not equivalent at all.

An **orthographic word** is something written with white spaces at both ends but no white space in the middle. Orthographic words are of minimal linguistic interest.

A **phonological word** is something pronounced as a single unit.

A **lexical item**, or **lexeme**, is a dictionary word, an item which you would expect to find having its own entry in a dictionary.

A **grammatical word–form** (GWF) (or **morphosyntactic word**) is any one of the several forms which a lexical item may assume for grammatical purposes.

Let's look at some examples. The item *ice cream* is two orthographic words, but a single phonological word (it's pronounced as a unit), a single lexical item (it's entered in the dictionary), and a single GWF (indeed, it hardly has another form, unless you think the plural *ices cream* is good English).

The singular *dog* and the plural *dogs* are each a single orthographic word, a single phonological word, and a single GWF, but they both represent the same lexical item (they would only get one entry in the dictionary). The same is true of *take*, *takes*, *took*, *taken* and *taking*: five orthographic words, five phonological words, five GWFs (at least), but only one lexical item. The two lexical items here would be entered in the dictionary as *dog* and *take*; these are the **citation forms** of these lexical items, the forms we use in naming them or talking about them.

The contraction *hasn't* is a single orthographic word and a single phonological word, but it's two lexical items (*have* and *not*), and two GWFs (*has* and *not*). The phrasal verb *make up* (as in *She made up her face*) is two orthographic words, two phonological words, but only one lexical item (because of its unpredictable meaning, it must be entered separately in the dictionary). And it has several GWFs: *make up*, *makes up*, *made up*, *making up*. The very different sense of *make up* illustrated by *She made up a story* would be regarded by most linguists as a different lexical item from the preceding one (a separate dictionary entry is required), but this lexical item exhibits the same orthographic, phonological and grammatical forms as the first.

Consequently, when you are talking about words, it is essential to specify exactly which sense you have in mind, and it may be preferable to use one of the more specific labels.

The study of words is *lexicology*.

*See:* **part of speech**
*Further reading:* Katamba, 1994: ch. 2; Matthews, 1991: ch. 2.

**word-formation**  The process of constructing new words from existing materials. There are many ways of constructing new words, and English uses almost all of them.

In *compounding*, two (or more) existing words are simply combined. There are several different patterns available for doing this, as in *blackboard, redneck, overthrow, olive green, scare-crow* and *forget-me-not*. Sometimes an **affix** is also present, as in *blue-eyed* and *flat-earther*.

In **derivation**, affixes are added to an existing word, as in *prehistory, rewrite, unsafe, washable, prohibition* and *finalize*. Multiple affixes are possible, as in *misdirection, illegitimacy, transformational* and *existentialism*.

In *clipping*, a piece is removed from a longer word, as with *bra, gym, flu, phone* and *cello*. In *blending*, pieces of two words are combined, as in *smog* (*smoke* plus *fog*). In *back-formation*, a new word is extracted from a longer word that appears to contain an affix but historically does not, as with *pea* from earlier *pease* and *edit* from earlier *editor*. *Reanalysis* involves changing the structure assigned to a word and extracting a piece that formerly was not a part of it, as when *hamburger* (*Hamburg* + *-er*) was reanalysed as *ham* + *-burger*, yielding the *-burger* now used in *cheeseburger* and *vegeburger*.

Combining the initial letters of a phrase into a single word yields an *acronym* if the result can be pronounced as a word (as with *laser*, from *light amplification by the stimulated emission of radiation*), but an *initialism* if it must be spelled out letter by letter, as with *FBI* and *BBC*.

Most of our technical terms are constructed by gluing together Greek and Latin *combining forms* of appropriate meaning: so, far example, the recently discovered creatures which flourish at or above the temperature of boiling water have been named *hyperthermophiles*, from three Greek elements meaning 'high-heat-lover'.

*See:* **affix**; **derivation** (sense 1); **morphology**
*Further reading:* Adams, 1973; Bauer, 1983; Katamba, 1994: ch. 4.


**writing system**  A conventional system for representing a language with permanent marks. Though human beings have been able to speak for many tens of thousands of years, writing systems were invented only a little more than 5,000 years ago, in the Near East. True writing was preceded by *precursors* which were adequate for recording only certain types of information, such as taxes due and paid. In a true writing system, however, any utterance of the language can be adequately written down.

There are several conceivable ways of constructing a writing system. We might attempt to provide a separate symbol for every different word-form of a language. This would mean, for example, that separate symbols would have to be provided for all of *drive*, *drives*, *driving*, *drove*, *driven*, *driver*, *drivers*, *driveway*, and so on. But the number of symbols required would be astronomical, and every new word or word-form entering the language would require a new symbol, and so such a system is completely unworkable.

Or we could provide a separate symbol for each *morpheme* in the language. Thus *drive* would have its own symbol, but *drives* would be written with the symbol for *drive* plus the symbol for present-tense *-s*, and *driver* with the symbol for *drive* plus that for *-er*, and so on. This is called a *logographic* system (though it might better be called a *morphemographic* system), and it actually works fairly well with a language whose words show little or no variation in form for grammatical purposes. Chinese is such a language, and still today Chinese is written in a logographic script – though naturally the number of different characters required still runs into many thousands. But note that Chinese does not provide a separate character for every word. There is a character for the word *huǒ* 'fire' and another for the word *chē* 'vehicle', but the word for 'train', *huǒchē*, literally 'fire-vehicle', is simply written with a combination of these two characters.

A third possibility is to provide a separate symbol for every distinct syllable in the language. Japanese does this. So, the Japanese word *ikura* 'how many?' is written with one symbol for /i/, a second for /ku/, and a third for /ra/, and similarly for every other word (except that Japanese uses Chinese characters to write many words). This kind of writing system is a **syllabary**, and it really only works well with a language which has only a small number of distinct syllables – no more than a few dozen. When a language permits very many different syllables, then either the number of symbols required becomes huge, or the system must be *defective* in some way – for example, a single symbol may be used to represent a number of distinct but somewhat similar syllables. The **Linear B** syllabary used to write Mycenaean Greek was like this: for example, the same symbol was used to write *to*, *tho*, *tos*, *thon*, and other syllables.

Finally, we can provide a separate symbol for each **phoneme** in the language – that is, for each distinctive consonant and vowel. Such a writing system is an **alphabet**, and alphabetic writing, the last type to be invented, is now by far the world's most frequent type of writing. The first alphabets, invented by speakers of Semitic languages thousands of years ago, were in fact defective, in that they provided **letters** (as alphabetic symbols are called) only for consonants; it was the Greeks who constructed the first complete alphabet by adding letters for vowels. In an ideal alphabetic writing system, every consonant and vowel in the language has its own consistent letter, and the spelling of a word is completely predictable from its pronunciation, but in practice few alphabetic scripts approach this ideal. In English, with its exceptionally complex and irregular spelling system, the spelling of a word typically exhibits only a modest correlation with its pronunciation (note the spellings of *rite*, *write*, *right* and *wright*, the verb *lead* and the name of the metal *lead*, and curiosities like *debt*, *knight*, *buy*, *pharaoh* and *autumn*), and our supposedly alphabetic system has become more similar to the Chinese logographic script, in which the representation of each simple word has to be learned as a unit.

Mixed systems are possible. The enormously complex Japanese writing system mostly uses Chinese characters to represent the stems of words, but a Japanese syllabary to represent grammatical words and grammatical endings, and it uses a second syllabary for various special purposes, such as writing words of foreign origin. The ancient Egyptian hieroglyphic writing system was almost numbingly complex, using a mixture of characters of various types to provide clues about both pronunciation and meaning.

In principle, any language can be written in any writing system, though not always with the same degree of success. Several central Asian languages have, during the last century, been successively written in the Arabic alphabet, in the Roman alphabet and in the Cyrillic (Russian) alphabet, depending on which way the political winds were blowing; Korean is sometimes written in Chinese characters but at other times in the local Han'gul alphabet; Chinese and Japanese are both sometimes written in the Roman alphabet for special purposes, but both the Chinese and the Japanese have so far resisted pressures to change over completely to the Roman alphabet. Turkish, in contrast, abandoned the Arabic alphabet in the 1920s in favour of the Roman alphabet.

Note carefully that every writing system ever used represents an attempt at recording utterances in a particular language. There has never been a real writing system which attempted to represent 'ideas' or 'thoughts' directly, without the mediation of a particular language, and suggestions to the contrary are ignorant and fantastic. (A few philosophers have occasionally tried to invent such systems, but they don't work.)

The study of writing systems is sometimes called ***graphology*** (not to be confused with the psychological interpretation of handwriting, of the same name).

*See:* **orthography**; **punctuation**; **spelling**

*Further reading:* Coulmas, 1996; Crystal, 1997a: section V; Daniels and Bright, 1996; Fromkin and Rodman, 1998: ch. 12; O'Grady *et al.*, 1996: ch. 15; Robinson, 1995; Sampson, 1985.

# BIBLIOGRAPHY

Adams, Valerie (1973) *An Introduction to Modern English Word-Formation*, London, Longman.

Aitchison, Jean (1998) *The Articulate Mammal*, 4th edn, London, Routledge

—— (1991) *Language Change: Progress or Decay?*, Cambridge, Cambridge University Press.

—— (1994) *Words in the Mind*, 2nd edn, Oxford, Blackwell.

—— (1996) *The Seeds of Speech*, Cambridge, Cambridge University Press.

Akmajian, Adrian, Demers, Richard A., Farmer, Ann K. and Harnish, Robert M. (1995) *Linguistics: An Introduction to Language and Communication* Cambridge, MA, MIT Press.

Allan, Keith (1986) *Linguistic Meaning*, 2 vols, London, Routledge.

Allen, Donald E. and Guy, Rebecca F. (1974) *Conversation Analysis: The Sociology of Talk*, The Hague, Mouton.

Anttila, Raimo (1988) *An Introduction to Historical and Comparative Linguistics*, 2nd edn, London, Macmillan.

Ashby, Patricia (1995) *Speech Sounds*, London, Routledge.

Asher, R.E. and Simpson, J.M.Y. (eds) (1994), *Encyclopedia of Language and Linguistics*, 10 vols, Oxford, Pergamon.

Austin, J.L. (1962), *How to Do Things with Words*, Oxford, Clarendon Press.

Bach, Emmon (1974) *Syntactic Theory*, New York, Holt, Rinehart and Winston.

Baldi, Philip (1983) *An Introduction to the Indo-European Languages*, Carbondale and Edwardsville, IL, Southern Illinois University Press.

Bates, Elizabeth (1976) *Language and Context: The Acquisition of Progmatics*, New York, NY, Academic Press.

Bates, Elizabeth, Benigni, L., Bretherton, I., Camaioni, L. and Volterra, V. (1979) *The Emergence of Symbols: Cognition and Communication in Infancy*, New York, NY, Academic Press.

Bates, Elizabeth, Bretherton, Inge and Snyder, Lynn (1988) *From First Words to Grammar*, Cambridge, Cambridge University Press.

Bauer, Laurie (1983) *English Word-Formation*, Cambridge, Cambridge University Press.

—— (1988) *Introducing Linguistic Morphology*, Edinburgh, Edinburgh University Press.

—— (1998) *Vocabulary*, London, Routledge.

Beekes, Robert S.P. (1995), *Comparative Indo-European Linguistics*, Amsterdam, John Benjamins.

Bennett, Paul (1995) *A Course in Generalized Phrase Structure Grammar*, London, UCL Press.

Berko Gleason, Jean (1997) *The Development of Language*, 4th edn, Boston, MA, Allyn and Bacon.

Berlin, Brent and Kay, Paul (1969) *Basic Color Terms: Their Universality and Evolution*, Berkeley, CA, University of California Press.

Bhatia, V.K. (1993) *Analysing Genre: Language Use in Professional Settings*, London, Longman.

Bickerton, Derek (1981) *Roots of Language*, Ann Arbor, MI, Karoma.

—— (1984) 'The language bioprogram hypothesis', *Behavioral and Brain Sciences* 7: 173–221.

—— (1990) *Language and Species*, Chicago, IL, University of Chicago Press.

—— (1996) *Language and Human Behaviour*, London, UCL Press.

Blake, Barry (1994) *Case*, Cambridge, Cambridge University Press.

Blake, N.F. (1996) *A History of the English Language*, London, Macmillan.

Blakemore, Diane (1992) *Understanding Utterances*, Oxford, Blackwell.

Bloomfield, Leonard (1933), *Language*, New York, NY, Holt, Rinehart and Winston.

Bodmer, Frederick (1944) *The Loom of Language*, London, Allen & Unwin.

Bonvillain, Nancy (1993) *Language, Culture, and Communication: The Meaning of Messages*, Englewood Cliffs, NJ, Prentice-Hall.

Borsley, Robert D. (1991) *Syntactic Theory: A Unified Approach*, London: Arnold.

—— (1996) *Modern Phrase Structure Grammar*, Oxford, Blackwell.

Bourne, J. and Cameron, Deborah (1989) 'No common ground: Kingman, grammar and the nation', *Language and Education* 2–3: 14–60.

Bradford, Richard (1997) *Stylistics*, London, Routledge.

British Dyslexia Association (1996) *Getting the Message Across: Dyslexia: A Hundred Years of Progress?,* Birmingham, Questions.

Brown, Gillian and Yule, George (1983) *Discourse Analysis*, Cambridge, Cambridge University Press.

Brown, Keith and Miller, Jim (1991) *Syntax: A Linguistic Introduction to Sentence Structure*, 2nd edn, London, HarperCollins.

Brown, Penelope, and Levinson, Stephen (1987) *Politeness: Some Universals in Language Usage*, Cambridge, Cambridge University Press.

Burke, Peter (1993) *The Art of Conversation*, Cambridge, Polity Press.

Burton-Roberts, Noel (1986) *Analysing Sentences*, London, Longman.

Butler, Christopher S. (1985) *Systemic Linguistics: Theory and Applications*, London, Batsford.

Caplan, David (1992) *Language: Structure, Processing and Disorders*, Cambridge, MA, MIT Press.

Carr, Philip (1993) *Phonology*, London, Macmillan.

Carter, Ronald (1997) *Investigating English Discourse*, London, Routledge.

Carter, Ronald, Goddard, Angela, Reah, Danuta, Sanger, Keith and Bowring, Maggie (1997) *Working with Texts: A Core Book for Language Analysis*, London, Routledge.

Catford, J.C. (1977) *Fundamental Problems in Phonetics*, Edinburgh, Edinburgh University Press.

Catford, J.C. (1988) *A Practical Introduction to Phonetics*, Oxford, Oxford University Press.

Chambers, J.K. (1995) *Sociolinguistic Theory*, Oxford, Blackwell.

Channell, Joanna (1994) *Vague Language*, Oxford, Oxford University Press.

Cheshire, Jenny and Stein, Dieter (eds) (1997) *Taming the Vernacular: From Dialect to Written Standard Language*, London, Longman.

Clark, John and Yallop, Colin (1995) *An Introduction to Phonetics and Phonology.* 2nd edn, Oxford, Blackwell.

Coates, Jennifer (1983) *The Semantics of the Modal Auxiliaries*, London, Croom Helm.

—— (1993) *Women, Men and Language*, 2nd edn, London, Longman.

—— (1996) *Women Talk*, Oxford, Blackwell.

Collins Cobuild (1990) *English Grammar*, London, HarperCollins.

351

Comrie, Bernard (1976) *Aspect*, Cambridge, Cambridge University Press.

—— (1985) *Tense*, Cambridge, Cambridge University Press.

—— (1989) *Language Universals and Linguistic Typology*, Oxford, Blackwell.

Comrie, Bernard, Matthews, Stephen and Polinsky, Maria (1997) *The Atlas of Languages*, London, Bloomsbury.

Cook, Vivian (1996) *Chomsky's Universal Grammar*, 2nd edn, Oxford, Blackwell.

Corbett, Greville (1991) *Gender*, Cambridge, Cambridge University Press.

Corder, S. Pit (1975) *Introducing Applied Linguistics*, London, Penguin.

Coulmas, Florian (1996) *The Blackwell Encyclopedia of Writing Systems*, Oxford, Blackwell.

Coulthard, Malcolm (1985) *Introduction to Discourse Analysis*, 2nd edn, London, Longman.

Cowper, Elizabeth A. (1992) *A Concise Introduction to Syntactic Theory*, Chicago, IL, University of Chicago Press.

Croft, William (1990) *Typology and Universals*, Cambridge, Cambridge University Press.

Crowley, Terry (1992) *An Introduction to Historical Linguistics*, 2nd edn, Oxford, Oxford University Press.

Crowley, Tony (1989) *The Politics of Discourse: The Standard Language Question and British Cultural Debates*, Basingstoke, Macmillan [published in the USA as *The Politics of Standard English*].

—— (1996) *Language in History*, London, Routledge.

Cruse, D.A. (1986) *Lexical Semantics*, Cambridge, Cambridge University Press.

Cruttenden, Alan (1986) *Intonation*, Cambridge, Cambridge University Press.

Crystal, David (1975) *The English Tone of Voice*, London, Arnold.

—— (1988) *The English Language*, London, Penguin.

—— (1995) *The Cambridge Encyclopedia of the English Language*, Cambridge, Cambridge University Press.

—— (1996) *Rediscover Grammar*, 2nd edn, London, Longman.

—— (1997a) *The Cambridge Encyclopedia of Language*, Cambridge, Cambridge University Press.

—— (1997b) *English as a Global Language*, Cambridge, Cambridge University Press.

Culicover, Peter (1997) *Principles and Parameters*, Oxford, Oxford University Press.

Culler, Jonathan (1986) *Ferdinand de Saussure*, 2nd edn, Ithaca, NY, Cornell University Press.

Dahl, Östen (1985) *Tense and Aspect Systems*, Oxford, Blackwell.

Daniels, Peter T. and Bright, William (eds) (1996) *The World's Writing Systems*, Oxford, Oxford University Press.

de Beaugrande, Robert (1994) 'Text linguistics', in Asher and Simpson (1994), vol. 9, pp. 4573–4578.

de Beaugrande, Robert and Dressler, Wolfgang (1981) *An Introduction to Text Linguistics*, London, Longman.

Denes, Peter B. and Pinson, Elliot N. (1993) *The Speech Chain: The Physics and Biology of Spoken Language*, 2nd edn, New York, NY, W.H. Freeman.

Deuchar, Margaret (1984) *British Sign Language*, London, Routledge.

Dunkling, Leslie (1995) *The Guinness Book of Names*, Enfield, Guinness.

Duranti, Alessandro (1997) *Linguistic Anthropology*, Cambridge, Cambridge University Press.

Eco, Umberto (1976) *A Theory of Semiotics*, Bloomington, IN, Indiana University Press.

Edwards, John (1994) *Multilingualism*, London, Penguin.

Elgin, Suzette Haden (1983) *What Is Linguistics?*, Englewood Cliffs, NJ, Prentice-Hall.

Fabb, Nigel (1997) *Linguistics and Literature*, Oxford, Blackwell.

Fairclough, Norman (1989) *Language and Power*. London, Longman.

—— (ed.) (1992) *Critical Language Awareness*, London, Longman.

—— (1995) *Critical Discourse Analysis: The Critical Study of Language*, London, Longman.

Ferguson, Charles A. (1959) 'Diglossia', *Word* 15: 324–340. Reprinted in Pier Paolo Giglioli (ed.) (1972) *Language and Social Context*, London, Penguin, pp. 232–251.

Fernando, C. (1996) *Idiom and Idiomaticity*, Oxford, Oxford University Press.

Fletcher, Paul and Macwhinney, Brian (eds) (1995) *The Handbook of Child Language*, Oxford, Blackwell.

Fodor, Jerry A. (1983) *Modularity of Mind: An Essay on Faculty Psychology*, Cambridge, MA, MIT Press.

Foley, John (1993) *The Guinness Encyclopedia of Signs and Symbols*, Enfield, Guinness.

Foley, William A. (1997) *Anthropological Linguistics: An Introduction*, Oxford, Blackwell.

Fowler, Roger (1996) *Linguistic Criticism*, 2nd edn, Oxford, Oxford University Press.

Fox, Anthony (1995) *Linguistic Reconstruction*, Oxford, Oxford University Press.

Frawley, William (1992) *Linguistic Semantics*, Hillsdale, NJ, Lawrence Earlbaum.

Fromkin, Victoria and Rodman, Robert (1998) *An Introduction to Language*, 6th edn, Fort Worth, Harcourt Brace.

Garman, Mike (1990) *Psycholinguistics*, Cambridge, Cambridge University Press.

Garnham, Alan (1985) *Psycholinguistics: Central Topics*, London, Methuen.

Giegerich, Heinz J. (1992) *English Phonology: An Introduction*, Cambridge, Cambridge University Press.

Givón, Talmy (1993) *English Grammar: A Function-Based Introduction*, 2 vols, Amsterdam, John Benjamins.

—— (1995) *Functionalism and Grammar*, Amsterdam, John Benjamins.

Gleason, H.A. (1961) *An Introduction to Descriptive Linguistics*, 2nd edn, New York, Holt, Rinehart and Winston.

Goatly, Andrew (1997) *The Language of Metaphors*, London, Routledge.

Goodluck, Helen (1991) *Language Acquisition: A Linguistic Introduction*, Oxford, Blackwell.

Gramley, Stephan and Pätzold, Kurt-Michael (1992) *A Survey of Modern English*, London, Routledge.

Green, Jonathon (1996) *Chasing the Sun: Dictionary-Makers and the Dictionaries They Made*, London, Jonathan Cape.

Greenbaum, Sidney and Quirk, Randolph (1990) *A Student's Grammar of the English Language*, London, Longman.

Greenberg, Joseph H. (1963) 'Some universals of grammar with particular reference to the order of meaningful elements', in J.H. Greenberg (ed.), *Universals of Grammar*, Cambridge, MA, MIT Press, pp. 73–113.

Grimes, B.F. (ed.) (1992) *Ethnologue: Languages of the World*, 12th edn, Dallas, TX, Summer Institute of Linguistics.

Grinder, John T. and Elgin, Suzette Haden (1973) *Guide to Transformational Grammar: History, Theory, Practice*, New York, NY, Holt, Rinehart and Winston.

Grundy, Peter (1995) *Doing Pragmatics*, London, Arnold.

Gumperz, John J. and Levinson, Stephen C. (eds) (1996) *Rethinking Linguistic Relativity*, Cambridge, Cambridge University Press.

Gussenhoven, Carlos and Jacobs, Haike (1998) *Understanding Phonology*, London, Arnold.

Haegeman, Liliane (1994) *Introduction to Government and Binding Theory*, 2nd edn, Oxford, Blackwell.

Halliday, M.A.K. (1989) *Spoken and Written Language*, Oxford, Oxford University Press.

—— (1994) *An Introduction to Functional Grammar*, 2nd edn, London, Arnold.

Halliday, Michael A.K. and Hasan, Ruqaiya (1976) *Cohesion in English*, London, Longman

Harris, Randy Allen (1993) *The Linguistics Wars*, Oxford, Oxford University Press.

Hawkins, John A. (1983) *Word Order Universals*, New York, NY, Academic Press.

Hawkins, Peter (1984) *Introducing Phonology*, London, Hutchinson.

Hock, Hans Henrich (1986) *Principles of Historical Linguistics*, Berlin, Mouton de Gruyter.

Hock, Hans Henrich and Joseph, Brian D. (1996) *Language History, Language Change and Language Relationship: An Introduction to Historical and Comparative Linguistics*, Berlin, Mouton de Gruyter.

Hockett, Charles F. (1958) *A Course in Modern Linguistics*, New York, Macmillan.

—— (1960) 'The origin of speech', *Scientific American* 203 (September): 88–96.

Hofmann, Th. R. (1993) *Realms of Meaning*, London, Longman.

Hofstadter, Douglas R. (1979), *Gödel, Escher, Bach: An Eternal Golden Braid*, Hassocks, Harvester.

—— (1985) 'A person paper on purity in language', in D.R. Hofstadter, *Metamagical Themas*, New York, NY, Basic Books, pp. 159–167. Reprinted in Deborah Cameron (ed.) (1990) *The Feminist Critique of Language: A Reader*, London, Routledge, pp. 187–196.

Hogg, Richard and McCully, C.B. (1987) *Metrical Phonology: A Coursebook*, Cambridge, Cambridge University Press.

Holm, John (1988–89) *Pidgins and Creoles*, 2 vols, Cambridge, Cambridge University Press.

Holmes, Janet (1992) *An Introduction to Sociolinguistics*, London, Longman.

Honey, John (1997) *Language Is Power: The Story of Standard English and Its Enemies*, London, Faber and Faber.

Horne, Kibbey M. (1966) *Language Typology: 19th and 20th Century Views*, Washington, DC, Georgetown University Press.

Horrocks, Geoffrey (1987) *Generative Grammar*, London, Longman.

Huddleston, Rodney (1984) *Introduction to the Grammar of English*, Cambridge, Cambridge University Press.

Hudson, Richard A. (1984) *Invitation to Linguistics*, Oxford, Blackwell.

—— (1995) *Word Meaning*, London, Routledge.

—— (1996) *Sociolinguistics*, 2nd edn, Cambridge, Cambridge University Press.

—— (1998) *English Grammar*, London, Routledge.

Hughes, Arthur and Trudgill, Peter (1996) *English Accents and Dialects: An Introduction to Social and Regional Varieties of English in the British Isles*, 3rd edn, London, Arnold.

Hurford, James R. (1994) *Grammar: A Student's Guide*, Cambridge, Cambridge University Press.

Hurford, James R. and Heasley, Brendan (1983) *Semantics: A Coursebook*, Cambridge, Cambridge University Press.

Hyman, Larry M. (1975) *Phonology: Theory and Analysis*, New York, NY, Holt, Rinehart and Winston.

Ilson, Robert (ed.) (1986) *Lexicography: An Emerging International Profession*, Manchester, Manchester University Press.

Ingram, David (1989) *First Language Acquisition: Method, Description and Explanation*, Cambridge, Cambridge University Press.

Jackendoff, Ray (1993) *Patterns in the Mind: Language and Human Nature*, New York, NY, Harvester Wheatsheaf.

Johnson-Laird, Philip H. (1983) *Mental Models: Towards a Cognitive Science of Language, Inference and Consciousness*, Cambridge, Cambridge University Press.

—— (1993) *The Computer and the Mind: An Introduction to Cognitive Science*, 2nd edn, London, Fontana.

Kaplan, Ronald and Bresnan, Joan (1982) 'Lexical-Functional Grammar: a formal system for grammatical representation', in J. Bresnan (ed.), *The Mental Representation of Grammatical Relations*, Cambridge, MA, MIT Press, pp. 173–281.

Katamba, Francis (1989) *An Introduction to Phonology*, London, Longman.

—— (1994) *English Words*, London, Routledge.

Kempson, Ruth M. (1977) *Semantic Theory*, Cambridge, Cambridge University Press.

Keyser, Samuel Jay and Postal, Paul M. (1976) *Beginning English Grammar*, New York, NY, Harper & Row.

Kilby, David (1984) *Descriptive Syntax and the English Verb*, London, Croom Helm.

Klaiman, M.H. (1991) *Grammatical Voice*, Cambridge, Cambridge University Press.

Klima, Edward S. and Bellugi, Ursula, (1979) *The Signs of Language*, Cambridge, MA, Harvard University Press.

Knowles, Gerald (1987) *Patterns of Spoken English*, London, Longman.

Krauss, Michael (1992) 'The world's languages in crisis', *Language* 68: 4–10.

Kreidler, Charles W. (1989) *The Pronunciation of English*, Oxford, Blackwell.

—— (1998) *Introducing English Semantics*, London, Routledge.

Labov, William (1972) *Sociolinguistic Patterns*, Philadelphia, University of Pennsylvania Press.

—— (1975) *What Is a Linguistic Fact?*, Lisse, Peter de Ridder Press.

—— (1994) *Principles of Linguistic Change, Vol. 1: Internal Factors*, Oxford, Blackwell.

Ladefoged, Peter (1971) *Preliminaries to Linguistic Phonetics*, Chicago, IL, University of Chicago Press.

—— (1993) *A Course in Phonetics*, 3rd edn, Fort Worth, TX, Harcourt Brace Jovanovich.

Ladefoged, Peter and Maddieson, Ian (1996) *The Sounds of the World's Languages*, Oxford, Blackwell.

Lakoff, George (1987) *Women, Fire, and Dangerous Things*, Chicago, IL, University of Chicago Press.

Lakoff, George and Johnson, Mark (1980) *Metaphors We Live By*, Chicago, IL, University of Chicago Press.

Landau, Sidney I. (1984) *Dictionaries: The Art and Craft of Lexicography*, New York, NY, Charles Scribner's Sons.

Langacker, Ronald W. (1987–91) *Foundations of Cognitive Grammar*, Berlin, Mouton de Gruyter.

—— (1990) *Concept, Image and Symbol: The Cognitive Basis of Grammar*, Berlin, Mouton de Gruyter.

Large, Andrew (1985) *The Artificial Language Movement*, Oxford, Blackwell.

Lass, Roger (1984) *Phonology*, Cambridge, Cambridge University Press.

Laver, John (1994) *Principles of Phonetics*, Cambridge, Cambridge University Press.

Leech, Geoffrey (1974) *Semantics*, London, Penguin.

Leeds-Hurwitz, Wendy (1993) *Semiotics and Communication: Signs, Codes, Culture*, Hillsdale, NJ, Lawrence Earlbaum.

Lehiste, Ilse (1970) *Suprasegmentals*, Cambridge, MA, MIT Press.

Lehmann, Winfred P. (ed.) (1967) *A Reader in Nineteenth-Century Historical Indo-European Linguistics*, Bloomington, IN, University of Indiana Press.

—— (1992) *Historical Linguistics*, 3rd edn, London, Routledge.

—— (1993) *Theoretical Bases of Indo-European Linguistics*, London, Routledge.

Leith, Dick (1997) *A Social History of English*, 2nd edn, London, Routledge.

Lepschy, Giulio (1970) *A Survey of Structural Linguistics*, London, Faber and Faber.

—— (ed.) (1994) *History of Linguistics, Vol. II: Classical and Medieval Linguistics*, London, Longman.

Levinson, Stephen (1983) *Pragmatics*, Cambridge, Cambridge University Press.

Lockwood, W.B. (1969) *Indo-European Philology*, London, Hutchinson.

—— (1972) *A Panorama of Indo-European Languages*, London, Hutchinson.

Lodge, R. Anthony (1993) *French: From Dialect to Standard*, London, Routledge.

Lucy, John A. (1992) *Grammatical Categories and Cognition: A Case Study of the Linguistic Relativity Hypothesis*, Cambridge, Cambridge University Press.

Lucy, John A. and Shweder, Richard (1979) 'Whorf and his critics: linguistic and nonlinguistic influences on colour memory', *American Anthropologist* 81: 581–615.

Lyons, John (1968), *Introduction to Theoretical Linguistics*, Cambridge, Cambridge University Press.

—— (1991) *Chomsky*, 3rd edn, London, Fontana.

—— (1995) *Linguistic Semantics: An Introduction*, Cambridge, Cambridge University Press.

McArthur, Tom (1986) *Worlds of Reference: Lexicography, Learning and Language from the Clay Tablet to the Computer*, Cambridge, Cambridge University Press.

McCarthy, Michael (1991) *Discourse Analysis for Language Teachers*, Cambridge, Cambridge University Press.

McCarthy, Michael and Carter, Ronald (1993) *Language as Discourse: Perspectives for Language Teaching*, London, Longman.

McCrum, Robert, Cran, William and MacNeil, Robert (1992) *The Story of English*, 2nd edn, London, Faber and Faber/BBC Books.

McMahon, April (1994) *Understanding Language Change*, Cambridge, Cambridge University Press.

Macwhinney, Brian and Bates, Elizabeth (eds) (1989) *The Crosslinguistic Study of Linguistic Processing*, Cambridge, Cambridge University Press.

Mallory, J.P. (1989) *In Search of the Indo-Europeans*, London, Thames and Hudson.

Malmkjær, Kirsten (ed.) (1991) *The Linguistics Encyclopedia*, London, Routledge.

Martin, Robert M. (1987) *The Meaning of Language*, Cambridge, MA, MIT Press.

Matthews, Peter (1979) *Generative Grammar and Linguistic Competence*, London, Allen & Unwin.

—— (1981) *Syntax*, Cambridge, Cambridge University Press.

—— (1991) *Morphology*, 2nd edn, Cambridge, Cambridge University Press.

Maybin, Janet and Mercer, Neil (1996) *Using English: From Conversation to Canon*, London, Routledge/Open University.

Mey, Jacob (1993) *Pragmatics*, Oxford, Blackwell.

Miles, Dorothy (1988) *British Sign Language: A Beginner's Guide*, London, BBC Books.

Milroy, James (1992) *Linguistic Variation and Change*, Oxford, Blackwell.

Milroy, James and Milroy, Lesley (eds) (1993) *Real English: The Grammar of English Dialects in the British Isles*, London, Longman.

Newmeyer, Frederick J. (1983) *Grammatical Theory: Its Limits and Possibilities*, Chicago, IL, University of Chicago Press.

Nida, Eugene (1975) *Componential Analysis of Meaning*, The Hague, Mouton.

Nofsinger, Robert E. (1991) *Everyday Conversation*, Newbury Park, Sage.

O'Grady, William, Dobrovolsky, Michael and Katamba, Francis (1996) *Contemporary Linguistics: An Introduction*, London, Longman.

Ouhalla, Jamal (1994) *Introducing Transformational Grammar*, London, Arnold.

Owens, Robert E., Jr. (1996) *Language Development: An Introduction*, 4th edn, Boston, MA, Allyn and Bacon.

Padden, Carol A. (1988) 'Grammatical theory and signed languages', in Frederick J. Newmeyer (ed.), *Linguistics: The Cambridge Survey. Vol. II: Linguistic Theory: Extensions and Implications*, Cambridge, Cambridge University Press, pp. 250–266.

Palmer, Frank (1971) *Grammar*, London, Penguin.

—— (1974) *The English Verb*, London, Longman.

—— (1976) *Semantics: A New Outline*, Cambridge, Cambridge University Press.

—— (1979) *Modality and the English Modals*, London, Longman.

—— (1986) *Mood and Modality*, Cambridge, Cambridge University Press.

—— (1994) *Grammatical Roles and Relations*, Cambridge, Cambridge University Press.

Palmer, Gary B. (1996) *Toward a Theory of Cultural Linguistics*, Austin, TX, University of Texas Press.

Partridge, Eric (1961) *A Dictionary of Slang and Unconventional English*, 5th edn, London, Routledge.

—— (1970) *Slang To-Day and Yesterday*, London, Routledge.

Pavlinić, A.M. (1994) 'Migrants and migration', in Asher and Simpson (1994), vol. 5, pp. 2491–2495.

Peer, W. van (1994) 'Text', in Asher and Simpson (1994), vol. 9, pp. 4564–4568.

Piattelli-Palmarini, Massimo (ed.) (1979) *Language and Learning: The Debate Between Jean Piaget and Noam Chomsky*, London, Routledge.

Pinker, Steven (1994) *The Language Instinct: The New Science of Language and Mind*, London, Allen Lane/Penguin.

Polanyi, Livia (1985) *Telling the American Story: A Structural and Cultural Analysis of Conversation*, Norwood, MA, Ablex.

Propp, Vladimir (1968) *Morphology of the Folktale*, Austin, TX, University of Texas Press.

Pullum, Geoffrey K. (1991) *The Great Eskimo Vocabulary Hoax and Other Irreverent Essays on the Study of Language*, Chicago, IL, University of Chicago Press.

Pullum, Geoffrey K. and Ladusaw, William A. (1996) *Phonetic Symbol Guide*, 2nd edn, Chicago, University of Chicago Press.

Radford, Andrew (1988) *Transformational Grammar: A First Course*, Cambridge, Cambridge University Press.

Rampton, Ben (1995) *Crossing: Language and Ethnicity Among Adolescents*, London, Longman.

Richards, Jack C., Platt, John and Platt, Heidi (1992) *Dictionary of Language Teaching and Applied Linguistics*, 2nd edn, London, Longman.

Roach, Peter (1991) *English Phonetics and Phonology: A Practical Course*, 2nd edn, Cambridge, Cambridge University Press.

Robins, R.H. (1997) *A Short History of Linguistics*, 4th edn, London, Longman.

Robinson, Andrew (1995) *The Story of Writing*, London, Thames and Hudson.

Romaine, Suzanne (1988) *Pidgin and Creole Languages*, London, Longman.

—— (1994) *Language in Society: An Introduction to Sociolinguistics*, Oxford, Oxford University Press.

—— (1995) *Bilingualism*, 2nd edn, Oxford, Blackwell.

Ryan, Marie-Laure (1991) *Possible Worlds, Artificial Intelligence and Narrative Theory*, Bloomington, IN, Indiana University Press.

Saeed, John I. (1997) *Semantics*, Oxford, Blackwell.

Sampson, Geoffrey (1975) *The Form of Language*, London, Weidenfeld & Nicholson.

—— (1980) *Schools of Linguistics*, London, Hutchinson.

—— (1985) *Writing Systems*, London, Hutchinson.

—— (1997) *Educating Eve: The 'Language Instinct' Debate*, London, Cassell.

Schiffrin, Deborah (1994) *Approaches to Discourse*, Oxford, Blackwell.

Sebba, Mark (1997) *Contact Languages: Pidgins and Creoles*, London, Macmillan.

Sebeok, Thomas (1984) *Encyclopedic Dictionary of Semiotics*, 3 vols, Berlin, Mouton de Gruyter.

—— (1994) *An Introduction to Semiotics*, London, Pinter.

Sells, Peter (1985) *Lectures on Contemporary Syntactic Theories*, Stanford, CA, CSLI.

Siewierska, Anna (1991) *Functional Grammar*, London, Routledge.

Silverman, David (1993) *Interpreting Qualitative Data*, London, Sage.

Simpson, Paul (1993) *Language, Ideology and Point of View*, London, Routledge.

—— (1996) *Language Through Literature: An Introduction*, London, Routledge.

Sinclair, J.M. (1991) *Corpus, Concordance and Collocation*, Oxford, Oxford University Press.

Sinclair, J.M. and Coulthard, R.M. (1975) *Towards an Analysis of Discourse: The English Used by Teachers and Pupils*, Oxford, Oxford University Press.

Smith, Cath (1990) *Signs Make Sense: A Guide to British Sign Language*, London, Souvenir Press.

Sommerstein, Alan H. (1977) *Modern Phonology*, London, Arnold.

Sperber, Dan and Wilson, Deirdre (1995) *Relevance: Communication and Cognition*, 2nd edn. Oxford, Blackwell Publishers.

Stainton, Robert J. (1996) *Philosophical Perspectives on Language*, Peterborough, ON, Broadview.

Steinberg, Danny D. (1993) *An Introduction to Psycholinguistics*, London, Longman.

Stillings, Neil A. *et al.* (1987) *Cognitive Science: An Introduction*, Cambridge, MA, MIT Press.

Sturrock, John (1993) *Structuralism*, 2nd edn, London, Fontana.

Szemerényi, Oswald J.L. (1996) *Introduction to Indo-European Linguistics*, Oxford, Clarendon Press.

Tannen, Deborah (1991) *You Just Don't Understand: Women and Men in Conversation*, London, Virago.

361

Tarleton, R. (1988) *Learning and Talking: A Practical Guide to Oracy Across the Curriculum*, London, Routledge.

Tench, Paul (1996) *The Intonation Systems of English*, London, Cassell.

Thibault, P.J. (1994) 'Intertextuality', in Asher and Simpson (1994), vol. 4, pp. 1751–1754.

Thomas, Jenny (1995) *Meaning in Interaction*, London, Longman.

Thompson, Geoff (1996) *Introducing Functional Grammar*, London, Arnold.

Thornborrow, Joanna and Wareing, Shân (1998) *Patterns in Language: An Introduction to Language and Literary Style*, London, Routledge.

Tobin, Yishai (1990) *Semiotics and Linguistics*, London, Longman.

Toolan, Michael (1988) *Narrative: A Critical Linguistic Introduction*, London, Routledge.

—— (1994a) 'Narrative: linguistic and structural theories', in Asher and Simpson (1994), vol. 5, pp. 2679–2696.

—— (1994b) 'Narrative, natural', in Asher and Simpson (1994), vol. 5, pp. 2696–2701.

Trask, R.L. (1994) *Language Change*, London, Routledge.

—— (1995) *Language: The Basics*, London, Routledge.

—— (1996) *Historical Linguistics*, London, Arnold.

Trudgill, Peter (1995) *Sociolinguistics*, 2nd edn, London, Penguin.

Trudgill, Peter and Hannah, Jean (1994) *International English: A Guide to the Varieties of Standard English*, 3rd edn, London, Arnold.

Turner, G.W. (1973) *Stylistics*, London, Penguin.

Ungerer, F. and Schmid, H.-J. (1996) *An Introduction to Cognitive Linguistics*, London, Longman.

Wallman, Joel (1992) *Aping Language*, Cambridge, Cambridge University Press.

Wardhaugh, Ronald (1987) *Languages in Competition*, Oxford, Blackwell.

Weinreich, Uriel, Labov, William and Herzog, Marvin I. (1968) 'Empirical foundations for a theory of language change', in W.P. Lehmann and Yakov Malkiel (eds), *Directions for Historical Linguistics*, Austin, TX, University of Texas Press, pp. 95–188.

Wells, John (1982) *Accents of English*, 3 vols, Cambridge, Cambridge University Press.

Whaley, Lindsay J. (1997) *Introduction to Typology: The Unity and Diversity of Language*, London, Sage.

Whorf, Benjamin Lee (1956) *Language, Thought and Reality: Selected Writings of Benjamin Lee Whorf*, J.B. Carroll (ed.), Cambridge, MA, MIT Press.

Wierzbicka, Anna (1996) *Semantics: Primes and Universals*, Oxford, Oxford University Press.

Yule, George (1996) *Pragmatics*, Oxford, Oxford University Press.

# INDEX